Twayne's United States Authors Series

Sylvia E. Bowman, *Editor*

INDIANA UNIVERSITY

James Michener

TUSAS 60

(Second Edition)

James Michener

JAMES MICHENER

By A. GROVE DAY

University of Hawaii

SECOND EDITION

TWAYNE PUBLISHERS

A DIVISION OF G. K. HALL & CO., BOSTON

Day, Arthur Grove, 1904-
  James Michener.

  (Twayne's United States authors series   ; TUSAS 60)
  Bibliography: p. 175 - 86.
  Includes index.
  1.   Michener, James Albert, 1907-   —Criticism and
interpretation.
PS3525.I19Z6   1977   813'.5'4   76-55700
ISBN 0-8057-7184-0

Dedicated to
CARL STROVEN
Senior Professor of English and Librarian
University of Hawaii
and Friend of
More Than Fifty Years

Contents

About the Author

A. Grove Day, Senior Professor of English, Emeritus, at the University of Hawaii, has known James A. Michener for more than a quarter of a century and has frequently conversed and corresponded with this author. Dr. Day collaborated with Michener on *Rascals in Paradise* (1957), which narrated the biographies of ten violent and colorful figures from Pacific history. Dr. Day, who served for five years as chairman of the Department of English at the University of Hawaii, has published more than a score of books dealing with the history and literature of Western America and the Pacific region. In all, he has authored, coauthored, edited, or coedited fifty books. In addition to *James A. Michener*, the original edition of which was published in 1964, he has contributed four titles to Twayne's World Authors Series: *Louis Becke* (1966), *Robert D. FitzGerald* (1974), *Eleanor Dark* (1976), and, in collaboration with Edgar C. Knowlton, Jr., *V. Blasco Ibáñez* (1972).

Preface

Everyone who reads, goes to the movies, or looks at television is aware that James A. Michener is one of the most popular writers of our generation. The reader recalls that Michener's first book, *Tales of the South Pacific,* was hailed as the best World War II novel from the Pacific, was awarded the Pulitzer Prize for fiction, and was made not only into a smash Broadway musical play but also into a film. He knows that Michener is a world traveler who has written a hundred articles for magazines as well as other books—*Return to Paradise, Sayonara,* and big novels like *Hawaii, The Source, The Drifters,* and *Centennial.* All his books—more than a score of them—are still in print in English, and his words have entertained millions around the world not only in that language but in translations into many other languages.

Aside from the first edition of this book and aside from reviews in periodicals, no critical attention has been given to Michener (for instance, only two brief articles are listed under his name in the annual *PMLA* bibliographies). The first special problem tackled in this revised biocritical volume, then, is: How much can be done in making a second definitive critical estimate in what is still a pioneering study? One man's answer, based on my rereading of some four million words by Michener—as well as on a personal relationship extending over a quarter of a century—is found in the following pages.

A second question that arises—the answer to which would be of great fascination not only to the general reader but to the aspiring writer and the student of literature—is: What is the "secret" of Michener's broad, sustained popularity as an author? Is it merely good luck, or his gift for the right word, or his sense of timing that enables him to anticipate what millions of readers will enjoy at the time his book appears on the market? Is it, perhaps, the result of a painstaking apprenticeship in the craft of writing and the application of a highly retentive memory and a fine intellect to the task of reporting the world with skill, versatility, and warmth? Is it—as appears again and again on the following pages—that through all of Michener's work runs a strong theme associated with the biggest question in the world today: How can we best get along with our human brothers of all races and creeds by avoiding stupid prejudice and eradicating bias? Michener has never known who his parents were; and, since he has been unable to solve the mystery of his own origin, he has been freer than most American writers of his time to put himself in the shoes or sandals of the billions of people on earth who are not of Anglo-Saxon and Christian ancestry. Some additional comment about Michener's "secret" appears in the final chapter.

Although I have a high opinion of James A. Michener's contribution to our literature, I am less concerned with booming the Michener shares on some sort of literary stock exchange than with trying to help his many readers discover his ideas and appreciate the richness of many other qualities of his works. As a writer and professor myself, I am as involved as anyone with the glaring fact that too many people read but do not comprehend—and that many who comprehend do not appreciate.

One contribution of the present volume, if rather a pedestrian one, is the Bibliography, which is the only one compiled on Michener with any attempt at completeness. Those who wish to follow my reading trail will find in this compilation the signposts. Another unique aspect of this book is that my lengthy friendship with Michener has given me the opportunity to record a number of his remarks from personal letters and from conversations that occurred in Honolulu, in Bucks County, and in other spots between. Seldom has a critic been free to obtain such full access to all the materials related to his author and, at the same time, been so free to express value judgments about their worth.

Grateful acknowledgment is made to the author and to Random House, Inc., for permission to use throughout this volume quotations from the copyrighted works of James A. Michener. Special acknowledgment is also made to the author and the Macmillan Company for permission to use quotations from *Tales of the South Pacific*, copyright 1947. I am most of all indebted to Mr. Michener for blanket permission to quote from any of his printed works or manuscripts.

A. Grove Day

University of Hawaii

Chronology

1907?   February 3 (?), James A. Michener born in New York City.
1921   Hitch-hiked through forty-five states.
1925   Graduated from Doylestown, Pennsylvania, High School.
1929   Bachelor of arts in English and history, *summa cum laude*, Swarthmore College (Phi Beta Kappa).
1929-   Master, Hill School, Pottstown, Pennsylvania.
1931
1930 - Graduate research at University of Pennsylvania, University of Virginia, Ohio State University, Harvard University, University of St. Andrew's (Scotland), University of Siena (Italy). Lippincott Traveling Fellowship.
1933
1933 - Teacher, George School, Doylestown, Pennsylvania.
1936
1935   Married Patti Koon.
1936 - Associate Professor of Education, Colorado State College of Education.
1939
1937   Master of Arts, Colorado State College of Education.
1940   *Unit in the Social Studies* (with H. M. Long).
1941 - Associate editor for the Macmillan Company.
1949
1942   Enlisted as apprentice seaman, United States Naval Reserve.
1944 - Active duty in United States Naval Reserve in South Pacific; discharged 1946 with rank of lieutenant commander.
1946
1947   *Tales of the South Pacific* (Pulitzer Prize for fiction).
1948   Divorced from Patti Koon; married Vange Nord.
1949   *The Fires of Spring;* play *South Pacific* opened on Broadway; ran for 1,925 performances.
1950   Awarded Doctor of Humane Letters, Rider College, first of many honorary degrees received.
1951   *Return to Paradise; The Voice of Asia.*
1953   Named president of Asia Institute; *The Bridges at Toko-Ri.*
1954   Fund for Asia founded; *Sayonara.*

1955   *The Floating World.* Divorced from Vange Nord; married
        to Mari Yoriko Sabusawa.
1956   Toured Asia while preparing television feature; covered
        Hungarian revolt.
1957   *The Bridge at Andau; Rascals in Paradise* (with A. Grove
        Day); *Selected Writings;* appointed to Federal Advisory
        Arts Commission; plane ditched in Pacific off Iwo Jima (Oc-
        tober).
1958   *The Hokusai Sketchbooks;* began working on novel about
        Hawaii.
1959   *Japanese Prints; Hawaii;* gift of Japanese print collection to
        Honolulu Academy of Arts.
1960   Active campaigning for John F. Kennedy in presidential
        campaign.
1961   *Report of the County Chairman.*
1962   Campaigning as candidate for House of Representatives
        from Pennsylvania Eighth District (unsuccessful); *The
        Modern Japanese Print.*
1963   *Caravans;* began working in Israel on *The Source.*
1965   *The Source.*
1967   Led foundation to establish Bucks County (Pennsylvania)
        Arts Festival; joined Americans for Permanent Peace in the
        Middle East; received Einstein Award from Einstein
        Medical College.
1967 - Secretary, Pennsylvania Constitutional Convention; presi-
1968   dent, Pennsylvania Electoral College.
1968   *Iberia;* Michener Collection of Contemporary American
        Paintings dedicated at University of Texas (Austin).
1969   *Presidential Lottery.*
1970   *The Quality of Life;* gift of $100,000 to Swarthmore College
        for black studies and race relations programs; appointed
        member United States Advisory Commission on Informa-
        tion.
1971   *Kent State; The Drifters;* gift of $100,000 to Kent State
        University for arts program.
1972   Visited China and Russia as news correspondent with party
        of President Richard Nixon.
1973   *A Michener Miscellany;* Michener Library dedicated at
        University of Northern Colorado (Greeley).
1974   *Centennial;* received seventeenth honorary degree at

Chronology

        Yeshiva University, New York.
1975   Represented President Gerald Ford at Okinawa World Ex-
        position; appointed to national Bicentennial Advisory Com-
        mission; attended White House dinner for Emperor
        Hirohito of Japan and Empress; sponsored conference on
        "The First Novel: An Endangered Species."
1976   *Sports in America;* represented the United States in
        Australia and New Zealand.
1977   Awarded Medal of Freedom by President Gerald Ford

CHAPTER 1

Citizen of the World

UNTIL he was forty, James Albert Michener had done almost everything except publish a book. His main apprenticeship came from adventuring in life rather than in growing up face to face with a typewriter.

Even to seek his own parentage was an adventure, a forlorn hope. The standard reference works solemnly state that the author was born on February 3, 1907, in New York City, son of Edwin and Mabel (Haddock) Michener. The father was a Quaker farmer of English extraction; the mother came from a North Ireland family settled near Wilmington, Delaware.

These books are in error.

"Although the extensive Michener clan has always welcomed me, and although I have appreciated their friendship and have maintained close association with them," James Michener frankly told me, "I am not a Michener. I am not related to them. Actually, I do not know who my parents were, or where or when I was born. I never had a birth certificate. The problem became acute in 1931, when I wished to get a passport for travel in Europe. At that time my foster mother, Mabel Michener, took me to a local notary public and told him that I was a foundling whom she had taken care of since birth. The notary said I would not be able to get a passport on that statement, so in my presence he and my mother worked out a statement to the effect that I was the son of Edwin and Mabel (Haddock) Michener, and on these terms I got the passport.

"The same problem recurred in 1942 when I wished to enlist in the Navy. Again my mother testified that I was a foundling, and again it was found advisable to revert to the passport story, which was already in the government files. So again I became the son of Edwin Michener.

"The facts in the case are very clearly set forth in the official

Michener family history.[1] This establishes that Edwin Michener was
dead long before I was born. The date, locale and parentage of my
birth I have never known."

Although near destitution herself, Mabel Michener, whom he
always knew as his mother, took in waifs and raised them along with
her own son, Robert. Six of her children went through high school,
and three of them through college. Among these latter was the
solemn-eyed James. His earliest recollections include lone trips to
Philadelphia, where he was sent to pick up and deliver bundles of
women's shirtwaists. Mabel Michener's chief income came from em-
broidering buttonholes in these shirtwaists.

I   *From Poorhouse to the Pacific*

Jim grew up in dire poverty. When illness struck the family, he
used to weather the bad times by moving into the county poorhouse
near Doylestown. There, among sad-faced, bearded wrecks who
shared a hoarded smear of margarine with him, Jim learned a sym-
pathy for unfortunate people that was to color his whole attitude
toward the world.

There were happy times, too, when he got off in a shady corner
with a book (he does not remember when he learned to read), or
paddled beneath a red, plank-covered bridge over the straggling
Neshaminy Creek, hunting for hellgrammites to use for fish bait. He
spent much time rambling around Bucks County, which lies
northwest of Philadelphia — a county whose Indian, colonial,
Quaker, and Pennsylvania Dutch history is reflected in such names
as Perkasie, Washington's Crossing, Quakertown, and Trum-
bauersville (Levittown was a mass-housing development still in the
future).

Jim went to Doylestown Grammar School, but at the age of fourteen he succumbed to the burning desire for travel that has never let
him rest. He bummed his way around the United States, and in this
way he saw every state except Washington, North Dakota, and
Florida. On the road he enjoyed the food and friendship of some fifty families, whose hospitality made him an "incurable optimist"
about human nature. On his return home he delivered newspapers,
was a hotel watchman, wrote a sports column at the age of fifteen,
and acted as a spotter of short-change "artists" at Willow Grove
Park, an amusement center near Philadelphia, where, stationed near
the bandstand, he became acquainted with John Philip Sousa and
Victor Herbert.

Jim was graduated in 1925 from Doylestown High School, where he had been noted for prowess in basketball, baseball, tennis, and acting. Thanks to a flypaper memory that later was to bring him success as a world correspondent and interviewer, he maintained high marks in all his courses. A scholarship took him to Swarthmore College, a celebrated institution under Quaker auspices.

As a young student of art, Michener, like many others, burned with curiosity to view the celebrated collection of European paintings held privately in the guarded gallery of Dr. Albert Barnes, the terrible-tempered Philadelphia collector who had made his fortune through the patented eye remedy Argyrol. Michener wrote the doctor a letter from Pittsburgh, posing as a culture-struck steel-mill worker with an unpronounceable name. Garbed to fit the part, he was admitted to view the collection and even got a free lecture from its owner on the relationship between Matisse and Brahms.

During one summer vacation from college Michener joined the traveling tent shows of Chautauqua, that long-enduring institution of rural enlightenment which had first drawn crowds at the New York lake of that name in the 1870s. Young Jim's caravan was one of the last to tour the American countryside. One of his roles was leading man opposite pundit Drew Pearson's sister, in a teenage vehicle called *Skidding*—it was from this play that the immensely popular Andy Hardy screen series was adapted. Michener's greasepaint experience on the road may well have increased his observation of dramatic techniques, although he is humble about his thespian powers.

Jim Michener graduated from Swarthmore in 1929, *summa cum laude*, with a bachelor of arts degree in English and in history. He was suspended several times "for girl troubles," but he won membership in Phi Beta Kappa, oldest of scholastic honor societies. He also served as Ivy Orator, with a wildly optimistic address on the subject of "On and Ever On," which he delivered not long before the stock market crash of 1929.

Young Michener chose the career of teacher, and throughout his life, although he has long since put his classroom service behind him, he has devoted much of his writing to informative purposes. Behind the novelist often lies the scholar, the editor, the professor.

For a while Michener served as master at Hill School, Pottstown, Pennsylvania. A traveling scholarship, the Lippincott Award, enabled him to make his first trip abroad. His headquarters were at gray, venerable St. Andrew's University in Scotland, but he also

studied art at the British Museum in London and Sienese painting at
Siena. Later he shipped as chart-corrector on a Mediterranean
collier. He is one of the few American authors holding papers as an
able-bodied seaman in the British merchant marine. Before returning to his homeland, he also traveled up and down the Hebrides,
helping to collect some of the rare songs and ballads remembered in
those northern islands. His *wanderjahre* were also filled with a
voracious reading of European authors.

When Michener returned to the United States, a salary of twelve
hundred dollars during the depression years didn't look too bad. He
taught from 1933 to 1936 at George School, a Quaker institution
near Doylestown. The next year he gained a master's degree in
teaching from the Colorado State College of Education at Greeley,
on the staff of which he served as associate professor from 1936
through 1939.

Michener used to drive fifty-five miles to Denver to the Baker
Federal Theater to see a Works Progress Administration repertory
company perform the plays of Shaw, O'Neill, Sinclair Lewis, and
others at a ticket cost of thirty-five cents. Here he continued his love
affair with the American theater, until this activity of keeping actors
on the federal payroll was abolished as a gigantic boondoggle. "Of
all that Colorado has offered me, nothing was more important to my
life than this theater," Michener says in justification for such federal
support of creative people. "Somebody estimated the other day that
on dramatic works that have been derived from my stories, the
federal government has collected not less than ten million dollars in
taxes, and on the personal income derived from them another twenty
million dollars at least. . . . So for every dollar that the government
'wasted' in 1936, it got back $300 from me alone."[2]

Michener, who in all had attended nine universities in Europe and
America, was visiting professor in the School of Education at Harvard University from 1939 to 1940. Several years earlier he had
begun his writing career in the educational press. Between 1936 and
1942 he published some fifteen articles "with lots of footnotes"; they
were mainly concerned with teaching social studies in America's
schools.

He is proudest, perhaps, of "The Beginning Teacher," chosen by
the National Council for the Social Studies to lead off their tenth
yearbook. His skill in making a story prove a point is shown in a short
piece called "Who is Virgil T. Fry?" It is supposed to be told by the
successor of a mysterious high-school instructor who had been con-

demned by all his colleagues and finally discharged by the school board, but who had been loved by all his students because he inspired them to learn much and to discuss their ideas freely. "Who is Virgil T. Fry?" first appeared in *Clearing House* in 1941; over the years it was twice reprinted therein, was printed twice by *Educational Digest*, and appeared also in *Scholastic* and in the *NEA Journal*. All these articles he, like the customary professor-writer, gave for publication without a nickel of payment; but, as he says, "I did learn how to write a sentence." This mastery of writing with clarity and popular appeal brought Michener the offer of a position in a textbook publishing house.

Anticipating conflict with the Axis powers, Michener published a warmly patriotic essay, "What Are We Fighting For?" one month before the United States was plunged into World War II. When the Japanese attacked Pearl Harbor on December 7, Michener was an editor in the offices of the Macmillan Company of New York. As a practicing member of the Society of Friends, he might well have been excused from serving in the armed forces. But he was a "fighting Quaker," like General Smedley Butler and Richard Nixon, and in 1942 he volunteered for service in the United States Navy.

Again his skill in writing brought him to the attention of superiors. He was sent to officers' training school; and, as a result of his European experience, he was given a special course qualifying him for carrier service in the Mediterranean theater. But his ability to draft reports brought about his assignment to Washington. There he requested active duty. Interviewed by a lieutenant (junior grade), Michener was told, "You will be sent to the Pacific."

"I dislike seeming to be insubordinate," he responded, "but have you read the note at the bottom of my dossier, stating that I have been trained for Mediterranean service?"

"You will go to the Pacific!" repeated the officer. And thus, almost by chance, James A. Michener first went to the ocean that later was to become almost synonymous with his name.

II   *Bus Ride to Random House*

Then began a wartime period of acting as supersecretary for aviation maintenance in the Solomon Islands and points north and south. As troubleshooter and atoll-hopper, Michener was able to visit some fifty islands and to observe the activities that were to be narrated so authentically in *Tales of the South Pacific*. Freedom to enter many areas came, perhaps, because he did nothing to controvert the widespread idea that he was a relative of the powerful Vice-Admiral Marc A. Mitscher.

Then, as he relates, "A slack spell came and I was stranded on an island with nothing to do. Each afternoon I went up to a deep cacao plantation where I drafted outlines of some stories that had disturbed me. Each night I went to a big, empty building with a dozen mosquito bombs and typed out the material I had been thinking about." This was the beginning of his first novel.

Later Michener was assigned to flying duty and became senior naval historical officer for the area from New Guinea to Tahiti. While on this assignment he wrote extensive histories of naval operations ashore at Bora Bora and Tongatabu, of which he says: "Long after I'm dead somebody will find those histories gathering dust in Washington, and they'll be published as affectionate little records of the absurd." He has always made light of his accomplishments in uniform. "My war record was quite undistinguished and all I accomplished could have been done much better by a capable girl secretary, except for one week in Tahiti." Actually he was discharged from the navy with a fine battle record and the rank of lieutenant commander. He returned to the post of associate editor in the high school text division at Macmillan, where a brilliant future was promised him.

By the end of 1946, however, he had sold two of the South Pacific chapters to the *Saturday Evening Post;* and *Tales of the South Pacific* was published in February, 1947, under the imprint of his own house. This crucial event was marked by few people other than the author. The rare first edition of the *Tales* makes an odd item for collectors. Probably no future Pulitzer Prize book has ever appeared in a more sleazy format. The book was considered to have such slight hopes that the publisher used up an overstock of chalky paper whose surface was different on either side, and these pages were draped in a shoddy binding. New chapters were started right under the last line of the previous ones, and "Fo' Dolla'," which was to inspire one of the most successful musical comedies of our generation, began six lines from the bottom in order to conserve paper, thus saving a few dollars.

Contrary to popular belief, *Tales of the South Pacific* was never a best-seller. It sells today about the same number of copies annually that it did at the start. Orville Prescott of the *New York Times* was not the only reviewer to anticipate the high reading pleasure that was to come. Prescott's reception was to be warmly remembered by

Michener; the review stated that *Tales* was "one of the best works of fiction yet to come out of the war . . . a substantial achievement which will make Mr. Michener famous. It is original in its material and point of view, fresh, simple and expert in its presentation, humorous, engrossing, and surprisingly moving . . . it is not primarily a book about combat and so deserves to escape from the present general dearth of interest in war books."[3]

On May 3, 1948, the Pulitzer Prize Committee at Columbia University gave a five hundred dollar award to *Tales of the South Pacific* as "a distinguished novel, preferably dealing with American life, by an American author." The book still caused no great stir and might have shared the quiet fate of such predecessors as *His Family* or *Years of Grace*. Luckily, Kenneth McKenna, an actor turned Hollywood motion picture executive, tried to sell Michener's book to his studio, but was told, "You could never make a picture out of this." To support his judgment, McKenna sent it to his brother Jo Mielziner, the famous stage designer, who took it to Richard Rodgers and Oscar Hammerstein II. They, as everyone knows, made it into the musical comedy *South Pacific*, which opened on Broadway in April, 1949, and ran for a total of 1,925 performances and which in its film version will run for years in many parts of the world.

"Two nights before their show opened," recalls Michener, "these men telephoned me. In addition to my royalty, which they were required to pay, they voluntarily gave me a part of the ownership, which they were not required to do and which I did not request. As a result, I was free to travel and to write as I pleased."

Michener remembered what sudden success had done to men like Thomas Heggen, who had committed suicide soon after his first novel, *Mr. Roberts*, had been well received. Michener determined to keep his head. The income from the musical show he reinvested in what he called "literary plant expansion." Assured for the first time of a modest living, he was able to write as he chose without regard for book markets.

The beginning book writer had another anchor to windward. Early in his career, DeWitt Wallace, the founder of the immensely successful *Reader's Digest*, spotted Michener as a promising and popular author. Wallace not only gave Michener lucrative assignments through the years but offered him an annual subsidy without strings attached in order to make sure that Michener would not stop writing through hard times. Reminded recently of this cushion against adversity, Michener hastily replied: "But I never accepted it." A selection of *Digest* articles, *A Michener Miscellany: 1950 - 1970*, was published in 1973; and the Micheners attended in 1972 a White House party that honored the Wallaces on the fiftieth anniversary of their publication.

Michener's successive volumes, ones which show that he was not content to spend his life writing and rewriting South-Seas fiction, are actually amazingly varied. One after another he wrote (1) a tender growing-up novel set mainly in Pennsylvania and New York; (2) a travel volume in unique form—half hard reporting, half regional short stories; (3) a political book consisting of vignettes of Asian personalities; (4) an intense, bitterly controlled novel of the Korean War; (5) a novella of Japan in antique style; (6) a philosophical study of Japanese art; (7) a collaboration on biographies of ten violent and colorful figures from Pacific history; (8) a fiery report on the Russian suppression of the Hungarian revolt of 1956; (9) three other scholarly volumes of Japanese prints; (10) a voluminous novel of several generations in the lives of several racial groups in the Hawaiian Islands; (11) a report on the author's participation in the Kennedy campaign of 1960; (12) a romantic travelogue about a group of Americans and Asians in Afghanistan in 1947; (13) a massive collection of stories of people living in the Holy Land through millenia; (14) a personal view of Spanish life and history; (15) a warning concerning the dangers inherent in the Electoral College system of choosing an American president; (16) a series of essays on environmental reform; (17) a large, documented account of the shootings in May, 1970, at Kent State University; (18) a novel narrating the misadventures of an international group of uprooted young people drifting through Europe and Africa; (19) a monumental novel about the westward movement and the development of the state of Colorado through eons of time; and (20) a collection of essays about the sports scene in the United States. And, at the age of three score and ten, he had in mind fifteen or twenty topics for other books that he might enjoy writing.

Freedom of choice and versatility of performance could hardly go farther than this. During much of this period, Michener's most strenuous efforts were devoted to acting as a roving reporter for such magazines as *Life, Holiday,* and *Reader's Digest.* For these publications, the world was his beat. And his skill in writing developed more and more to the point where all his various endeavors paid generous rewards. His versatility also required fresh treatment by the reviewers of each new book. Since there was no such thing as "another typical Michener book," each had to be read and discussed.

His second novel, *The Fires of Spring*, is a tender story of growing up in America, a *Bildungsroman* if not a *Künstlerroman*, the type of semiautobiographical work that it is customary for beginning writers to evolve. It was therefore surprising to be assured by Michener that not one word of it was written before he finished *Tales of the South Pacific*.

The Fires of Spring marked another crisis in the author's career. He had to change publishers. Macmillan, despite having a Pulitzer prizewinner on its staff, declined the second novel but not because of lack of merit. Michener had a future there as a senior editor, and it was amicably suggested to him that this did not include writing novels on the side. Michener chose to submit the manuscript to Random House. His action began an association which over the years grossed millions of dollars for that house. The acumen of the editorial team headed by Bennett Cerf under the Random imprint was well known in writing circles, but, typically, Michener's decision had a human rather than a calculated basis.

"I had visited the Random House offices," Michener once told me, "and had noted that their receptionist was a charming young Negro girl (she later appeared in the musical *Carmen Jones*). Most publishing houses at that time did not even employ Negroes in their shipping rooms. I imagined that Random's choice of a receptionist might cost some patronage, and I felt that an outfit willing to risk prejudice by such an act of faith would be a good one to associate with. So I got on a Fifth Avenue bus at Washington Square, rode up to 50th Street, and handed that Negro girl the manuscript of *The Fires of Spring*." Since that day, Random House has sold millions of copies of books by James A. Michener.

III   *Hardly a Cardiac Cripple*

Michener's appearance, at the summit of his Pulitzer and *South Pacific* fame, was that of a stocky fellow of medium height, with bespectacled, warm, brown eyes; a placid Quaker smile; and one of the highest foreheads in modern American literature. He spoke slowly, precisely, in a voice like that of a teacher aiming at the back row of seats; and, at our first meeting, I was reminded that he had once been a professor of education. He kept in good physical shape, broke some amateur records for skin diving in Hawaiian waters, and neither smoked nor drank (except for a friendly beer). He was at this time "returning to Paradise," accompanied by his second wife, to write a series of articles for *Holiday* magazine.

Michener's first marriage, to Patti Koon in 1935, had ended in divorce in 1948. In September of that year he had married twenty-six-year-old Vange A. Nord, a *Time Magazine* writer and an interior decorator. They lived in a flat at 85 Charles Street in Greenwich Village, on the walls of which were hung a Van Gogh print, an Italian Renaissance panel, and José Clemente Orozco's portrait of Emiliano Zapata.

As soon as it became financially possible, however, the Micheners acquired a forested hilltop acreage near Pipersville, twelve miles from his boyhood home at Doylestown. Bucks County had meanwhile become a fashionable refuge for such country gentry as Oscar Hammerstein, George S. Kaufman, Pearl Buck, S. J. Perelman, and Moss Hart; and Michener took pride in having been a "native" of that region. He and his wife designed a dwelling combining comfort and artistic charm, complete with swimming pool and caretaker's cottage.

Jim's job as a world reporter frequently interrupted construction. Work on a garage building was delayed when he was called upon to revisit the South Pacific for eight months. Back home again, he got the garage built; but before he could get his car into it the *New York Herald Tribune* asked him to tour Asia on an assignment. Home once more, he started to paint the garage—but then a ten-thousand-mile lecture tour of the United States interfered.

Michener's knowledge of Asia brought him recognition and responsibilities. In April, 1953, the regents of the Asia Institute, the only graduate school in the United States then devoted exclusively to training in Asian affairs, named him president. Both he and James M. Landis, appointed as chancellor to succeed retiring founder Professor A. U. Pope, served without salaries, and an appeal for funds was issued to support the school, which had twenty-five candidates for the master's degree.

A year later, on February 7, 1954, Michener helped to found the Fund for Asia, a national nonprofit organization designed to provide technical aid in Asia by private agencies in the United States. He attended the Bandung Conference of non-Caucasian nations and spent several months in Afghanistan in 1955. He arrived in Afghanistan just as civil war seemed inevitable. When he reached the capital, national mobilization was announced, and for one terrifying moment it looked as if he was going to be one of the conscripts. For eleven weeks he lived in a land of tension; but Asia, he found, had somehow learned to solve its disputes short of war. In Saigon in July of that year, when demonstrators mobbed and pillaged his hotel, Michener was able to save his possessions from the rioters by announcing that he was an American and a friend.

The Fund for Asia lasted only two years; in December, 1956, Michener, as president, announced that it would end its activities because "recent world events in the Middle East and Hungary had made its discontinuance advisable."[4]

Working on a *Life* feature concerning the marriage of a G.I. and a Japanese girl, Michener was in Chicago in December, 1954. Two days before Christmas he attended a luncheon of friends of the Pfeiffer family and was introduced to Mari Yoriko Sabusawa, assistant editor of the American Library Association *Bulletin*. One of the first things she said to the author was that she did not like the ending of *Sayonara*. An interracial marriage need not always be a tragedy, she maintained.

Michener learned more about Mari. She had almost missed the luncheon because of another invitation. She had lived in Chicago for a decade, working and studying political science at the University of Chicago. She had been born, however, in 1920 in Las Animas, Colorado. After the Pearl Harbor attack, she was one of the first Japanese-Americans to be sent to an internment camp in California, the one set up at the Santa Anita race track. She had preferred treatment: "I lived in Equipoise's stable." One of the first to be released, she went to Antioch College in Ohio, where classroom work was intertwined with practical experience on the job. And she ended the war in Washington doing top-secret work for the government.

Less than a fortnight after Michener met Mari, his wife Vange Nord Michener sued for divorce on the grounds of "indignities" and complained that the writer was seldom home. The divorce was completed on the last day of August. She received custody of a Japanese boy that had been adopted by the childless couple.

James Michener and Mari Sabusawa were wed on October 23, 1955, in the Hilton Chapel at the University of Chicago. She was thirty-five; he, forty-eight. She was listed as Presbyterian, Michener as a Quaker; the minister was a Baptist. Newspapers commented that the bride did not greatly resemble the stately actress Hana-ogi of *Sayonara:* "Michener's bustling, bright-eyed American Madame Butterfly is neither tall nor exotic, has no theatrical background and cannot dance."

As a writer, Michener felt that this marriage would present no problems. "If I were a banker, say, in the South, I might encounter some difficulty." He predicted more such marriages, since the United States is becoming more and more international. Mari also felt that, since marriage is a personal thing, people who love each other should go ahead and marry. None of her relatives made objections. All her mother asked was: "Is he a good man? Will you be happy with him?"

The couple left for a honeymoon around the Pacific, passing through Hawaii on the way to Australia, where Michener had some writing assignments. Six months later, after a tour of East Asia, they returned via Hawaii. This time Michener, accustomed to travel with one seabag, arrived in Honolulu with his wife and thirty-eight pieces of luggage. He settled in his Waikiki apartment on the eighth floor of the Ainahau Apartments at 260 Lewers Road. He then began an intense collaboration with A. Grove Day on the completion of the volume called *Rascals in Paradise*.

One Saturday night in June, 1956, during a Honolulu Press Club dinner in his honor, Michener was presented by Admiral Felix Stump with the Navy Gold Cross, highest award given to a civilian and the first ever given to a writer, in recognition of his many services to the Navy.

In July, 1956, the Micheners went to the West Coast and drove across the country to Bucks County. By heavy use of airmail facilities, the collaboration on the big biographical volume was finished.

Michener was soon back in Asia, on a task that few American authors had previously faced. He was asked by the National Broadcasting Company to prepare a special ninety-minute television report called "Assignment—Southeast Asia." To make this color documentary, he traveled with camera crews for five weeks through Java, Bali, Malaya, Cambodia, Viet Nam, Thailand, and Burma. They interviewed fifteen major leaders, fifty or sixty personalities, and some three hundred anonymous men-in-the-street. Michener felt that presenting this film to the American public was harder than writing a book but that doing so had tremendous satisfactions.

In Amsterdam, homeward bound, he was asked by *Reader's Digest* to cover the Hungarian revolution which had erupted on October 23. The Russians had reoccupied the country on November 4, and the brutal suppression of the population was such a dramatic story that Michener was soon on his way to Vienna and to the bridge at Andau. He spent four weeks interviewing, day and night, hundreds of refugees and wearing out two interpreters. To see for himself the effects of Red domination, he accompanied Freedom Fighters on rescue expeditions, and helped people through the border swamps, across rivers and canals, and past false Austrian flags put up by the Russians to try to detour the fleeing Hungarians. Despite such hindrances, two hundred thousand of them escaped from tyranny, and Michener's resulting book was the first to document this international episode.

Early in 1957 Michener was given another global assignment—to write about the activities of the Strategic Air Command that protects the free world around the clock and around the world. In order to write about the men who fly the big nuclear bombers, Michener wanted to fly one himself; but an Air Force doctor, discovering a minor heart ailment resulting from the Hungarian episode, refused him permission to sit at the controls. Typically, Michener boarded a commercial plane to Honolulu, hunted up a medico who was a personal friend, obtained a clean bill of health, and soon had the thrill of piloting a Strategic Air Command bomber at forty thousand feet.

Since then, avoiding the temptation to be a cardiac cripple, he has skin dived to a depth of sixty-five feet, traveled around the world half a dozen times, engaged in two major revolutions, explored the deserts of Central Asia and climbed the lower Himalayas, written a dozen books, fought a couple of yearling bulls in Mexico, campaigned energetically for election to the Congress of the United States, lived for months on an archeological site in the deserts of Israel, collected several hundred masterpieces of painting by prominent modern American artists, and traveled to Russia and China as a news correspondent with President Nixon's party. In Michener's sixty-ninth year, he visited Japan at a showing of the Japanese print collection he had donated to the Honolulu Academy of Arts in 1959; and he soon thereafter flew to South Australia and then toured the islands of New Zealand.

IV *Campaigning at Clambakes and Coffee Hours*

In the first half of 1957, Michener had three books on the stands: *The Bridge at Andau;* the *Rascals in Paradise* collaboration completed the previous year; and *Selected Writings*, a Modern Library anthology. In June he was awarded two honorary degrees: a Doctor of Laws from Temple University and a Doctor of Letters from the American International College. In October he was appointed by

Secretary of State John Foster Dulles to a Federal Advisory Arts Commission.

An unsought adventure came to Michener early in October, 1957. He and twelve others took off in a C-47 transport from the plateau airfield of Iwo Jima, a stop on his trip from Guam to Japan. Almost at once, one of the engines failed and the other began to falter. The plane crashed into a heavy sea at eighty-five knots and sank in three minutes. During this time the occupants had quickly boarded a life raft. A small boat sent to pick them up had its engine fail a mile away from the drifting raft. The castaways paddled closer to the rescue launch but without making contact. Finally a Japanese sailor tied a rope around his waist and swam from the launch, through shark-ridden waters, to the raft, where he was pulled in with a great deal of hearty affection. No lives were lost. At the time of the crash, Michener, seeing the smallness of the raft, abandoned all his possessions, including the manuscript of *Hokusai's Manga*, which was to have been published in Japan, and a fat book of notes for a novel which he had been considering writing about Hawaii.

James Michener has never permanently resided in any spot other than Bucks County, Pennsylvania, where he had been picked up in the street as an abandoned waif. Several times, however, in order to do research and write about a region of the earth such as the Hawaiian Islands, the nation of Israel, or the state of Colorado, he and Mari have established a temporary home in which a typewriter was always handy. In 1958, therefore, the Micheners took an apartment on Lewers Road in the heart of Waikiki. There Jim began work, in consultation with research assistant Mrs. Clarice B. Taylor, on his voluminous novel *Hawaii*. He started the final writing of this long-planned book on May 1 and worked at it steadily for ten months. He did not leave the islands during this time except for a four-day appearance at the Pan-Pacific Festival in San Francisco.

Despite his daily labors at his writing table, Michener plunged into local politics. He had forsaken his many years as a staunch Republican and become a peacemaker in the faction-ridden Democratic party of the islands. His old fascination with sociology and politics drove him to attend dozens of coffee parties and rallies complete with flower leis and hula dancers. His strong advocacy of statehood for Hawaii had made him influential, and the liberalism which had caused him to shift to Adlai Stevenson in 1956 led him to see in the Democrats of Hawaii the champions of the underdog. He traveled to islands other than Oahu in 1959 and strongly pleaded for the election of John A. Burns for governor several days after Burns himself had decided that he could not win. (Burns did achieve the governorship in the Democratic landslide of 1962.)

Michener's Republican friends were puzzled by his advocacy of a party that seemed to them recklessly trying to destroy the new state that was undergoing its first election—some of them felt that he was swayed by his wife. The ending of the novel *Hawaii* presents the outcome of an election as Michener would have wished it. The reality was the election of Republicans as governor and lieutenant-governor, with a bare majority of Republicans in the state Senate to offset a big majority of Democrats in the House. A series of five articles that Michener wrote for the Honolulu *Star-Bulletin*, including one with the title of "How to Lose an Election," is an outspoken postmortem by Michener the realistic political scientist.

In the spring, with his novel *Hawaii* finished, Michener shipped aboard a sailboat which was beating its way back from Honolulu to Los Angeles, following its participation in the biennial trans-Pacific yacht race. The writer told himself that, since he had written so much about the Pacific, he should cross it in a small vessel to see what it was like at close quarters. He found out. The yacht took twenty-two days of buffeting, with the rail under water most of the trip. It was a tedious, wet passage; and even the professionals were seasick.

On land again, he and Mari drove across the country and found not much improvement in conditions. "We did strike very bad weather driving home and on the stretch from Wichita to Kansas City were on a sleet-covered highway where we did about ten miles an hour all day," he wrote me. "It was rather harrowing but interesting to be back in the middle of weather as weather should be." The couple might well have yearned for Hawaii, but some time would pass before they could return. Christmas was spent in Mexico, for Michener was doing a piece about bullfighters.

In November the novel *Hawaii* had been published. Even before this novel, some six million copies of Michener's books had been sold in twenty-four languages. At once the new novel hit the best-seller lists and stayed at or near the top for no less than twenty months. Even before publication, the film rights were sold for six hundred thousand dollars against a ten per cent share in the gross—the highest price paid at that time for a picture property.

During the following summer, Michener diverted himself by playing the typecast role of "the perfesser" in a production of *South*

Pacific at New Hope, Pennsylvania. He also began campaigning for the election of John F. Kennedy for the presidency of the United States, an experience to be related in *Report of the County Chairman*.

A furor arose in Honolulu in April, 1961, when an interview with Michener reprinted from the *New York Post* quoted his amplification of a paragraph in the forthcoming book. He had mentioned three reasons why he had decided to leave Hawaii and return to his residence in Pennsylvania. Among these was the statement that, despite Hawaii's great achievements in racial harmony, "on the day-to-day operating level at which my wife and I had to live, we met with more racial discrimination in Hawaii than we did in eastern Pennsylvania, and my wife understandably preferred to live permanently in the latter place."[5]

Queried by transatlantic telephone in Seville, Spain, where he was working at the time, Michener stated that he would still like to return to Hawaii some day and that the decision to leave came from himself and not from his wife. A letter of amplification from Michener to Clarice Taylor, which was published in Honolulu in July, helped slightly to put the misunderstanding into its proper place, but the passions of many good people in Hawaii, most of whom had not read the novel nor *Report of the County Chairman*, were slow to cool.

In November, 1959, Michener had denied to reporters the rumor that he intended to run on the Democratic ticket for governor of Hawaii the following year. Anticipating the local irritation that might be caused by *Hawaii*, he warned his would-be electorate: "I feel that writers do not make good elected officials because writers have to probe into so many aspects of community life—and when they do, they are bound to make more enemies than friends."[6] However, within the next two years he found himself back in Pennsylvania, about which he had *not* written; and he changed his mind about participation. During nine months in 1962 Michener devoted most of his waking hours to campaigning as a Democrat for a seat in the United States Congress from Pennsylvania's eighth district.

His motives were explained in an article he wrote for the *Saturday Evening Post:*

On the surface, I would seem to be the least likely candidate for public office that a major party could find. But three significant factors didn't appear on the surface. (1) I used to teach American history and took the subject very seriously. (2) I have lived in many foreign nations that did not have good government, and I have come to respect self-government as one of the highest attainments of man. (3) As a boy I lived in dire poverty and was rescued by scholarships, fellowships, and the generosity of our nation. I owe a debt to America which is constantly in my mind and which I have always been willing to repay, either by volunteering for military service or by helping out in government. . . .

I'm running for one of the 435 most important jobs in the United States and the opposition has a right to belt me with every fact they can turn up. They won't say anything worse than book reviewers have said in the past.[7]

Michener's experience in the rough-and-tumble of politics in Hawaii had prepared him well for the strenuous job of fighting for a Pennsylvania seat that had been held by Republicans for twenty-six years. His opponent had been reelected four times, but Michener and his wife did not yield to tradition. They zigzagged around Bucks and Lehigh counties in a small station wagon, attending union picnics, clambakes, book club meetings, Pennsylvania-Dutch tall-story contests, dedications of new firehouses, and various coffee hours, asking for votes. Michener found that many people were curious about meeting his Japanese-American wife; and, when they did so, they often decided to vote for her husband. And he was frequently diverted on the stump by questioners who wanted to ask him about his novel *Hawaii*. "I'm going to charge the Hawaii Visitor's Bureau half of my campaign expenses," he joked, following a session at a ladies' tea party. "Four-fifths of them told me they had read the book and wanted to climb on the first boat available to the islands."[8] But political experts who had predicted that Michener could win only by a miracle were proved correct. However, when he lost by only seventeen thousand votes, he could feel that his months of effort had not proved fruitless.

V *A Bicentennial Rite of Passage*

During the hot political campaign, Michener found time to continue his interest in painting—an interest stemming at least from his high-school days. Income from the sale of the film rights to *Hawaii*, for example, enabled him to support the avocation of collecting art in a serious manner. "The only way I know to get any pleasure out of a large income," he told me, "is to buy paintings, keep and enjoy them for a while, and then donate the collection to a museum in return for tax considerations." During a visit at his Bucks County home, I found the rooms—even the kitchen—stacked with valuable "on-approval" canvases by contemporary painters, and guests were polled on the question of which ones should be purchased for posterity. Sixty of his acquisitions were exhibited in Little Rock, Arkansas, in May, 1961; and one hundred of them were shown in Allentown, Pennsylvania, the following year. Michener's purchasing continued; and in September, 1968, the chancellor of the University of Texas announced that a major collection of two hundred and fifty modern paintings by American artists, valued at three million dollars, had been donated by the Michener Foundation, one formed by Jim and his wife Mari. The collection has since been shown in Australia, New Zealand, Poland, Germany, Rumania, Russia, and six Latin American nations.

Caravans, a novel deriving from Michener's visit to Afghanistan in 1955, appeared in 1963. In that year he left his Bucks County base for an extended stay in the Jewish state of Israel in order to gather material for the volume to be published in 1965 as *The Source*. As he had done in Hawaii, he saturated his mind with a mass of information about the chosen region. This novel, extending in time from about twelve thousand years ago to 1964, focuses on an imaginary "tell," or archeological site, on which one settlement after another had been erected and had vanished because of the comings and goings of conquerors of many historic breeds. In a series of chapters, each a complete story in itself but linked to others by theme, the dramatic history of the Holy Land is revealed, as well as its influence on the development of Western civilization itself.

Michener's concern for the future of the Middle East, which had extended over at least a decade (he had written in 1955 about Islam, the misunderstood religion of three hundred and fifty million Muslims), expanded after the success of *The Source*. He was honored in April, 1967, by receiving the Einstein Award of the Einstein Medical College as a member of a group known as Americans for Permanent Peace in the Middle East, and in June he published a letter to the *New York Times* hailing the reunion of Jerusalem under Israeli rule., An article on the problem of the Arab refugees and possible solutions, published in the *Times* in September, 1970, was lauded by several writers and won him various awards. During a press briefing in Moscow in May, 1972, when Michener was part of the newspaper corps attending President Nixon's visit to Russia, the Russian officer in charge responded to a question concerning the status of Soviet Jews by flippantly quoting from a satirical, forty-year-old novel. Michener and another correspondent caused a Russian response of "hysteria" by walking out of the meeting.

Michener was awarded his seventeenth honorary degree by Yeshiva University, New York, in 1974. The following March, he was one of a group of about a hundred persons gathered in Paris to protest the failure of UNESCO to maintain its universality by banning Israel's participation. Again in 1975, in a December letter to the *Times*, Michener and other signers scored the United Nations resolution equating Zionism with racism, and proclaimed a "Decade of Action to Combat Racism."

"Today I think of myself as a somewhat older social studies teacher," Michener wrote in 1970;[9] and, indeed, another lifelong interest has been his advocacy of enlightened politics and civic responsibility. Elected secretary of the 1967 - 1968 constitutional convention of the State of Pennsylvania and president of the Pennsylvania Electoral College, he served with distinction in these important posts. During his studies he became alerted to the incredible danger inherent in our constitutional system of choosing a president of the United States by means of the Electoral College system. The result was the publication in 1969, after the election of Richard Nixon, of *Presidential Lottery*. Michener's concern about national unrest during the Vietnam conflict and such upheavals as the trial of the "Chicago Seven" in 1968 led to an assignment to cover the shootings in May, 1970, of students at Kent State University in northeastern Ohio, and the resulting publication of a large, documented book, *Kent State*, in 1971. The alienation of young people is even more heavily emphasized in the big novel *The Drifters*, published the same year. Part of the setting of *The Drifters* is Spain, a country about which Michener had published a big nonfiction volume, *Iberia*, in 1968.

When not working at his typewriter on such books, Michener served in various public capacities. In 1970 a group headed by Dr. Wallace Sterling met frequently to plan for a noble celebration of the coming national bicentennial in 1976. When Michener was assigned to put these ideas into form for presentation to Congress, dissident members of the group leaked the plans to a few legislators who scuttled every promising possibility and reduced the vision to one trifling fair in Philadelphia. Disappointed, Michener turned to the idea of making his own private celebration; and, in the spring of 1970, he began his field research for the volume that would be published in the autumn of 1974, after more than three years of effort, under the terse title of *Centennial*. However, in the spring of

1975, when he accepted an appointment on the national Bicentennial Advisory Commission, he explained his reasons in a *Times* article stressing the importance of ritual observances such as the tribal
"rites of passage."

VI   A *Million Dollars to Spare*

Still active in campaigning, in 1972 Michener supported Edmund
S. Muskie, but he and the other committed delegates lost their bid in
the Pennsylvania Democrat primaries. Reviewing the election in
November, Michener concluded in a *Times* article that the
Democrat party had destroyed itself at the convention by failing to
achieve a balance between generations. Domination of the
procedure by ultraliberals and by youths resulted in the nomination
of Senator George McGovern, who was never seriously considered
by most voters as a responsible candidate; and the election of
Richard Nixon was assured.

Republican lack of confidence, however, which resulted in the
Watergate break-in and in the subsequent national constitutional
crisis, was studied by Michener. In July, 1973, he held an "am-
bivalent attitude" toward demands for impeachment or resignation
of Nixon, hoping for an eventually more responsible attitude by the
president. By November, he had shifted to a conviction that Nixon's
resignation was the only possible outcome; and he was therefore one
of the first to demand openly what became the first resignation of an
American president under threat of impeachment.

During the past decade, James Michener has emerged not only as
a world traveler, a superlative reporter, and a novelist read by
millions around the globe but also as a public pundit. His
pronouncements are eagerly awaited on such subjects as youth, the
aged, sex and pornography, rock music, language, the environment
(see his book *The Quality of Life*, 1970), copyright law, science,
television, women, the metric system, war, and racial prejudice (in
1970 he announced a gift of one hundred thousand dollars to be
devoted over a period of five years to a black studies and race
relations program at his alma mater, Swarthmore College). In spite
of such diversification of interests, he found time to publish in 1976 a
volume, *Sports in America*, which voices not only a spectator's
enthusiasms but also his lifelong enjoyment of active physical effort
(in that year he was still playing tennis weekly at his Bucks County
home).

Michener has appeared frequently on television, addressed impor-

tant gatherings such as the annual American Bar Association convention in Honolulu in 1974, attended such White House functions
as the dinner for Emperor Hirohito of Japan and the empress; and in
1970 he was appointed a member of the select and influential
United States Information Advisory Commission, which promotes
national policy through such international efforts as the Voice of
America broadcasts. Michener's concern for his creative fellows in
the arts is shown by his support of programs like the annual Bucks
County arts festival. In June, 1975, he was active on a panel headed
by David Rockefeller to produce a report aimed at improving the
curricula at all educational levels, especially through recognition of
the role of the arts. In the autumn of that year he organized a conference at Tarrytown, New York, entitled "The First Novel: An Endangered Species," which emphasized the plight of the beginning
novelist in the marketplace. Immediately thereafter he served as
President Ford's personal representative to the World's Fair at
Okinawa. In the spring of 1976 he and Mari were on the panel at a
writer's conference in Adelaide, Australia; and he then spent several
weeks revisiting wartime haunts in New Zealand and meeting with
fellow writers, as he had done throughout his publishing period.

Since the age of forty, then, James Michener's main activity has
been to build a career as an author. He is one of the few American
writers of our century to have all his works (including even his art
books) in print today; for a well-known publisher of paperbacks has
contracted for the entire list. Indeed, Michener's position as one of
the best-paid writers alive raises the question of his attitude toward
money and the creative person. As a poor boy who had often been
broke, he grew up unworried by lack of financial security. "I have
always insisted that the writer be properly paid for his labors, like
anyone else," he recently told me. "But what he does with his earn-
ings, after taxes, is his own affair. I don't think this attitude is in-
consistent." On the other hand, few writers are more generous in
writing for low fees to oblige a friend or to help a good cause, for
Michener works just as hard on an essay for which he gets nothing as
he does on the highest-paying assignment. For example, he gave
away a series of Korean War dispatches which were headlined
around the world. His four volumes of Japanese prints cost him a
large amount of money to publish; and all proceeds from the fourth
volume, about contemporary Japanese artists, which sold for one
hundred and fifty dollars a copy, went to the artists themselves.

"Yes, what we do with money is our privilege," he repeated. "Not long ago Mari and I sat down and calculated that our assets, not counting royalties in escrow, amounted to just about a million dollars. It's silly for two people to be responsible for having all that cash around. We decided to give it all away. To whom? Well, the money came from the arts. Logically, it should go back to the arts. And it will."

CHAPTER 2

Start in the South Pacific

MICHENER'S first book, *Tales of the South Pacific*, was
published early in 1947; it won the Pulitzer Prize for fiction
for that year. The book retains the freshness of having been written
on the spot at about the time of the action it relates, but the author
tried to present the scene as it would be remembered in the future.
"I wrote that book under extremely difficult circumstances," he
recalls. "I was in the Navy on Espíritu Santo in the South Seas. The
mosquitoes drove me batty and the humidity was terrible. It took me
a year and a half. . . . I was sure the people who were bitching so
much about the Islands would not remember them that way. I try to
anticipate history."[1]

Although never a best-seller, *Tales of the South Pacific* was quite
favorably received by the reviewers. In the Sunday edition of the
New York Times,[2] David Dempsey called it "truly one of the most
remarkable books to come out of the war in a long time. . . . The
book's only weakness—the interminable length of some of the tales.
Mr. Michener saw so much, and his material is so rich, that he simply could not leave anything out. . . . Fortunately, even when he is
uneconomical, Mr. Michener is never dull. Nor is his lengthiness
always a fault." Orville Prescott, who had been enthusiastic in the
daily *New York Times*, was even more so in the *Yale Review:* "These
Tales of the South Pacific are magnificently entertaining. But they
are more than that. Mr. Michener is an acute observer of human
character. An adroit literary artist, a man with a philosophy of life
which makes him tolerant of many human weaknesses but not of all,
he is certainly one of the ablest and one of the most original writers
to appear on the American literary scene for a long time."[3]

Michener has modestly stated that the Pulitzer Prize came to him
in 1947 because there was no competition and that he would not
have won it in any other year.[4] This idea is not borne out by the

facts: the year 1947 saw also the publication of Laura Hobson's *Gentleman's Agreement*, John Steinbeck's *The Pearl* and *The Wayward Bus*, Sinclair Lewis' *Kingsblood Royal*, Vincent McHugh's *The Victory*, David Davidson's *The Steeper Cliff*, Theodore Dreiser's *The Stoic*, John Horne Burns's *The Gallery*, A. B. Guthrie's *The Big Sky*, and Malcolm Lowry's *Under the Volcano*. In the minds of the judges there must have been a good deal of competition, particularly to cause them to choose for the first time "a book of short stories," as the *New York Times* reported, "even such related short stories as make up Mr. Michener's excellent book."[5]

Michener himself has always thought of the book as a novel because a strong theme and a changing but limited setting around the Pacific islands lend unity and because among the large cast are several recurring figures, especially Tony Fry, Bus Adams, and the narrator himself.[6] The nineteen chapters are also tied together by the giant anti-Japanese operation—called "Alligator" in the book —which slowly rises into a crescendo and a climax, and has its aftermath in the cemetery at Hoga Point.

It is true that the focus of narration sometimes shifts,[7] but this is the case with other books too. If *Moby Dick* is a novel, and it is, so is *Tales of the South Pacific*.

I   *Progeny of the* Bounty

Appreciation of Michener's first novel is increased if one studies the various chapters as the story unrolls. The opening sketch, "The South Pacific," stresses the beauties of the region to which war had come, as well as the differences between it and other theaters, such as Europe. For several years it was to be a war of waiting, "timeless, repetitive waiting." But it was also a war in which people were important—such as Bloody Mary, who sold dried human heads as souvenirs, and the old native who persuaded the Americans to let him make a parachute jump, and thereafter lived silent, a being apart. Especially were the American servicemen in the foreground of the picture: the mad commander who would summon a carpenter at two in the morning to sandpaper the floor of his hut; Admiral Bull Halsey, who grunted out during a defeat, "We'll be in Tokyo by Christmas!"; Admiral Millard Kester, a fictional creation whom we first see tearing off his pants and being immobilized by a jammed zipper; and Tony Fry, everybody's friend, whose old TBF, used in missions for ferrying liquor, had twelve beer bottles painted on its side. In three pages, the general tone of the stories to come is adumbrated.

The second piece, "Coral Sea," tries to reveal the significance of this battle during which the Japanese fleet was first turned back and the shores of Australia and New Zealand were rescued by American naval might from the shadow of invasion by a cruel enemy. This action, truly one of the decisive battles of history, is still annually celebrated in Australasia in a way that overwhelms visiting Americans, who for the first time begin to understand the deep feeling of gratitude for their salvation that our allies are glad to express.

But Michener avoids the temptation to offer a standard battle description here. The meaning of the trembling victory comes most significantly to an isolated group of allied airmen who are stuck in a malarial, bombed-out swamp on Vanicoro, with a portable radio receiver their only contact with the action. Of all the men, this crisis is most desperate for Leftenant Grant, a silent New Zealander whose rickety PBY has finally crashed in the bay and left him grounded. His wife back home has volunteered to mobilize other women with axes and pick handles to defend their menaced beaches. For three days, Grant sits silent at the radio. Then, when the great news comes through, he presents his surviving comrades with a bottle of Scotch; and, after a few fumbling words of a speech of celebration, he falls over—dead drunk.

One of the best stories about the Pacific ever written is "Mutiny." To Norfolk Island, a tiny dot between New Zealand and Noumea, goes the narrator, the "I" of *Tales of the South Pacific*, who is not necessarily Michener himself. He has been ordered by Admiral Kester to find out what is holding up a vital operation—the leveling of an airstrip that will be the only salvation of the supply planes flying between Australasia and New Caledonia to prepare for the Guadalcanal campaign.

A decision that should be made in an hour drags on for weeks. There is only one logical spot for the runway—but it happens to be the one spot that is covered by a two-mile avenue of towering Norfolk pines which had been planted "because God has been kind in His wisdom to bring us here" by descendants of the *Bounty* mutineers settled on this far isle. Tony Fry, charged with giving the order to bulldoze the strip, has apparently been led from his simple duty by the pleas of the Norfolk inhabitants, including Lucy, a simple-minded girl, and white-haired old Teta Christian, descendant of the man who had led the mutiny against Captain Bligh on the *Bounty*.

Profoundly, Michener uses history to reinforce the theme of his tale. Norfolk was one island in the Pacific never reached by man until Captain James Cook set foot there. It was later a prison island for the murderous hard cases that even the penal colony of Australia could not subdue; the impressive stone walls of the buildings erected by convict laborers were topped with broken glass to protect the jailers from the attacks of mutinous convicts. After the final mutiny, the island was emptied and then offered to the *Bounty* people who were invited to emigrate from their Pitcairn hideaway. And at the denouement, when the narrator—bemused like Fry into a delay to avoid destroying "the loveliest monument in the South Pacific," "a living cathedral" of unique, giant trees—is forced at last to issue the order for their destruction, Tony Fry in a gesture of defiance dynamites one of the bulldozers and credits the two women with its ruin. In this isle of mutiny, even an American naval officer reverts to passion and rebellion and takes a stand against the destruction that authority has decreed. Ironically, at the end, the lovely trees are blasted down; but not one of the grim, empty buildings of the penal settlement has had to be destroyed.

One of the tales from the Pacific war that Michener did not use concerns the interrogation of a Japanese prisoner. Asked which men were best at jungle fighting, he replied: "Japanese." For second best: "Australians." When asked about Americans, he answered: "Americans no jungle fighters. Cut jungle all down." "Mutiny" reveals the reluctance of at least one American to engage in the brutal, bulldozer sort of war that had to be used against the Japanese aggressors.[8]

"An Officer and a Gentleman" is handsome Ensign Bill Harbison, a college athlete from the mountain states and the husband of a Vassar girl. Stuck for months in a soft job as recreation officer on Efate, unable to obtain promotion ahead of the slow navy system, and unable to transfer to a theater of action, Bill has his main character traits revealed by the omniscient narrator. Competently doing his work in less than an hour a day, Bill spends his time writing to his wife, exercising his body, and relaxing his mind until the day when the nurses arrive. Then, starved for women's society, he first displays his "mother-complex" by dating Dinah Culbert. She enjoys the attention while it lasts, but remarks: "I pity the next girl he goes with!"

II *She Finds Her a Wonderful Guy*

The next girl is Nellie Forbush, later to be the heroine of the musical play *South Pacific*. She is a small-town girl, and she realizes the irony of the situation in which navy nurses find themselves. They are classed as officers but can seldom find their equals among the male officers. "Cut off by law from fraternizing with those men who would like to marry them and who would have married them in civilian life, they find their friendships restricted to men who are surprisingly often married or who are social snobs" (47).[9]

The joys of dating on a romantic island in the tropics when war is at a standstill and passions are free to rove have their expected outcome. At the climax, Bill's snobbishness is nakedly revealed: "The damned girl was proposing to him! What was happening here? He swallowed hard and looked at her, a common little girl from some hick town. . . . He knew Nellie was his for the asking, but damn it all she was nothing but a little country girl. Hell, he wouldn't look at her twice in the States" (51). On the way back to his quarters, he feels a thin line of fat menacing his athletic stomach: "Soft living. I better get back to kicking that football in the afternoon."

"The Cave" is an exploration of the meaning of courage. Three men are contrasted in the story. One is Lieutenant Commander Charlesworth, an Annapolis graduate, and the skipper of one of the PT boats at the Tulagi base who are trying with feeble, brave little vessels of plywood to fight off the big Japanese ships that menace the American forces on Guadalcanal. A second is Lieutenant Tony Fry, the reservist who arrives with plenty of whiskey and snuggles down in a cosy hangout inside a cave commanding a view of The Slot. Fry, to whom humanity is the most precious thing, jeers at navy protocol and confesses frankly his fear of death; but night after night he drags himself down to the dock and boards Charlesworth's frail craft "to see what the heroes are doing" and to duel with Jap destroyers. The heroes are busy holding a defensive line against suicidal odds, and Charlesworth is one of the bravest of them all.

Fry's mission is to receive the radio messages of a volunteer coast-watcher, an exiled Britisher who flits from island to island for two long months, risking betrayal and death daily in order to send revealing weather reports and observations of Japanese troop and plane movements. "The Remittance Man," as he humbly calls himself, is merely a Malaita trader who has married a Melanesian wife and who, for no sound motive that Fry can figure out, is living

every moment with a fear balanced only by the all-embracing importance of his messages to the allied battlers on Guadalcanal. He is
the third of the men who must face and solve the problem of how to
crawl out of his deep spiritual dugout, day after bloody day, and face
the terror.

"And so," remarks the narrator, now attached to Charlesworth's
staff, "arguing about the Remittance Man, we studied ourselves and
found no answers" (64). What keeps Fry interested is the question of
the power that holds the Remittance Man on his job, although court-
ing certain death. Even when the gruesome details of that death
have been ascertained by the navy men on a crazy submarine
scouting expedition, the question still remains. At the end, even
Charlesworth, who has won three medals for superhuman bravery
against Japanese ships, speculates on the personal history of the
Britisher whose sign-off words, "Good hunting, Americans!", has
led the way to the evacuation of Guadalcanal by the beaten
Japanese. The theme of the story is related to the title:

How does any man have the courage to go to war? . . . And I hated
Tony Fry for having raised such questions. I wanted to shout at him, "Damn
it all! Why don't you get out of the cave? Why don't you take your whiskey
bottles and your lazy ways and go back to Noumea?" . . . And then I understood. Each man I knew had a cave somewhere, a hidden refuge from
war. For some it was love for wives and kids back home. . . . For others the
cave consisted of jobs waiting, a farm to run, a business to establish, a tavern
on the corner of Eighth and Vine. For still others the cave was whiskey, or
wild nights in the Pink House at Noumea, or heroism beyond the call of
valor. (72)

And for Tony and Charlesworth, their "cave" was the contempla-
tion of the courage of another man: "The Englishman's great courage in
those critical days of The Slot buoyed their equal courage" (73). For
those who today may have to face a greater Guadalcanal, "The
Cave" is still a heartening parable.

"The Milk Run" is told to Tony Fry by Lieutenant Bus Adams, a
naval bomber pilot. Anything but a peaceful, routine mission is his
trip to Munda. The thrill of an authentic adventure northwest of
Guadalcanal is conveyed in offhand tones, complete with accurate
flyer talk. Shot down in the bay at seven-thirty in the morning,
without even a life raft, Bus Adams is a sitting duck for a Japanese
bullet. But, miraculously, he is protected for five hours by a circling
cover of New Zealand and American aircraft. His rescue becomes a

point of honor with Admiral Kester and the focus of a side battle in the war. Lieutenant Grant, the New Zealand flyer, lands his PBY next to Bus and takes him aboard. But at once the plane's wing is shot away, and all the men are in the water. Grant, protagonist of the "Coral Sea" chapter, remarks mournfully: "Second PBY I've lost since I've been out here." The windup of the affair preserves the life of Bus Adams at an estimated cost to the taxpayer of some six hundred thousand dollars. But as Bus remarks: "It's sure worth every cent of the money. If you happen to be that pilot."[10] To Americans, even in wartime, human life is precious.

"Alligator" is an interchapter with little story content. It foreshadows the big push for which all the painful waiting is a prelude. "Alligator" is the code name for this gigantic operation, and the audacity of the decision to attack Kuralei, a thousand miles northward behind enemy lines, is presented in factual prose. The narrator is the man selected by chance to carry from Pearl Harbor to Noumea, in a locked and guarded briefcase, the bulky mimeographed orders for the operation in which men would die or not die, families would be bereft, and women would or would not marry. "The intensity, the inevitability, the grindingness of Alligator were too great for any one man to comprehend" (93).

"Our Heroine" is Ensign Nellie Forbush, later to be glorified on Broadway by Mary Martin. After her sad affair with Bill Harbison, she asks to be transferred to an island to the north; and there she meets the charming Emile De Becque, the prototype of Ezio Pinza. The view from his hilltop is a delight to the girl from a small town near Little Rock, Arkansas,[11] and so is the view from the secluded pavilion in his cacao grove. She discovers that he left France because he had stabbed a local bully to death, but she listens to his proposal. Emile is all man, a leader of the French community and, as Bus Adams casually reveals to Nellie, a hero with the island women. In fact, he has no less than eight lovely but illegitimate daughters.

The shock of having her future husband the father of eight girls younger than herself affects Nellie less than the realization that the girls are not all white. Four of them are half Javanese; two, half Tonkinese; and two others, half Polynesian. "Emile De Becque, not satisfied with Javanese and Tonkinese women, had also lived with a Polynesian. A nigger! To Nellie's tutored mind any person living or dead who was not white or yellow was a nigger. And beyond that no words could go!" (111 - 12).

The fact that Emile had not married because he dreamed that

some day Nellie would come to the island and be the mistress of his household canot offset the shock. But on the way back to the hospital in his jeep, Emile defends her from four lurking American rapists. Charlie Benedict, back in Otolousa, Arkansas, does not have a chance against Emile. Nellie had left home to see the world and meet people, and she had come at the right time to the right place. "Out here," counsels her friend Dinah Culbert, "good people seem to get better and bad people get worse." And Nellie's mind is changed. "I got me a man!" she says joyously. Racial prejudice has been overcome by love. And the eight step-daughters are lovely.

III   Boars' Teeth and Religion

It is not only a fighting war but a waiting war. In "Dry Rot," Joe, the shoemaker from Columbus, Ohio, wants only to serve his time and keep out of trouble. For twenty-seven months on a frizzling coral atoll west of the Solomons, he fights off the temptation to go rock-happy. He survives the tortures of jungle fungus and peeling skin, lack of whiskey and even water, and monotonous duty; but, after Luther Billis passes through and adopts the lonely sailor, Joe is able even to enjoy the beauties of moonlight on the Pacific shore. The new skipper manages to give Joe a chance to take a free nip of whiskey now and then, and life seems glorious when Billis the Seabee manages to fix up Joe with a lovely pen pal, Alice Baker. Joe is about to mail his picture to Alice when the tragic news of her death arrives. "I got to get out of here!" is the sailor's desperate decision. Twenty-seven months is too long a time to fight off the screaming meemies.

The longest story in the book—and one of the three main sources for the musical play—is "Fo' Dolla'." In it we meet the memorable Bloody Mary; her slight, shy daughter Liat; and big, virile marine lieutenant Joe Cable. But first we meet Atabrine Benny, philosophizing druggist from Waco, Texas, who travels around the islands administering antimalarial pills to all the civilians. On a jeep ride with Benny, the narrator first encounters the redoubtable Mary, an indentured laborer from Tonkin, China: "She was, I judge, about fifty-five. She was not more than five feet tall, weighed about 110 pounds, had few teeth and those funereally black, was sloppy in dress, and had thin ravines running out from the corners of her mouth. These ravines, about four on each side, were usually filled with betel juice, which made her look as if her mouth had been

gashed with a rusty razor. Her name, Bloody Mary, was well given"
(139).

With an oval, yellow face and with almond eyes beneath a
peachbasket hat, Mary is sly and aggressive; but people are fond of
her. She is an even bigger "dealer" than Luther Billis. She can sell a
grass skirt, dyed with atabrine pills, for "fo' dolla'," and she sells a
shrunken human head for fifty. With a volley of foul language
taught her by idle soldiers, she can vanquish all the military police
on the island. But her first sight of Joe Cable leads her to an unwonted subjection to orders because she starts at once to do her best
to obtain Joe as an American son-in-law.

Thereafter we follow Joe Cable's emotions as he makes his first,
rhapsodic visit to Bali-ha'i. This little island, just off Vanicoro, is a
Michener invention. Bali-ha'i has passed into our language as a symbol for the island of all our dreams: "Like a jewel, it could be
perceived in one loving glance. It was neat. It had majestic cliffs fac-
ing the open sea. It had a jagged hill to give it character. It was
green like something every youthful, and it seemed to curve itself
like a woman into the rough shadows formed by the volcanoes on the
greater island of Vanicoro" (147 - 48). Bali-ha'i is a refuge on which
have been collected all the South Pacific women who might be in-
sulted by rude G.I.'s: bare-breasted Gauguin girls of Polynesia,
high-heeled French ladies, nuns of the hospital staff—and Liat.

The idyllic, impossible love affair of the officer from Philadelphia
and the slim Tonkinese virgin is told at length—and with many
variations on the theme of interracial tension. The story must be
long because the increasing frenzy of Cable and the impossibility of
their marriage must develop like a lingering illness. Desperate with
passion, Cable forgets his work and sees his sweetheart again and
again: but, as time runs out, it becomes tragically clear that Joe,
even if he has thrown over his Bryn Mawr fiancée, cannot marry
Liat. She is coldheartedly sold by Bloody Mary to Benoit, the sloppy,
lustful French plantation owner. And Joe Cable is summoned to embark on the big push that will, we suspect, lead him to glory and the
cemetery at Hoga Point.

While they waited and worked, the men in the Pacific thought of
their wives at home and wrote to them letters revealing a variety of
personalities. In "Passion" we are given three kinds of love letters.
One is from a naive young sailor with a strong libido, who frankly ex-
changes nostalgic letters with his wife that could get them both
arrested. Dr. Paul Benoway, the meditative medico of LARU-8, who

has just survived the crash of a flying boat and four days of sizzling torture on a life raft, tries to write to his wife about this highest adventure of his life. "On the fourth day," he says, with unwonted lyricism, "when I saw the sun again, I felt like an Aztec's human sacrifice who waits at the end of the fiftieth year to see whether or not the sun will rise. Like him, I knew that when the sun rises again the world is saved and there is still hope. But like the Aztec I also knew that with the rising of the flaming beacon my individual torture would begin" (190 - 91). His words sound phoney, and he tears up the paragraph.

But later, as a censor, he reads the letter of Lieutenant Bill Harbison. Bill has written up their raft experience as if it were a yarn from *War Aces* in order to make himself appear to be the perfect lover as well as the heroic pilot. Benoway yields to temptation, and copies into his own letter two pages from the flyer's passionate screed. But it does not sound like the pedestrian style of the good doctor himself; it seems silly. He tears up the plagiarized pages and sends his original epistle, signed "All my love, Paul."

"A Boar's Tooth" is a story about religion. Luther Billis gets Tony Fry interested in the lovely ivory bracelets made from the curved tusks of the Melanesian boars raised by the savages in their villages on the volcanic slopes. Billis describes the sacred pigs:

> "All their lives they live in that little circle, tied to the tree. . . . The last four years must be real painful."
> "Four years?"
> "Yeah, it takes about seven years to grow a good tusk. It begins to enter the face about the fourth year. This here pig lived about five years after the tusks started through the bone."
> "How horrible!" Fry said.
> "Seems funny to me," Billis said. "But everyone I show this to always thinks about the pig. What about the people? They was mighty proud of this porker. It was the best pig in the area. It was sacred." (209, 211)

That night, Fry is drawn into an argument with a soured fellow officer about the sacred-pig religion. Fry says:

> "Pain is at the center of all religions. Almost all beauty, too. Fine things, like human beings, for example, are born of pain. Of great suffering. Of intense, in-driving horror. Fine things never come cheaply. . . . Here you are, staked out on a jungle island. . . . What holds you fellows here? A three-foot chain to the stake of custom? . . . I think there must be

something ennobling in this vast and timeless waste. Not to me, but to somebody who follows me. . . . Well, fifty years from now somewhere. . . . Let's say in Des Moines, Iowa—some high school girl will suddenly catch a faint intimation of what we accomplished out here." (212 - 13)

The "big dealer" Billis promotes a trip from Espíritu Santo to Vanicoro to see a special pig-killing celebration. In the party is little Chaplain Jones. On the way to the island in the crash boat, the chaplain gives a lecture on the religion of the Santa Cruz group: "I don't know of anything in the world quite like this pig worship. . . . Primarily it's a monument to man's perversity. There is no place on earth where living is so easy as on these islands. . . . But there was one flaw. Amid all this luxury there was no reason for living. . . . They created, at one swoop, something to live for. Now believe me when I tell you that they took one of the commonest things in their acquaintance, one of the dirtiest: a jungle pig" (214 - 15).

No detail is omitted of the ceremony at which the pigs are clubbed to death and carefully butchered. Dr. Benoway gets sick at the sight. The most perfect of pigs—his tusks had made two complete circles, burrowing for years twice through the pig's living face and once through the jawbone—is killed and his tusks are given as souvenirs, one to Fry and the other to the chaplain. The chaplain gives his away to the doctor, saying: "The appurtenances of the religion are slightly revolting." Fry laughs: "I feel that way myself, sometimes, on Sunday in Connecticut" (222).

IV *"You Didn't Know What War Was"*

"Wine for the Mess at Segi," a story of a Pacific Christmastide, reveals the secret of how Tony Fry got his liquid refreshments. He and Bus Adams take a last ride in the antiquated plane christened the "Bouncing Belch" (ordinarily used to ferry beer cases), along with the unnamed narrator, who now returns and incidentally reveals himself as a Harvard graduate (Fry the wangler is from Yale).

The crazy odyssey of the trio covers thousands of miles, from the Japanese-held Shortlands group in the north to New Caledonia in the south, where the battered flyers, on their way home with twenty-two cases of prime whiskey, visit the four beautiful De Becque sisters. The final-landing decision that Bus Adams has to make—with Tony, the liquor, and a traded washing machine in the bomb bay—results in the destruction of the "Belch" but in a hearty

Christmas party for the Segi mess. Their Christmas present from the skipper is the news that they have been chosen to hit the next beachhead. Their shout of thanks can be heard half a mile away along the shore.

"The Airstrip at Konora" is a hymn of praise to the Seabees, the Construction Battalions of civilians who could do anything from mending a zipper to constructing a landing field on a crooked little Pacific atoll under enemy fire. Big Commander Hoag, a contractor from Georgia, is untinged with the prejudices that would keep lesser officers from getting the most out of their working teams. Ordered to build the field that will be the main steppingstone toward the capture of Kuralei, he is also charged with putting down the airstrip in fifteen days after the landing of the marines.

Hoag is able to handle not only modern machinery but men like Lieutenant Pearlstein, who detects the possibility that a hidden ravine on the atoll might threaten disaster and who, once proved right, is given the job of filling in the ravine with equipment that is put out of action again and again. Hoag has to manage Seabees like Luther Billis, who will volunteer to make a suicidal night landing on occupied Konora to spy out the land and who shortly after will go AWOL—disappearing for two days to win a bet and coming back with two captured samurai swords as souvenirs.

The story is also about the importance of coral in the island-hopping saga of America in the Pacific war. The problem of finding a surfacing material for the airstrip is solved by dredging live coral from the reef and watering it with milk trucks to keep the coral insects alive and the landing field springy and porous. On this lifesaving strip, Bus Adams, forced down in his shot-up SBD fighter plane, is the first to land—on the eve of the day when the flight of bombers arrives just in time to begin operations against Kuralei. The builder is not there to greet them. A crazed Japanese, using himself as a living grenade, has committed hara-kiri in order to destroy Commander Hoag, "a free man, a man of thought and dignity, a man for whom other men would die" (225). But above, the bombers wheel and come in for their landings; from here they will proceed to Kuralei, to Manila, and to Tokyo.

On the Konora airstrip, while waiting for the final giant push against Kuralei, Bus Adams recalls melodramatic events in the house of the Frenchman's daughters back at Luana Pori on New Caledonia. The tragedy of the coming battle is made more poignant by the remembrance of the soft arms of half-caste Latouche Barzan

and of her three beautiful sisters. This plantation paradise, lux-
uriously furnished with pilfered American comforts, keeps open
house for all the American warriors. Achille Barzan, Latouche's es-
tranged husband, is hiding in the hills from his own people; and Bus
easily takes his place in her bedroom. He forgets time and his wife
back in the United States until Tony Fry shows up; and then, with
Bus an invalid after a gallant fight with drunken Bill Harbison, Fry
and Latouche have an even more romantic affair. The unwanted
husband, Achille, is shot by Latouche in "self-defense" in a carefully
planned murder; and she and Tony are married in a Buddhist temple ceremony.

At the end, all the sisters have done right by themselves. Laurencin has married a Yankee colonel. "I wrote to my mother about
Laurencin," confides Colonel Haricot. "Her being half Javanese,
you know. Mom was very broadminded. Been giving money to missions all her life." Josephine marries a sailor, who had helped to win
the beachhead at Konora. Marthe's sergeant was not so lucky, but
she was young yet and could look higher. And, when Tony asks Bus
to witness his will leaving everything to Latouche De Becque Barzan
Fry as his lawful wife, we fear she too will find that her bruised heart
can quickly heal.

The success of operation Alligator now depends upon a strike
against the fortified island of Kuralei. The last four sections of the
novel are all chapters in this operation, told by our narrator. In "The
Strike," he is assigned to the naval supply depot which is the heart of
the staging operation. In midsummer heat, this area of two square
miles of huts and dumps buzzes night and day with feverish activity.
In command is Captain Samuel Kelley, a supply corps officer par ex-
cellence. Annapolis-trained and a strict disciplinarian, he arouses
animosity and causes backbiting among his men; but the crucial
work of preparing the fleet for the landing goes forward. What seem
to be painfully unnecessary precautions by Kelley turn out to be
vital when a hurricane strikes the supply huts; all goods have been
stored in such a way as to support the walls against the destruction of
the high winds.

The arrival of flyer Bus Adams to serve on the liaison staff arouses
more animosity from Kelley than might be expected simply because
Bus wears a baseball cap and refuses to defer to navy spit and polish.
Tension mounts. An ammunition ship explodes in the bay before the
eyes of four of the ship's officers who are drinking in the club ashore
and who thereafter demonstrate that they are living on borrowed

time. And one of them reveals the secret of Kelley's dislike of aviators. The incident is used skillfully by Bus to gain him a transfer to a fighting squadron. Next afternoon he is on his way north to share in the bombing of Kuralei.

In "Frisco" the narrator spends the night in an LCS off Kuralei during the first great Pacific bombardment. The fleet is in action all around them, and in the crew's recreation room the men get ready for the landing next day in which they will face the brunt of the Japanese shellfire. In their various ways, the men recall their last view of America and comment on the adventures of the cook and others with the girls of San Francisco, white and yellow. In one corner sits Norval, a twenty-three-year-old fireman. All during the grim night of bombardment, Norval sits in the corner with a file, honing his bayonet to a razor edge and sharpening his dagger and even the spikes of his baseball shoes. At dawn, "in the gray twilight of D-Day the first wave was going in. Fire raked them as they hit the coral. Jap guns roared in the gray dawn. Men, human beings on two feet, men, crawling on their bellies over coral, with minds and doubtful thoughts and terrible longings. . . . Men took over" (304).

"The Landing on Kuralei" is Michener's full-dress battle piece. The strategists had been outguessed by a clever Japanese officer who had fortified the promontory overlooking the two landing beaches to the south of the vital island fortress. After a bloody repulse at Red Beach and Green Beach, Admiral Kester is forced to put into action an alternative landing at what the men at once christen Sonova Beach. Tanks battle tanks, planes fight planes, shells from battlewagons fall on friend and foe. Amid the typhoon of lead, human beings crawl from trench to trench and after dark win the blockhouse with searing flamethrowers. The battle plan, at immense human cost, is on schedule after all.

Some of the men of the previous tales appear again. Those of LARU-8 are in a transport that suffers a direct hit. Dr. Benoway gets off with a wound in the leg. Bill Harbison, of course, had managed to get transferred back to the States four days earlier. And Tony Fry, beachmaster, although told to stay behind, rushes into battle to repel a surprise flank attack: "The Japs got him right away. Two slugs in the belly. He kept plugging along. Finally fell over" (316).

Fry and the rest had reached the end of the long line extending from safe civilian life in the States all the way out through Noumea and Guadalcanal and the landing craft to the storming of the blockhouse. "No matter where along that line you stood," realizes the narrator, "if you were not the man at the end of it, the ultimate man with his sweating hands upon the blockhouse, you didn't know what war was. . . . By the grace of God you would never know" (317). The battle drops to a lull as two buddies settle down for the night in their foxhole. The gist of their argument is: Was the landing as bad as they feared it would be? And would the other landings be even tougher? This section foreshadows the remaining years of World War II not described in this novel.

V   *Men Lost in a Strange World*

After the crescendo of "The Landing on Kuralei" comes the diminuendo of the final chapter, "A Cemetery at Hoga Point." The narrator, with nerves shaken by the baptism at Kuralei, is on leave, fishing off Konora. Set ashore near the American cemetery on the cliff, where under the waving flag lie two hundred and eighty-one dead heroes, he ponders the meaning of war and life. He chats with the philosophizing black caretaker, to whom the men in the graves are friends. The best-tended grave is that of Commander Hoag, "about de bes' man I met in all de Navy," for to him colored men and Jews and Italians were equally human and fine.

At Hoga Point there are no officers and enlisted men; there are only *men*. Here is the grave of First Lieutenant Joe Cable, USMCR: "He go after dem Japs plenty tough. . . . Finally he git his. Go down all in a lump. Dey tell me de colonel see him go. . . . I figger he pretty glad he let de lieutenant outen de brig. But maybe he ain' so glad, neither. 'Cause if he keep de young man locked up, he be alive now" (324 - 25). Liat's lover is merely one of the heroes at Hoga Point, about whom the caretaker—back home in Mississippi he used to call himself a "preacher"—can continue to speculate. For "Each man who lay on Hoga Point bore with him to his grave some promise for a free America. Now they were gone. Who would take their places?" (325).

Of his final chapter, Michener himself has commented: "Most perceptive readers of the book felt that the last story, 'A Cemetery at Hoga Point,' was the best thing in it, an opinion with which I am somewhat inclined to agree, for if I had any purpose in writing it was to extol the brotherhood that we seem able to attain only in cemeteries."[12] We know that he usually does have a purpose in his writing, and we can guess that the main theme of the book does have much to do with the idea that all men are brothers under the skin, and that the crucible of war hastens the process of revelation of character.

Awakening did come to many Americans during the tests of the Pacific war. They found they could be brave or cowardly; enduring or despairing; and, above all, blind to or able to see the common humanity beneath uniforms or dusky skins. The attitude toward interracial love evident in such stories as "Fo' Dolla'," "Our Heroine," or "Those Who Fraternize" was responsible for Michener's main expression of opinion when the musical play *South Pacific* came to be staged—in fact, his only expression.

"I had absolutely nothing to do with the Rodgers and Hammerstein musical and did not even attend any of the rehearsals, seeing the show for the first time in the final run-through," he said in 1956.[13] "I contributed no dialog, no additional story line, no staging ideas."

I recall that after the tryout in New Haven, a group of experienced theatrical people who wanted the play to be a success visited me to see if I could persuade Rodgers and Hammerstein to remove from the second act their song on race relations, "You Have to be Taught." Many others brought heavy pressure on them to eliminate this controversial number, but the authors replied sturdily that this one represented why they had wanted to do this play, and that even if it meant the failure of the production it was going to stay in. And as the well-wishers foresaw, many of the major reviews panned the song, as an interruption. But as the play matured it was found that this song was more often praised than any other. I think that courage and determination such as this count for something in art.

The play was banned in South Africa in 1964 as "a plea for the mixing of races."

The themes of the novel are made flesh in a wide variety of characters who under the stress of war in the tropics reveal themselves as brave or craven, broad-minded or prejudiced, passionate or cold. Michener gives a broader view of men and women in the Pacific, at play or on operations, than any other novelist of World War II. They are shown on PT boats, on landing craft, on battleships, on ammunition carriers, and on submarines; they are men of the Supply Corps or the Seabees or repair units; they are doctors and nurses; they are cacao planters or coast-watchers or Australian missionaries; they sit on lonely atolls or dash ashore in combat to die. Of special interest are men like Tony Fry, who says: "I like these islands. I've got some cash. Maybe life here is what I've been looking for. This Pacific will be the center of the new world. This is our future. Well, I'm part of it. This is for me" (276). Have other Tony Frys returned to the Pacific after the war to settle an American frontier in this ocean?

The action of the novel is varied as well. Plots of the different episodes range from almost nothing ("Alligator") to complicated melodrama ("Those Who Fraternize"). Although the novel culminates in combat, many chapters deal with other types of conflict.

Perhaps the most enduring value of *Tales of the South Pacific* is the use of setting. Michener's firsthand knowledge of almost all his scenes and his deep understanding of the history of the region enable him to utilize local color as a motivating force in the evolution of character.

Dealing with the earlier years of the war, when all the native glamor and jungle riot had not been leveled by the bulldozers, Michener was freer to depict the effect of the environment on Americans. He reveals also that he is aware of the provincialism both of the natives and of the Americans; and he uses it for plot purposes. Preoccupation with the exotic might open him to the charge of being a naive romanticist. However, his reportorial eye was so keen that through it we see the Pacific with a wealth of sharp detail. He can spend three paragraphs to describe a sunrise (183) or to render a hurricane (293). He can stop to depict with realistic care the colors of a cacao grove (102) or the horrors of a land-crab invasion (228, 234). He mentions that the men in the southern hemisphere see Orion upside down. Other men in a quonset hut on the morning of a hot day can hear the metal "expanding in little crackles. New men always thought it was rain, but it was the sun" (57). He can explode our preconceptions by the casual remark that Segi Point is "the only place out here I know that looks like the South Pacific" (80). Realistic treatment of exotic materials by a writer such as Michener is not mere dreamy romanticism.

Michener was surprised and pleased that his novel was selected for a Pulitzer prize; for, as he said, "if I held no great brief for the stories as art, I was indelibly convinced that they could never be challenged as a truthful and sometimes probing analysis of men lost in a strange world."[14] He had hopes, too, that his volume would be a "solid emotional source book of the Pacific," particularly for future work, by unknown authors. "Some very great novels are going to come out of the Pacific experience," he predicted in 1948.[15] In that

54

year appeared Norman Mailer's *The Naked and the Dead*, and thereafter such Pacific war novels as James Jones's *From Here to Eternity* and Ira Wolfert's twice-written *An Act of Love*. But in 1951 Michener stated that he thought the great novel of the Pacific war was still to be written.[16] Quite likely, *Tales of the South Pacific* is that book. Looking back thirty years later, I feel that the best picture of what that war was like is to be found on Michener's broad canvas. Who has painted a better one?

CHAPTER 3

Homeward Journey and Return

MICHENER, speaking in 1948 to some students at Washington and Lee University, was angered when one of them remarked: "It's easy for you to write. You've traveled." He responded that it was his intention never again to write about foreign lands. "The writer's job," he added, "is to dig down where he is. He must write about the solid, simple things of his own land."[1]

Michener was working at the time on a big book tentatively titled "The Homeward Journey" that was published early in 1949 as *The Fires of Spring*. It was truly about solid, simple American things. More than slightly autobiographical, it was the sort of book about growing up in the world that most writers turn out as a first novel. Unconventional as usual, Michener wrote his "first" novel second. As a freelance writer, Michener could have continued for several years to sell stories in the vein of his Pacific fiction; indeed, old-timers in Australia still tell him: "If you had kept at it, you could have become the twentieth-century Louis Becke."

"Yancy and the Blue Fish," which might easily have appeared in *Tales of the South Pacific*, appeared in the *Ladies' Home Journal*. It concerns a tattooed Georgian, a "mustang" officer risen from the naval ranks, who fights the war with vigor even though his worthless wife back home has run away and deserted their daughter. Yancy, helping to occupy the island of Emirau which flanked the Japanese bases at Kavieng, specializes in rescuing and resettling island people who have suffered under the Japanese. He is a leader in the establishing of a new village on the island of Mussau because he speaks Chinese, and it seems for a while that he is able to sublimate his love life only by his almost lunatic efforts to keep alive a transparent blue fish picked up on the reef. When he hears that his wife has returned home, Yancy forsakes the lovely Chinese refugee girl and tosses his fish bowl over the cliff.

56

Another *Journal* story, which could have been written by others familiar with the campus setting during the overcrowded postwar conditions under the earliest G.I. Bill, is "The Empty Room." The self-pitying dreams of a mourning faculty couple who lost a son in the war are broken by the demand that they house two young veterans. The complications are slick but plausible, and at times the sincerity of the theme overcomes the soapiness of the plot. The women's magazines lost nothing when Michener decided not to spend time writing short stories that others could do as well as he.

I *"People, Just as They Are"*

The Fires of Spring, like these two stories, was written before Michener's share in the Rodgers and Hammerstein musical play gave him an assured income. The book is indeed about Americans in America; and, although David's travels cover a number of states, it centers around his boyhood in Doylestown, Bucks County, Pennsylvania; his summers as a cashier in an amusement park near Philadelphia; his college career at an institution not too different from Swarthmore; his travels on the Chautauqua circuit; and his struggles in Greenwich Village to learn the craft of the writer.

David is deliberately a less interesting character than the people he encounters. Michener was aware, however, of the danger of portraying a pallid hero. And David is more than an average lad; few young Americans of his time were orphans living in a poorhouse, or self-supporting shortchange artists at the age of fifteen, or traveling actors or protégés of rich bootleggers.

Nonetheless, thousands of young Americans have found in this book frankness and a voicing of their own attitudes, to which they respond gratefully. Of *The Fires of Spring* the author has said: "I get more mail about it than about anything else I've ever written, and a good deal of the mail is almost illiterate. It has a tremendous appeal for young people, particularly for boys in military service or people away from home for the first time. . . . I am somewhat depressed by the fact that the IQ of the people who praise it to the skies, judging from their handwriting, would not be very high."[2] This book was also the Michener title most immediately recollected as enjoyable by John F. Kennedy.[3]

Critics who expected another *Tales of the South Pacific* were less enthusiastic than Michener's correspondents about *The Fires of Spring*. Orville Prescott reported: "Mr. Michener is fine with his host of minor characters. But the passionate women in David's life are less convincing, and David himself is of little interest. *The Fires of Spring* is somewhat sentimental and sententious."[4] A similar basic weakness in the lack of definition of David's character was noted by G. D. MacDonald, who added: "The first two sections with a poorhouse and amusement park background are brilliantly done."[5] William Du Bois agreed that "For all his haste, Mr. Michener's anger at life is sincere. It is a pity he did not let his notes age a bit longer—or, at least, that he did not take the time to dramatize his anger in believable terms."[6] Perhaps the fairest review was that of Horace Reynolds, who said, in part: "There are commendable things in this novel. Mr. Michener writes with gusto and a good sense of story. . . . The stream of American life through which the hero walks, seeking both its meaning and knowledge of himself, is well realized. . . . Mr. Michener is addicted to melodrama, violence, and coincidence, and his story does not have the clarity of outline, the control and reserve his character David finds in Henry James."[7]

In Part I, "The Poorhouse," David Harper, eleven-year-old orphan, is living with his aunt, Reba Stücke, in the county home. She beats him often, but the old inmates are usually kind to the boy; and the home is an exciting place where an alert, sandy-haired, freckled kid can observe life. Like Huck Finn, David is exposed to tragedy and violence. He twice discovers old men who have hanged themselves; a homosexual is found floating in the water tank; David wrestles with a madman, Luther; and he watches a mad woman eat flies. He has early experience of the paradoxes of sex—his friend Toothless Tom is caught peering at little girls on the bank of the swimming hole. David feels a fondness for Marcia Paxton, a Quaker girl, and with borrowed pennies treats her and her family to loganberry juice at Paradise Park.

Most of the year, David finds life satisfying. But "Spring in a country poorhouse is a time of pain. . . . The men do not await refreshing breezes. They await the haunting memories of their youth" (21).[8] In David, cheerful failures like Old Daniel see a promise of fulfillment that is worth all their encouragement. The boy's desire to write springs from his disillusion when he discovers that Hector and the other heroes of Troy could be beaten. "When I write a story," he explains, "the good people always win." Old Daniel forbears to deal the blow that would make the lad face too early the grim inexplicability of things as they are. Yet on his death-bed, Daniel does try to advise David and to explain to him that the earth is not an evil place: "But it's quite possible for a man in America to lead a good life and die in the poorhouse" (38).

In this limbo, roles are reversed. David is a child, but he is getting an education: "He was the man! He was the man who would avoid the terrible errors that had brought them to the poorhouse. And they were the children, looking forward to the distant day that would never dawn for them" (8).

Part II, "Paradise," shows David leading a double life. He is a ready learner in high school, especially when Miss Chaloner opens to him the magic door of mathematics; and he is also a star forward on the basketball team. In the summers he is a skilled cashier at Paradise Park, who has learned not to cheat unduly the company that hires him but who is an expert at shortchanging the yokels by all the arts of coins or bills. He resists the temptations of the little crook Max Volo and the pessimism of hardhearted Mr. Stone, to whom "people are cattle." He is a friend of Captain John Philip Sousa, of the bandmaster's singer Mary (later Mona) Meigs, and of the sensitive European musician Klementi Kol, who initiates David into art galleries and to the candors of Hardy, Balzac, and Oscar Wilde.

David still lives in the poorhouse; but, when working at Paradise, he is a man of the world. And at fifteen he falls in love with an unattractive little prostitute who lives in a den under the Coal Mine concession. He pays her way to spend the winter in Colorado to help her lung condition, but she goes off with a man to Florida instead. When she returns, he makes an assignation with her that would have been dangerous to his future. This human bondage is ended an hour before the meeting when Nora burns to death in an accidental fire. David does not play the Dutch bundling game enjoyed by his schoolmates like Harry Moomaugh. But Marcia Paxton's lips are cool, and Mary Meigs does not object too much when his boyish kiss musses her coiffure.

Recipient of a scholarship from a mysterious donor—in Part III, "Fair Dedham"—David enters Dedham College as a freshman. He goes through a busy period of further intellectual and emotional awakening. What seems to the reader like one year is really four years. At this Quaker college, which bears some resemblance to Swarthmore, David falls under the spell of the White Russian mathematics professor, Tschilczynski; but he finds that there is "no mathematical certainty in life" and that the professor does not have all the answers. Nor does David's pal Joe Vaux, the radical Bostonian Irishman. Iconoclastic young Mr. Thorpe broadens David's appreciation of modern art by disturbing his old convictions. But not even Doc Chisholm, who teaches David how to read a novel and to enjoy cowboy songs, can remain the true messiah, even though he points out that books are the spirit of man and "the spirit of man jes' plain ain't purty. Yew can call it magnificent or bewilderin' or powerful to the point of despair. But it ain't college-English purty. And yew ought to stop writin' as if it was" (237 - 38). David concludes not to be a mathematician but to study people: " 'People, just as they are.' And that was the beginning of his education" (238).

II   *Chautauqua and Greenwich Village*

David's progress as a scholar is disturbed by his affair with Mona Meigs, now a lovely vaudeville actress. She is the mistress of kind Kol Klementi, but she satisfies herself with the passion of young David when Uncle Klim is away on concert tours. When David and Mona are caught at last, they gaily go to a college "prom"; Kol, with his last illusion gone, shoots himself. When Mona decides to storm Hollywood, she gets David to borrow five thousand dollars from Max Volo, now a big-shot gangster. David's involvement with Max and the bacchanalian rout almost causes him to fail on his Chaucer paper, but he fights through his week of honors examinations and is awarded a *summa cum laude* amid cheers from "the only American college where the student body could get as excited about distinguished scholarship as it did about football" (266).

David is awarded a fellowship at the University of Chicago, and he starts to spend the intervening summer working on the Paxton farm near New Hope, with echoes of great poetry running through his head. It is clear that he and Marcia will soon marry and settle down, but David is not yet ready. He has not seen anything of his native land, broad America. "He did not want to be a college professor. He felt that surely somewhere there must be a more urgent life than that. Nor did he want to marry Marcia." When a phone call comes from Mona, David is ready to say farewell to Doylestown and to hit the road.

In Part IV, "Chautauqua," it is the summer of 1929 and the end of an economic era. It is also time for the last appearance of the traveling tent shows of the Chautauqua circuit. Mona has recommended David to be a low-paid juvenile actor, puppeteer's assistant, and general roustabout in the Cyril Hargreaves Troupe of Broadway Players. She is the ingenue and the mistress of sixty-six-year-old Director Hargreaves, who takes the role of Judge Hardy in *Skidding* and saves on cast salaries by handling a dozen other roles on the stage telephone.

If, as Michener suggests, growing up is the process of seeing things as they actually are, then the knowledge David gains from his fellow members of the troupe brings greater maturity. He admires dwarf Vito Bellotti, who plays the boy Andy Hardy and manipulates the strings of the puppet show while scanning the audience for a girl dwarf that he might be able to marry. David also admires the frank hedonism and lovemaking of Wild Man Jensen, ex-football star and truck driver. Most of all, he learns about life and the glamor of the stage from Emma Clews, for some reason called the Gonoph; aged forty-four and a dumpy theatrical veteran, she attaches herself to David and helps him see things as they are.

David rubs against the beauty, the harshness, and the mystery of America during the summer tour. He also begins to see life not through the eyes of others but through his own. The terrifying tornado episode tests his courage and reveals the truth that the world is "a superb flowing organization of people of which he was not the selfish center. Whether he lived or died was of no moment; and that discovery—which many young men never make—was the threshold by which David passed from callow youth to manhood" (317). But even when vengeful Hargreaves lies to Max Volo and gets David beaten up by the bootlegger's henchmen, the young man holds no grudge. He is learning that the motives of people are seldom unmixed strains of good or evil. And his jealousy of Jensen's acting ability strangely leads David to find a bride for Vito, the dwarf.

In Part Five, "The Valley," threads of lives are reentwined and at last unraveled. In the winter of 1931 David has come to Greenwich Village—"the hidden valley between the breasts of Manhattan"—to learn how to be a writer. Through Alison Webster, a pretty young redhead he had met during his Chautauqua days, he gets a job with Clay Publications, which turns out more than a score of pulp magazines—the "cleanest filth" purveyed to the mass of America's literates. He works for the gifted Morris Binder, born editor and armchair detective who loves music (he has rigged up, with half a dozen radios, a set foreshadowing the hi-fi of today) but who cannot attend concerts because he is subject to unexpected convulsive fits.

Alison writes for money and knows all the clever tricks, but David hates himself when he yields to the temptation to turn out anything insincere. She is on the way up but he is content to live in the bohemian boardinghouse of Mom Beckett on MacDougal Street, just off

Washington Square with its ghosts of Eugene O'Neill and Theodore Dreiser. Mom, a battling Amazon from Arizona, does not write books; she "lives them." In her lifetime she has fed more than forty writers as if they were stray animals; David, along with the rest, is termed a "horse's ass" for thus wasting his effort. Mom supports Claude, a bearded innocent who is "America's greatest poet," and pays for the publication of his verses; but she also makes him put together the meals whenever she has fired the Chinese cook.

After a year as assistant editor for Clay Publications, David is forced to join the jobseekers of March, 1932. There is no place for him in the depths of the depression, and he sweeps out the boardinghouse and lives on Mom's handouts, shared with Mona Meigs, who is again broke. She has deserted the dying old Hargreaves; David helps her and even the old actor. For a while he is happy with Mona, until she goes off to become Max Volo's "moll."

The next winter Reba Stücke dies, but her savings are tied up and David has to borrow fifty dollars to bury his mother's sister. In Bucks County he finds that Marcia Paxton, who had married Harry Moomaugh, is hurting the family name by getting a divorce. Mona Meigs dramatically returns to David to hide out from the gang murderers of Volo but then obtains publicity by putting "the finger" on the culprits. When her next "big chance" arrives, David submits to the abasement of masquerading as her chauffeur. He becomes encompassed in the vast ugliness of human life in a violent world. Yet it is the same world in which Max Volo secretly donated the cost of a fine young man's college education.

David, writing his novel at last and saving his pennies, lands in the hospital; and there he finds Marcia doing penance in the wards. When Miss Adams, Binder's secretary, nurse, and mistress, murders her boss because he is losing his mind, jobless David is thrust into the editor's chair. But he quits that post to go back to Mom's, finish his novel, and return to Bucks County. Ironically, his aunt's savings are given to Mona Meigs for another "big chance"—the Harpers do not wish to start their married life with poorhouse money. Journeying homeward, after a humble Quaker wedding, David and Marcia have found themselves at last.

III *Cleansed of the Autobiographical Itch*

Since *The Fires of Spring* is primarily the portrait of a literary artist as a young man, we expect and receive a number of comments about writers and writing. For instance, Doc Chisholm recommends to David the reading of "mordant novels"—those which cut away all pretense from the inner being of the reader. "Mordant novels are often ugly novels," he says. "There is sand and gristle in them, and Ah can't name four that are well written." He directs his students to *Moby Dick*, *Casuals of the Sea*, *Oblomov*, and *The Old Wives' Tale*. It is more than probable that Michener feels the best books are those which have not only strong themes but high intensity and impact on their audience.

The financial contrast between great writers such as Claude and a cheap hoodlum standing in the bar with a roll of greenbacks is also ironic. In this world, writing as an art has nothing to do with marketable writing such as manufactured by David for *Bare Confessions*, *Real Love*, and *Rodeo Yarns*. And Claude gives David the best distinction he has heard between a novel and a poem: "A novel is a golden kettle into which you pour all of experience. . . . A poet tries to say it all in a few lines." Good poems are "distillations of books" (398).

In a moment of dedication, David realizes: "Writing is like that. Seeing what no one has ever seen before and writing it down so simply that everyone will say, 'Of course! I knew that all along.' If I can see, I can write. . . . If I could see into the core of some one thing each day, say a horse eating oats, or a ferryboat, or the way a chair stands on the floor, I'd soon be so terribly filled with material that they couldn't stop me from writing. Not even with machine guns. . . . There's no reason why I couldn't write as well as Balzac" (420).

David creates whole chapters of the novel in his mind, feeling almost as good as if he had committed them to paper. The characters, still nameless, come to have greater reality for him than people he meets on the street. Once he spends a whole day trying to evolve a name for a woman. He conceives the idea that, if he could only find the right name, his book would be half written. Like a pregnant woman, he feels embarrassed to talk about the ideas he is carrying. He feels that too much talk might bring his offspring bad luck (452). Later he begins to experience

one of the most unbelievable phenomena of art. He had a novel completely written in his mind. . . . Yet he could not write!

How can it be that a man can even see the finished printed page in his eye, can taste the plaudits of a job well done, and yet be unable to push a pen across a paper or strike one reluctant key? . . . He had never previously bothered about drinking, but now when he could borrow money from Mom he wandered into one recently opened bar after another, explaining to anyone who would listen the details of his book. (465)

David gets most encouragement from gray, prim Miss Adams, the secretary of Clay Publications. She predicts he will be a fine writer, but she heavily edits his opening paragraph by knocking out words. He uses too many adjectives and adverbs, she says. "And David, please don't use words like *beloved*. If your little boy loves the barges, let him show it." But he objects strongly: "When I write I want everything that happens to be absolutely clear. If I think the reader won't catch it, I'm going to say it right out" (454).

Quite likely, the mature Michener would still be on David's side. Pope's maxim of "Be thou clear" appeals to him. Michener is less fearful of adjectives and adverbs than most American writers today. If he thinks that something is interesting or beautiful, he says so. For him, style is not the art of getting along without adjectives.

Did Michener try to pour into this "golden kettle," *The Fires of Spring*, more than the novel form can comfortably contain? The theme is strong, and is reinforced by many little homilies on life and love and education that caused reviewers to label the book "sententious."

The characters are numerous, and each bears almost an allegorical position in the progress of the young pilgrim in search of himself. There is pattern in their appearance—David's bondage to Nora is repeated in his enslavement to Mona, who turns out to be the heroine of his novel manuscript. Mona is in many ways supposed to be much like David, but she has sold herself from the start to the Bitch Goddess. Some of the characters stick in the memory—the aging actor Hargreaves, the pathetic Gonoph, Wild Man Jensen with his signal broom above the back of the truck. Other characters, however, seem to have been devised for plot purposes or drawn from the stock shelf. Again and again, the autobiographical urge is evident in David's responses, and his life, like that of some of the other characters, is too close to actuality to enable the novelist to handle it with suitable "distance."

The plot is also a bit too pat. The path of David as a lad who strives to grow up has often been trodden before. The arm of coincidence—for example, in the timing of the death of Nora or the murder of Binder—is sometimes stretched to the fracture point. The final wedding scene is almost a curtain call for the cast.

Primarily, this novel is memorable for the use of setting observed by the author as he lived through his own growing-up period. Michener never was the editor of pulp magazines, but it is possible for him to have seen and done most of the other things that David Harper sees and does. The college period and the Greenwich Village days have been handled better by other novelists. Most memorable of all are probably the early poorhouse scenes and the warm re-creation of life while traveling the roads of America with the brown tents of Chautauqua.

In this early novel, which still seems too uncontrolled to have been written by the author of *Tales of the South Pacific*, Michener—like Thomas Wolfe—looked homeward and used up the material which his early life had accumulated for him. *The Fires of Spring* is better than most *Bildungsromane*. Its greatest value, though, is that it purged its author of the autobiographical itch. Thenceforward, as a born reporter, he would gather and reproduce the lives of many people less close to him, and he would also achieve again and again what Keats called "negative capability." Villages either in Pennsylvania or Manhattan could not continue to engage the man who had roved through Europe and the Pacific.

IV *Kim Sing Gets the Baby*

The Pacific, in fact, still beckoned to Michener. Royalties from the musical *South Pacific* gave him a steady income and freedom to experiment as an author. Despite his vow never again to write about foreign lands, he accepted magazine commissions to revisit and to report on the scenes of his first novel. *Return to Paradise* is in part the book of a former serviceman who comes back to his wartime haunts after a lapse of five years. (Originally meaning Hawaii, the "Paradise of the Pacific," the term "Paradise" came to be extended to the whole Pacific region.)

This adventure, Michener felt, would be "intellectually honorable" if he tried to put his material into a form that had never before been used. He wrote a series of fact-crammed essays about all these places. Then he wrote a series of stories growing out of the themes of the essays. Thus the reader could see from each essay what Michener thought about the region, and from the companion story the reader could determine what the region thought about itself. This sandwich system of producing a volume that could not be wholly labeled either as fiction or as nonfiction was viewed with disfavor by everyone else connected with the enterprise; but Michener felt that for this particular purpose the device would justify itself. The format was paid the compliment of imitation by Eugene Burdick in 1961 in *The Blue of Capricorn*.

The resulting volume, avowedly a *tour de force*, was highly successful and was chosen in 1951 as an offering of the Book-of-the-Month Club. Michener was called "a Gunther with a dash or two of Dr. Kinsey" by Riley Hughes in the *Catholic World*,[9] but his work was termed by the *Chicago Sunday Tribune*[10] "a brilliant book and a worthy successor to *Tales of the South Pacific*." P. V. Farrell remarked: "Michener conveys the beauty and color of the islands, sensitively and perceptively. More than that, he carefully, imperceptibly, without grinding any axes, reaffirms the human dignity of even the most primitive savage and our responsibility to respect it. This is most welcome now, when the peoples of the world are suddenly being 'discovered' by Americans, variously as customers for creature comforts, decimal points in a Point IV program, birth control prospects, sandbags against Communism, or eventually, votes."[11] Robert Payne concluded: "It is when Mr. Michener describes his travels that he is most convincing, and the mature eye, selecting fragments of experience from the past and then setting them against the present, possesses a splendid power of evocation."[12]

Return to Paradise will be read with pleasure for years to come, and to one who knows anything about the Pacific Ocean area the descriptive sections will remain classic treatments. Michener was, moreover, fully aware of the tradition of South Sea fiction in which he was working.[13] "No writer need be ashamed of punishing his legs while trying to reach the footsteps of Conrad, Melville, Maugham, or James Norman Hall," he remarks in "The Mighty Ocean," the opening section.

His apprehension that his long journey around the Pacific might result in another heartbreaking trip of disillusion was not fulfilled. He had not lost his fascination with the atolls, the jungles, and the sprawling Australasian cities, nor his zest for making a travel essay into a clearly focused medium of illumination. Indeed, he deliberately made his nonfiction colorful and exotic, but he rigidly excluded from the stories the lush overwriting so common in the usual "South Sea stuff." He succeeded so well that, when films came to be made from several of these stories, the movie makers found that to feed their scenarios they had to purchase the rights not only to the fiction but to the companion factual essay as well!

In addition to the prologue and epilogue, the essay sections of
Return to Paradise cover nine regions. Most of the pieces appeared
in *Holiday* magazine with color illustrations. The guidebook information they contain is not too dated, but the scenes and peoples of
the places visited are the most memorable parts.

A section on the first region, "The Atoll," has been reprinted in
college rhetoric books as an example of inspired structural skill. It
was written, Michener told me, out of the practical necessity to explain to the ordinary reader just how an atoll was built and what it
was like to stand on one. It is followed by portraits of several "atoll
men" he has known, white wanderers such as the writer Robert
Dean Frisbie, for whose daughter's book Michener later found a
publisher. "Much romantic nonsense has been written about the
atolls," Michener concludes. "A thousand wastrels have befouled
the islands; a hundred sentimentalists have defamed them. But
there still remains this fact: when the great seas pound upon the
reef, when the stars shine down upon the lagoon, there is a
mysterious, fragile something that no amount of misrepresentation
can destroy."

Wartime memories helped Michener make vivid his return to
such hallowed spots as Guadalcanal, Espíritu Santo, New Guinea,
and Rabaul. His essays on Polynesia, Fiji, Australia, and New
Zealand served well to prepare me for my own year in the South
Pacific. The visitor to Fiji, for example, cannot but recognize—as he
drives around the rutted roads of Viti Levu—the "mynah birds," the
unsmiling Indian women in their rainbow saris, the scowling
shopkeeping Indian men, the grave children of the race that has out-
bred the happy Fijians in their own islands. Motivated by his hymn
of praise for the Huka Lodge of Alan Pye, high priest of New
Zealand fly fishermen, we spent some wonderful days in the
mysterious white cottage on the banks of the brawling Waikato
River near the volcanoes of the North Island.

Readers of Michener who learn that a planet can cast over the still
waters of the Pacific a glow almost as bright as a northern moon-path
will seek, and find, their own star-paths. For years to come, the
readers of *Return to Paradise* will be aroused to see for themselves
the Pacific wonderlands that are now opening up more and more to
visitors, even though the Tahiti that Michener revisited in 1950 is
already as lost as the "New Cytherea" of the bare-breasted Polynesian nymphs that greeted the seamen of Bougainville's day.

The stories accompanying the travel essays, because they were admittedly written to voice a theme about a place, were assumed by reviewers to have been mechanically turned out to fit this need. Actually, some of the "local-color" fiction in this book belongs with Michener's best.

"Mr. Morgan," which furnished the scenario for the superb Gary Cooper film "Return to Paradise," was one of the two stories in the book that appeared first in magazine form. The narrator is a young native of the island of Matareva. The clash between the sanctimonious and lustful churchwardens of Pastor Cobbett and the war-weary Yank, Morgan, who merely seeks a refuge, can arouse the reader's fighting spirit. Worth pointing out, however, is the fact that Morgan is a "moral zero" and the pastor, his opponent, does stand for a doctrine even though at first it is tyrannically enforced. This is not the usual island love story, either; Morgan does not realize how much Maeva could have shown him until she is dead of tuberculosis. Nor does it end with an American marriage in the second generation. Harry Faber,[14] pilot of the World War II C-47 saved by a night landing in the Matareva lagoon, does return to his paradise; but, because he is a "bird of passages," he is driven off by Morgan in the role of irate parent. Morgan's daughter Turia weds a native lad when she is properly pregnant. After the ceremony, Morgan spends his time talking things over with another old man, the saintly Pastor Cobbett.

"Povenaaa's Daughter" also is one of Michener's best stories. It is an easygoing evocation of postwar Tahiti, when the Americans returned to the islands—in yachts. The seventeen-year-old heroine, Teuru of Raiatea, is ordered by whiskery, drunken Povenaaa to go along with the more experienced Hedi to Papeete to find a rich American. But, instead, Teuru's charms are showered on unworthy objects. First she brings home a young French poet, Victor, who insults Teuru by asking her to marry him. He goes back to France, and she goes back to Papeete. Next she brings home the small, old British sculptor Earl Weebles, who dies and is buried by the straits of Raiatea after having created great statues of the Polynesian people who set out from there on voyages of high discovery. Next Teuru, going to Papeete for the third time, fails to make a smug marriage as did Hedi, but she rehabilitates the gin-soaked beachcomber Johnny Roe. Povenaaa is pleased when at last she brings home to Raiatea an American—but this one has spent all his travelers' checks and Povenaaa still cannot buy that secondhand jeep on Bora Bora. When Teuru finally has an American baby on the way, Kim Sing, local

Chinese vanilla planter, wins it on a cast of the dice; and Johnny
goes back to America on a yacht. The ending is happy: Kim Sing
gets the baby and the mother too, in a proper island marriage. And,
of course, it turns out that, since all Polynesian first babies are given
away to a friend, Teuru is not really skinny old Povenaaa's daughter
after all.

This story is long because time must be allowed for Teuru to pass
through her various involvements with men of four nationalities.
Space is also required for the creation of the atmosphere of Papeete
and Raiatea, regions that will never again be the same as they were
right after World War II.

V *What He Learned in Paradise*

In Michener's essay on Fiji, his almost universal charity for the
nationalities of the world clearly does not extend to the immigrant
East Indians who had come to those islands and, by raising large
families, had outnumbered the native Fijians. "Soon," Michener
predicted in 1950, "they will outnumber all the other races combined, and it seems inevitable that Fiji must one day become a
colony owned, populated, and governed by Indians."[15] His story
"The Mynah Birds" likens the restive, revolutionary Indians to the
greedy, quarrelsome Asian birds which have invaded many a
peaceful Pacific island and driven out the native avifauna. But
Ramcheck Billimoria, the Indian fanatic, is contrasted with the lovely Indian girl, Pata Cadi, whom he stabs because she has been going
with an American airport engineer, Joe Harvey.

The story also gives occasion for Michener to contrast a British official, of the sort that has effectively administered overseas
possessions for generations, with the brash American State Department representative Louis Richardson McGurn, one of the breed
that must now take over such administration in many far-flung man-
dates. The irony lies in the fact that Sir Charles's family admires
American things, but McGurn is trying so hard to be more British
than the British that he even legally drops his last name because it
has Boston Irish origins! McGurn, trying to hold civilization
together, considers Joe Harvey to be the new American barbarian
who will damage our nation in the eyes of the world, but at least Joe
is a warm human being. McGurn may become human only if his
British sweetheart can extract the stuffing from his shirt and get him
to relax at a yangona party.

"The Story" is set on postwar Guadalcanal. The narrator, a writer, is besieged like all writers by people who want to collaborate with him by telling him a wonderful plot which he will write down, dress up, and sell for a fortune. Such a person is cadaverous Larcom, marked by many years of living in the tropics. Like Captain Handy in James Norman Hall's great story, "Occupation: Journalist," Larcom has a story to sell, and it is a mixture of trite romance and raw reminiscence from his patchwork past. The climax is supposed to come when an American Marine from Brooklyn, who had found a Solomon Island valley of gold and then lost it, flies in frenzy into a mountainside. As he burns to death, the valley shines in a golden glow.

The author rejects the offer to buy the story but during later encounters with Larcom it transpires that there actually was a Brooklyn American and a valley, not to mention a Jewish father seeking the body of his flyer son. It further develops that Larcom had played a heroic role as a coast-watcher on Bougainville, and that he had cherished a promising son, murdered by the Stern Gang in Jerusalem. The story of Larcom's life is more dramatic than any literature Larcom could fabricate. And again Michener's sympathies for men and women of all races is woven into the narrative.

Interracial tension is prominent in the Espíritu Santo story, "The Good Life." The narrator, a British civil servant of the Anglo-French Condominium ruling the New Hebrides, gingerly participates in the gay life of the French cacao planter, Perouse, whose home much resembles that of De Becque in "Our Heroine." Perouse likes to live at peace not only with his imported Australian or French girl guests but also with the Tonkinese laborers such as Nguyen Bo, whose family works hard to improve its lot. Perouse becomes unpopular by figuratively labeling as a "murderer" anyone who thinks he can keep backward races backward much longer. A riot on the eve of Bastile Day results in the literal murder of Nguyen Bo and his wife and in the maiming of Perouse. But Perouse survives to carry on his ideas of the "good life" through a slow evolutionary improvement and through the immediate adoption of Nguyen Bo's beautiful teenage daughters. "The Good Life" is the only story in the book in which no American character appears.

The New Zealand essay is reinforced by a lengthy story, "Until They Sail," which was finally made into a film by a British company. It covers the lives of members of a Christchurch family from the eve of World War II through V-J Day. Captain Harry Neville, his wife, and their five children form a unified group which is slowly broken down through the war years. The menfolk are killed or wounded on the far edges of the Empire; and, through the volunteer gallantry of its soldiery, New Zealand is left undefended before the Japanese threat.

Then the American legions arrive, and the four Neville girls become involved, one after another, with varied samples of Yank lovers. Anne, the eldest and most prim, has a baby by a handsome lieutenant, whose family after he dies in the war invites Anne and the child to live in Oklahoma City. The youngest, little Evelyn, grabs even at a horrid New Yorker G.I. named Max Murphy. Delia, who has married a ne'er-do-well New Zealander later captured in Malaya, spends most of her time staying with American officers and cheering them up "until they sail" for places like Tarawa and Okinawa. And widowed Barbara, whose husband had died in Egypt, finally joins the ten thousand New Zealand women who married Americans and gets herself a sensible major from Chicago. Again the twin ideas of undergoing wartime shake-ups in settled opinions and of avoiding racial and national prejudices are underlined in this tale from the home front in southernmost Polynesia.

However, as a companion piece to an excellent essay on Australia, Michener does not even attempt a local-color story with a setting on that continent-sized nation. "The Jungle" starts on a vessel in Sydney Harbor, but no effort is made to dramatize any section of Australia as "Until They Sail" dramatizes New Zealand. Instead, an Australian couple, Captain Alec McNair and his dumpy, subjugated, prematurely aged wife, who has the ridiculous name of Citronella, are contrasted with an American couple. The husband, a former PT boat skipper named John Millstor, is taking his wife with him on a sentimental pilgrimage back to Guadalcanal in McNair's trading vessel.

Millstor, who has been slowly dominated by his wife, has lost the virile mastery shown by McNair. In the sociological jungle that is modern marriage, John is the giant kauri pine of Malekula which has slowly been destroyed by the thousand aerial roots of the parasitic strangler fig, his wife. She cuckolds him with McNair almost before his eyes, and his shame is only ended when in a hurricane he sacrifices his now meaningless life in an attempt at he-man heroism. But are we supposed to accept the McNairs as having hacked a better pathway through the matrimonial jungle? This story is disturbing because the Pacific setting merely makes overt the action of the enemy—which this time is "the American wife, tall, straight, thin limbed, carefully beautiful."

Least satisfying of all the stories to me is "The Fossickers." Perhaps the spirit of New Guinea is too primitive, too nebulous for any civilized writer to encompass. At any rate, Michener merely assembles slowly a cast of four foreigners—an evil Australian adventurer, an unlovely English woman anthropologist, a Dutch ex-administrator, and an American cameraman—and takes them up the Sepik River and into a native village. Then the first three start for the distant hills with a girl (daughter of the anthropologist and the village chief) who will lend comfort to the Dutchman. We are supposed to anticipate their fates. But the ending is just a beginning.

In "What I Learned," his epilogue to *Return to Paradise*, Michener concludes that, whatever the South Pacific has been in the past, it will be most important in the future as the meeting ground between America and Asia: "It is the highway between Asia and America, and whether we wish it or not, from now on there will be immense traffic along that highway. . . . Asia must inevitably become more important to the United States than Europe." After spending a year reexploring the South Pacific, Michener directed himself to a wide exploration of Asia.

CHAPTER 4

Around and About Asia

W HEN Joseph Conrad was a boy in the middle of Poland, he pointed to a map of darkest Belgian Congo and said, "When I grow up I shall go *there*." When Jim Michener was a boy in Pennsylvania, he came upon an article on Central Asia in the *National Geographic* magazine and made a similar vow. The result of Michener's dream was that he has lived in more Asian countries than probably any other American—or, for that matter, any Asian. His next three books all dealt in different ways with various parts of the same great continent. The titles are *The Voice of Asia* (1951), *The Bridges at Toko-Ri* (1953), and *Sayonara* (1954). *Caravans*—a novel with its setting in Afghanistan, an Asian country visited by Michener for some months in 1955—is also considered in this chapter although the book was not published until 1963. Another book, *The Floating World* (1955), a scholarly study of the art of the Japanese print which required two years of his working time, is mentioned in a later chapter, which also considers three other books about Asian art.

I *Proconsuls, Rajahs, and Mem-sahibs*

Feeling that an understanding of Asia, a region more than five times the size of the United States, was absolutely crucial to Americans, Michener set off to talk to as many Asians as he could. Of some one hundred and twenty interviewed, he reported in *The Voice of Asia* on fifty-three individuals or groups. Some of the interviews lasted eight or ten hours. Michener did not edit the thoughts which he chose for inclusion. A helpful technique, after an hour or two of recording answers to simple questions, was for the interviewer to say, "Perhaps you have some questions you would like to ask me." Then the problems that were really bothering the Asian would be reflected in the questions he fired at the American.

Michener's method upon arriving in a new country was to state to the newspaper reporters that he wanted to learn as much as possible about it. He would then hole up in his hotel room and for three days write down his notes on the previous country. The local residents would become crazed by the sound of his typewriter and deduce that he was writing a dastardly exposé of their land without having talked to a single person. They would then insist on arranging for him a series of interviews—ones he could never have obtained for himself—to give him a proper perspective.

"I talked with people of almost every conceivable calling," the author noted. "And I can say that this overwhelming experience of friendship, understanding and brotherhood has left me changed . . . . They are yellow, many of them, but they are also individual human beings who can be approached by every single psychological avenue used to persuade Americans" (11).

The volume contains six vignettes from Japan, five from Korea, four from Formosa, four from Hong Kong, six from Singapore, four from Indonesia, three from Thailand, two from Indochina (which then was still being painfully retained by France), three from Burma, thirteen from India, and three from Pakistan. At the end of each section, Michener appended his "observations" about what he thought Americans should know factually about that region. The book ends with a section on "America and Asia" which embodies the author's more general conclusions about the continent, and it suggests some main lines for the guidance of Americans while thinking about their future attitude toward the revolutions in Asia. These "rules" should be even more pertinent today, when a decline of United States power can be averted only through "intelligence, tolerance, and hard work."

The Voice of Asia was very well received. "Highly recommended as a thoroughly painless, thoroughly serious, study of current history," was the verdict of H. P. Linton.[1] Marcus Duffield reported that "Ninety per cent of the interviews and all of Michener's 'observations' reflect his intelligent way of searching for greater understanding of the mind of Asia."[2] Robert Trumbull concluded: "Michener, both as a straight reporter and in his analytical passages, succeeds in giving a picture of complex Asia today that is clear and accurate, on the whole."[3]

Much water has flowed down the Mekong River during the quarter of a century since 1951—an era during which the United States became more involved with Asian affairs than ever before.

Michener continued to write about the people of most of the countries between Israel and Indonesia, as a study of the Bibliography
will show. He was among the first contingent of journalists to enter
the People's Republic of China, and during his sixty-ninth year
made two more trips to Asia. It is easy to look back, in these post-
Vietnam days, and remark that, if more writers like Michener had
visited Asia more often and had written more candidly about these
countries, America might have been spared the decade-long involvement with an unwinnable land war in Asia.

Not only the "observations" in *The Voice of Asia* but such portraits as "The Proconsul" (General MacArthur, treated in a less than
worshipful tone) and "The Man Without a Country" (Anthony
Brooke, last of the white rajahs of Sarawak, whose final abdication
statement Michener helped to write) may have historical value.

The lasting value of *The Voice of Asia* does not lie, though, in its
political acumen. The sketched profiles will endure as long as we
cherish portraits of real human beings of other cultures than ours.
"The New Japanese Woman," "Boy-San," "The Hard Way," "The
American," "The Buddhist Monk," "Three Rupees, Sahib," "The
Hungry Old Man," and "The Grace of Asia" will well repay
rereading. Especially heartwarming are the vignettes dealing with
those favorite Michener subjects—racial conflict and outmarriage
problems. On these topics one appreciates "Reasonable Doubts at a
Strip Tease," "The Marginal Man" (the Eurasian), "The School-
teacher," and "The Sheikh's Women." On the subject of India's
reforms in the area of these topics, the first five articles under that
country are devoted to the new woman and the attempt to shatter
the caste system. Michener is also fond of quoting an interview on
one side and then another on just the opposite side; both seem
equally convincing. Panel pieces of this sort are "The Optimist" and
"The Cynic."

An edge of satire is found in "The New Mem-sahibs," which the
author terms "The most widely read single piece of writing I have
done."[4] Because it showed how an ordinary American wife could set
up housekeeping in Asia and immediately acquire the fatal
arrogance that got the British kicked out of that continent, it has
been distributed by American corporations to new employees.

II *Voluntary Men in Korea*

Michener's concern with Asia, where he served as news correspondent during the Korean War, extended also to the field of fiction.

The Bridges at Toko-Ri burst upon the public complete in an edition
of five million copies in *Life* magazine for July 6, 1953, followed
three days later by publication of the hardbound book. Its creation
was not so lightninglike. Actually, Michener had planned a novel on
Korea two years before, but he "couldn't get it off the ground." Six
months later, he worked on a version about the Marine Corps, but
put it aside as being too trite in plot. He turned then to work on the
novel that later became *Sayonara;* but in February, 1952, he wrote a
complete outline of the Toko-Ri story. He laid it aside three times,
and might not have completed it for two or three years. But some of
the editors of *Life* came to him and asked for a novelette. He related
the plot, and the piece was commissioned on the spot. "The story I
told them that day wasn't changed by so much as a comma when I
came to put it down," the author said later. "When I talked to them,
the hard work had been done."[5]

To brief himself further on the operation of the jet-fighter planes,
however, Michener spent eight days on an aircraft carrier. Three of
the pilots he met there did not return—family men with children.
Undoubtedly the technology of the story and the character of Harry
Brubaker were strengthened by this close research.

Both in magazine and hardbound form, the reception of *The
Bridges at Toko-Ri* was friendly. Riley Hughes, who had considered
Return to Paradise the work of a combination John Gunther and Dr.
Kinsey, said: "Mr. Michener's book deserves to be read as a splendid
tribute to what he calls 'the voluntary men,' the men 'on whom the
world has always depended.' "[6] Quentin Reynolds said bluntly:
"Anyone who can read this magnificent novel without being moved
should run—not walk—to the nearest psychiatrist's couch."[7] James
Kelly in the *Saturday Review* reported: "Mr. Michener turns in his
best performance. Always an acute observer of human character,
usually a serious-minded and formidably informed reporter, he has
been less at home as a fictioneer. But *The Bridges at Toko-Ri*, a
honed-down story of action, ideas, and civilization's responsibilities,
moves forward with the inevitability of literature."[8]

Several reviewers thought that the descriptions of machines were
better than those of men. "Sure, his pilots are good Americans and
two-dimensional human beings, yet what they do and feel and say
sounds too frequently more like the Voice of America than fine art,"
said H. D. Webster.[9] "Mr. Michener has Kipling's dangerous gift of
making engines live," said Robert Payne, and added, "Mr.
Michener is not so fortunate with his human characters. . . . Is

Brubaker iron or jelly? . . . In these last pages Mr. Michener nearly makes up for the early failure. . . . He has entered more com-
passionate depths than ever before."[10] Charles Poore concluded: "It
has streaky faults of over-emphasis, but *The Bridges at Toko-Ri* will
stand with the best of Michener's tales of the Pacific. His ability to
breathe new life into familiar characters made from his familiar
blend of pathos, homily, hilarity, engine grease and valor serves him
well again."[11]

The novelette, only a hundred pages long, is divided into three
sections: "Sea," "Land," and "Sky." It opens with an exciting
episode concerning the aircraft carrier *Savo*, driving toward the
deadly shore of Korea in order to take aboard returning bombers.
One of them has been hit and has to ditch near the carrier. But the
crew of the ship's helicopter go to the rescue. Mike Forney, Irishman
from Chicago who wears a kelly-green stovepipe hat to give
reassurance to downed pilots, takes the chopper to the spot and his
buddy, Nestor Gamidge, drops into the icy water and hooks the flyer
to the sling.

The survivor, almost frozen, is Harry Brubaker; a veteran of
World War II, twenty-nine years old, and a successful Denver
lawyer, he does not want to be fighting a war in Korea. Revived, he
reports to Admiral George Tarrant, who tells him that Harry's wife
and two small daughters have managed to get to Japan in time to
share his forthcoming leave. And after that, the admiral knows, he
must send his best men against the almost impregnable batteries surrounding the crucial four bridges across the canyon at the enemy
center of Toko-Ri. Will the American flyers knock out those bridges
and make the commissars finally decide to quit the war? Or has
America become too indifferent to stick out the struggle and make
the sacrifices? Will America have to make her last stand against the
Russians on the banks of the Mississippi?

During the "Land" interlude in Japan, in "the greatest liberty
port in the world," Brubaker's idyll with his family is quickly dis-
rupted when he has to travel to Tokyo to get Mike and Nestor out of
jail. The Irishman, fighting over his Japanese sweetheart, has
caused a riot that demands Harry's time and money to settle; but he
can do nothing less for the pair that hauled him out of the deadly
sea. The admiral explains to Nancy Brubaker about the bridges,
because she at least must have some conception of what the war is
about, even though most Americans neither know nor seem to care.

In the final panel of the story, Harry and "Cag"—commander of

the air group, an Annapolis professional slated for high promotion—streak over Korea in their Banshee jets to photograph the ap-
proaches to Toko-Ri in preparation for the bombing mission. Two
hundred Communist guns bombard Cag's plane as it enters the
valley and runs the gauntlet through the pinpointed course,
resolutely clicking its camera shutters. Once again, miraculously un-
scathed, "Cag" makes a photo run before returning with Harry to
the *Savo*.

The sight of the bridges recalls to Brubaker all the doubts that
might cause him to request permission to stay safely on the ship next
morning, when the big strike would take place. But he is the best of
the admiral's flying team. He is on the spot in Korea: "Might as well
do the job." He calms his fear of physical cowardice by standing
close to the plane catapult without flinching when its eleven-ton
steel piston flashes at his face.

The climax of the book comes when the pilots dress for the final
mission and take off for the strike. Despite the snowstorm of flak
they complete the destruction of the bridges at Toko-Ri. But while
he is returning to the carrier, a random bullet in his engine brings
Harry's Banshee down in the paddy fields. Even though Mike and
Nestor come to his aid, there is no hope for the airmen in this mud,
for they are surrounded by snipers and grenade throwers. Mike and
Nester die first. Finally the sky is empty, and Harry Brubaker is
"alone in a spot he had never intended to defend in a war he had not
understood." Only in the last fraction of a second before his death
does he understand. The admiral, who had looked on Harry as a sur-
rogate for his own son, is left to marvel: "Why is America lucky
enough to have such men? . . . Where did we get such men?"

What Harry understood in the last second of his life is the theme
of this novelette—that all through history free men have had to fight
the wrong war in the wrong place and that the bravest few cannot
shift the burden of sacrifice to anyone else. The "voluntary men,"
on whom finally civilization must depend, cannot say: "Hold back
the enemy but make someone else do it." Their wives, like Nancy
Brubaker, may say, "If the government dared to ask women like me,
this stupid war would end tomorrow"; but the men must fight the
war because victory is more important than family. As at the climax
of *Tales of the South Pacific*, Michener points out that only a few
men are ever the spear point at the end of a long line of defenders,
and only these ultimate men can know what war really is.

Perhaps the role of Brubaker is too heroic to be highly convinc-

78   JAMES MICHENER

ing. Other characters in the novelette stand by themselves. Beer
Barrel, gigantic Texas farmer who mounts the carrier's deck to wave
down the planes with his paddles while making microsecond
decisions on life and death, remains in the memory. Coming aboard
lugging two golf bags weighted down with cans of beer, he is a dis-
grace to the uniform but the sole hope of returning pilots who fear a
crash. As the admiral says: "He flies against his bridges every day."
Beer Barrel has one kind of bravery that a navy must have.

Other brave men are those of the helicopter crew. And another is
the air group captain, "Cag." He must be ready to take the highest
responsibility of command. For a while, it seems that he will back
away from what he knows is right. But after Brubaker's death,
"Cag" talks back to the admiral: "I don't care any longer what kind
of fitness report you turn in on me because this was a good mission."
He is ready for responsibility now.

Michener's concern for human brotherhood is exemplified again
in the scene in the private pool at the hotel, where two families,
American and Japanese, introduce themselves and paddle about
naked in the sulphur bath, conversing without enmity.

The best part of this book is probably the description of what it
was like to live on a carrier and to fly a jet plane in war. "It was terrible and supreme to be there, whistling into the morning brilliance,"
Harry realizes as he flies on the photo mission toward the Communist bridges. Reading of such exultation, one forgets Michener's
wry confession that each time he himself flies in a combat jet he
becomes violently airsick.

The use of propeller planes to "windmill" the giant carrier and to
keep it from crashing against the quay, burning out expensive
engines in the process, brings a shudder to the taxpaying reader.
Two pages of detail describing Brubaker as he dresses in his pilot's
"poopy suit" for winter flying conclude with a simile: "Harry
Brubaker, who was about to soar into space with a freedom no
previous men in history had known, was loaded down with such in-
tolerable burdens that at times he felt he must suffocate; just as
many citizens of his world, faced with a chance at freedoms never
before dreamed of, felt so oppressed by modern problems and re-
quirements that they were sure they must collapse" (99 - 100).[12]
Even the chance, fatal bullet in the Banshee's turbine carries with it
an image: "Like the society which had conceived the engine, the
turbine was of such advanced construction that even trivial disrup-

tion of one fundamental part endangered the entire structure" (122 - 23).

Full utilization by moviemakers of the resources of the United States Navy, as well as an outstanding cast, resulted in a full-color version of *The Bridges at Toko-Ri* that was one of the finest films of 1955.

III   *Madame Butterfly in Swingtime*

Meanwhile, Michener had published a novel about Japan, which had come to be his favorite foreign land. *Sayonara* is not only a love story about a modern-day Butterfly but also a love letter from the author to a country that had been his greatest enemy only a few years before. As Pearl Buck put it: "The book is, for me, this author's best work, and it can and should be read for any or all of several reasons: as a moving story, told in spare strong prose; as illuminating description, original and unusual, of a rarely beautiful country; as a powerful portrayal of Americans and Japanese as they must now live together upon Japanese soil. But deeper than this, if anyone cares to go deeper, is the authentic explanation of why, if we Americans do not change, we can never win in Asia."

Sayonara appeared early in 1954, after having run in three issues of *McCall's* magazine. Of it Bradford Smith wrote: "He artfully conveys a sense of the sensitiveness, the artistic quality of Japanese life."[13] John Metcalf labeled it "his most serious and accomplished writing yet."[14] Although Frank Gibney remarked that "There are only a few flashes in it of the sympathetic observer and the fine literary reporter that Michener has proved himself to be,"[15] Fanny Butcher concluded: "*Sayonara* is written with a sensitive feeling for beauty of materials and expressions and it has a quality rarely found in modern fiction—moral conviction."[16]

The story of *Sayonara* was such that it soon had several Hollywood studios going into court to argue that the film rights belonged to them. In the book, Major Lloyd "Ace" Gruver, twenty-eight-year-old son of a four-star general, has just shot down his sixth and seventh MiGs in Korea, and is sent to Japan to rest and recover. His father's friend General Webster has arranged a cushy job for him near the general's daughter Eileen, a Vassar graduate to whom Ace is more or less engaged.

A stuffy West Pointer, anticivilian, anti-Japanese, Ace gets involved in helping Joe Kelly, a tough kid in his unit who wants to marry a Japanese girl. Ace realizes that any such involvement would ruin his own career; but he soon falls deeply in love with Hana-ogi, a tall, cool girl, the greatest dancer in Japan, who plays men's parts in the Takarazuka theater near the marines' dormitory where Ace lives. He learns that her peasant father, who sold her into the theater life, had been killed by an American bomb; and her brother had been executed as a war criminal for his behavior toward American prisoners. But the flyer's bold approach wins her, and they set up a little house by a canal in Osaka, near the home of the Kellys—for Joe has overcome all the red tape and found happiness with his wife Katsumi.

Breaking with Eileen and her battle-ax mother, Ace risks ruin to experience what some half a million American men have sought—the devotion of a Japanese sweetheart. "Did I love Hana-ogi because I was afraid of American women?" he asks himself (134). Again the spoiled, bossy, selfish coldness of these women alienates their men, just as it does in "The Jungle" story in *Return to Paradise.* "I almost cried with pain to think that something had happened in American life to drive men like Mike Bailey and me away from such delectable girls" (138). He decides that the dedication of Katsumi and Hana-ogi to their menfolk is deeper than anything Eileen could offer. Eileen certainly would never erase the irritations of the day by scrubbing her husband's back in a big Japanese tub.

The rhapsody of the little house by the canal cannot last. Ace is put under house arrest by General Webster; and, when his father arrives and slanders Hana-ogi, Ace strikes him. Ace remembers that his father once persuaded him not to give up his West Point career, so he is hardly touched by his father's dictum that "Strong men have the guts to marry the girls who grew up next door." He and Hana-ogi move into the tiny home of the Kellys, and here Ace learns more about the Japanese women: "They had to do a man's work, they had to bear cruel privations, yet they remained the most feminine women in the world" (146). Some of them, naturally, were far from perfect as wives; in fact, "they were exactly like the wives of America; some were gentle mothers, some were curtain dictators and some few were lucky charms who brought their men one good thing after another" (168).

Hana-ogi is one of the real charms, he feels, especially after he wanders with her through the Japanese countryside and understands the soil from which she came. She has taken the name of a celebrated actress, "the most renowned prostitute in the entire history of Japan" (140), whose life is a perennial subject for the color prints whose strange artistry Ace comes to appreciate.

Ace decides to marry Hana-ogi and destroy his future. Paradoxically, he discovers that the age-old story of Butterfly is quite wrong. "Always the yellow girl tried to seduce these clean-cut men away from their decent white sweethearts" (203). He pleads with the girl to marry him, and it is she who refuses.

The Kelly family is blasted by an army order requiring Joe, a prospective father, to return to America and to desert his legal wife. Rescued by their Japanese neighbors from an anti-American mob, Ace and Joe still face tragedy. Joe and Katsumi take the romantic Oriental way out, and die in a love pact—ironically, just one day before the cruel order is rescinded. Ace is not even able to say *sayonara* face to face with his lost sweetheart, who leaves with her theatrical troupe. He returns to America, to promotion, to a glittering future, and to Eileen. "And you, Japan," he says in farewell, "you crowded islands, you tragic land—*sayonara*, you enemy, you friend." But he lives in an age when soldiering is the only honorable profession, and "the only acceptable attitude toward strange lands and people of another color must be not love but fear" (243).

The theme of this novel is clearly that many an American has found a profound satisfaction in marriage with an Oriental wife to whom her husband's needs are supreme. But in a profession as rigid as the military, such a marriage is not possible; prejudice is still too strong.

Again Michener found difficulty in creating an entirely convincing main character, for Ace Gruver is unbelievably prejudiced at the opening and unbelievably converted at the end. Heroic, he sounds conceited, probably because of the first-person narration. He seems more a victim than a chooser, less an actor than a patient. Nor does Hana-ogi really come through to the Western reader as an appealing, credible companion. Their love affair seems forced, like the early-blooming chrysanthemums given to Ace by the friendly flower vendor. Oddly, the most plausible characters are those sketched with strong dislike: despotic Mrs. General Webster, whose bigotry is embodied into army orders; or Lieutenant Colonel Craford, Southern autocrat who brands Ace a "nigger lover." Again some of the supernumerary characters, inhabitants of a strange country, are given with typical Michener sensitiveness—an old peasant farming his tiny plot of land with his fingers, a highly educated Japanese museum curator and scholar, a henpecked husband who flings away all his yen into a sparkling pinball machine.

The setting of the novel makes much of the Japanese cities and byways, the little paper-walled houses of Osaka, the glamor of the Takarazuka girls during a performance of "Swing Butterfly," the peaceful shrines of Kyoto, the puppet theater revealing the celestial charm of ritual suicide. Michener's growing interest in Japanese prints, which was to result in his gathering of a notable collection and the publication of four books on the subject, is revealed in his remarks about the appeal of the old Hana-ogi drawings.[17]

The humor of culture clashes is shown in such scenes as the one in which Ace braves the terrors of the post-exchange lingerie department to buy "weekies" for Katsumi, who desires to be as American as possible for her G.I. husband. And the question of how two lovers without a common language can communicate is feelingly sketched in several pages, making attractive the overuse of a few handy words and Hana-ogi's *l*-less pidgin. She can say, "Rots peopre nebber rub nobody," but it is better when she dances out the story and uses her genius of mimicry to reveal her love.

The popular appeal of *Sayonara*, at its lowest level, might simply be an answer to the question: "What's it like with an Oriental girl?" At the highest level, it is again a warm exemplum on Michener's perennial theme of universal equality, of love as the catalyst of interracial tranquility. Less than two years after the publication of *Sayonara*, Michener himself married in Chicago a girl of Japanese ancestry.

IV *"Absolutely Everything About Afghanistan"*

Afghanistan—a wild country in which Michener traveled in 1955—is the setting of the novel *Caravans*, which appeared in 1963. Since the story covers some months in the year 1946, it might be considered historical fiction; for, to write it, Michener had to do research and imagine a region that would emerge after World War II into a much less primitive nationhood than he describes. The book published in 1963—eight years after Michener had crisscrossed Afghanistan with notebook in pocket—was probably a more manufactured product than one he might have issued soon after his journeys from the Khyber Pass to Herat. The plot is contrived to give Mark Miller, the narrator, a maximum opportunity to describe the scenes visited by Michener, and much of the book is devoted to geography (a study that he has called "the queen of sciences").

Mark Miller, a product of Groton, Yale, and the United States

Navy, is a young man attached to the American Embassy in Kabul, the capital of the kingdom. Blond and handsome, he is a Jew who does not look like one. In March, 1946, he is sent forth to seek the missing daughter of a leading citizen of Dorset, Pennsylvania. She had married an Afghan engineer who had studied in Philadelphia, but she has left him and vanished in the desert inhabited only by wandering tribes called Kochis, whose caravans range from Persia to India and from Baluchistan to the Russian provinces north of the Oxus. By a series of accidents Mark and Ellen—a beautiful and intelligent blonde from Bryn Mawr College—join such a nomad camel caravan and spend the summer months tramping through the snowy defiles of the Hindu Kush in the heartland of Asia. Ellen sways the souls of one man after another, and Mark enjoys an idyll with the adolescent daughter of the tribal chieftain before the inevitable ending of this romantic interlude.

Kabul, the isolated capital, is in 1946 an outpost where diplomats of a dozen nations mingle with Afghan authorities and where a multiracial cast of characters may logically assemble. Among the Afghanis are Shah Khan, a power in the government; his son Moheb, leader in the new national spirit; and Nur Muhammad, a smart young Afghan assigned as Miller's local aide. At Qala Bist, site of a proposed irrigation project, Miller meets Nazrullah, the husband abandoned by Ellen, and Dr. Otto Stiglitz, a refugee from Germany. In a stirring confrontation in an abandoned caravanserai in the desert, Stiglitz, a Nazi who had tortured a thousand German Jews during the war, fights with Mark; but Stiglitz is saved from being strangled by the arrival of Ellen and the caravan of Zulfiqar. Michener's concern for the recognition of universal brotherhood is later epitomized by a sunset scene in a mountain gorge when Miller rubs shoulders in prayer with the ex-Nazi, who is now determined to serve humanity, and with an illiterate camel driver who chants the greatness of the Muslim God. Another character is the American engineer John Pritchard, whose efforts to modernize Afghanistan compete with Russian aid projects and result in his brave death in the desert.

Mark Miller, narrator, is almost altogether lacking in character in the active sense. A patient rather than an agent, he slides along in the stream of events without real opposition from anyone.[18] The most enigmatic figure, however, is Ellen Jaspar of Pennsylvania; for she finds America unbearable. The testimony of her music professor seems plausible: "Ellen Jaspar is sick with the disease that is beginning to infect our ablest young people. She has disaffiliated herself from the beliefs that gave our society its structure in the past, but she has found no new structure upon which she can rely for that support which every human life requires" (79). Having abandoned her lawful husband for the caravan chief Zulfiqar, she joins, in a melodramatic switch, the stateless German. "He's already convicted and dead," she tells Miller. "I've rejected all the lives I've known, so I'm dead too. I can live only at the bottom . . . at the bottom dregs of an insane world. Where hope is being reborn." The ghosts of teachers in the cave at the Vale of Bamian are applauding her, she declares, when she says that "they know that society becomes corrupt and that men must reject it if they are to remain free. They know that life, to replenish itself, must sometimes return to the dregs, to the primitive slime" (276). When Ellen and Stiglitz are banished from the caravan, Miller concedes that they had indeed "converted themselves into non-people, those rejected dregs on which the world rebuilds" (304). He still does not understand Ellen's belief that "The non-people don't accomplish. They exist, and from them the world takes hope" (313). Yet in the end Miller must consider her motivation as simply "rejection" (324). Ellen Jaspar is probably an unfinished sketch for characters who were to appear eight years later in Michener's more extended study of disaffiliated youth, *The Drifters*.

In order to explain the historicity and authenticity of *Caravans*, Michener appends a "Note to the Reader" that identifies the real and imagined settings and that presents his credentials for writing this novel. He also indicates the progress made in the kingdom of Afghanistan between 1946 and 1963, and he justifies several gory scenes in the book on the ground that they had happened this way. His travels gave him excellent material for informative essays, as well as a lecture on the country that I consider one of the most scholarly brief presentations that I have ever audited; and such material was then reworked into a smooth tale suitable for a home magazine for ladies. But the imagined cast fails to people the realistic landscape. As one reviewer of the novel concluded: "What dominates it—indeed, frequently shoulders the action right off the stage—is information, facts, explanation. . . . Michener tells you, it sometimes seems, absolutely everything he has learned about Afghanistan, whether it holds things up or not. As a result, it is much like reading a bound set of the *National Geographic*, without the pictures."[19]

CHAPTER 5

Oceania, Andau, And Bucks County

T HE Pacific, where Michener had first won his laurels,
  still beckoned. He returned to this region for the materials for
two more books—*Rascals in Paradise* and the big novel *Hawaii*. The
first of these was the only book Michener wrote in collaboration, and
it happened that I was chosen to be the junior author.

Michener was an editor at Macmillan when the manuscript of *The
Spell of the Pacific* arrived, a big anthology edited by Dr. Carl
Stroven and myself. Michener was so enthusiastic about the project
that he offered to write an introduction, and we were delighted to
accept. Soon we met in Honolulu, and thereafter kept in touch with
each other. On November 15, 1954, hearing that I was soon to leave
for a year in Australia as a Fulbright senior research fellow,
Michener wrote me, in part: "I would enjoy collaborating with you
on a book to be called something like *Wild Men in Paradise*. It
would consist of about eight long, accurate, provocative, and poetic
biographical essays on some of the worthies of the Pacific. . . . We
would certainly have maximum color as one criterion, but we would
also want to cover those typical and inherently interesting men
whose lives have a chance of evoking large speculative problems."
He named ten prospective subjects.

Naturally, I accepted with great gusto and suggested more than a
dozen other candidates for biography, and a month later sent along
six more. The final selection of ten persons, from our omnibus list of
several dozen, included only four from Michener's original proposal.

Early in February, 1955, Michener and the Bennett Cerfs were in
Hawaii. Sitting in swim suits on Waikiki Beach in front of the Royal
Hawaiian Hotel, Cerf, Michener, and I discussed our project as a
possible Random House book; and we informally reached agreement on contract terms.

Rascals in Paradise was titled, it happens, before a line of the book

had been written. Bennett Cerf picked up a word I used to describe
some of our prospective biographees. Despite the joint efforts of the
collaborators to find a better title—since several of our men were not
rascally at all—the editors resisted all suggestions to change. The title was finally attached to the opening chapter, which appears as
"Rascals in Paradise: The *Globe* Mutineers," but we still get comments that Captain Bligh and Will Mariner were really quite
honorable fellows.

I   *Two Authors, One Book*

The day after the Waikiki pact, Michener sat down with me in his
tidy, impersonal hotel room, and we selected ten characters about
which chapters would be written. Of these, two turned out to be un-
suitable and were later replaced. Our plans were made at this time to
divide up the chapters for the purpose of writing the first drafts. I
then embarked on a ship heading for Fiji, New Zealand, and
Sydney; and Michener took a plane on his way to spend some
months in Afghanistan.

The ten characters were chosen with a view to maximum coverage
over time and space in the world's biggest ocean. In addition to Sam
Comstock (1802 - 1824), murderous harpooner of the *Globe,* they
comprised the French Marquis de Rays, chief monster of the New
Ireland colonization frauds (1880); Coxinga, master pirate of all time
(died 1662); Walter Murray Gibson (1822 - 1888), the power behind
the throne in the reign of King Kalakaua of Hawaii; Captain
William Bligh, who was involved not only in the *Bounty* episode but
in three other mutinies and in five major courts-martial (1754 -
1817); Doña Isabel Barreto, our only lady subject, wife of Don
Alvaro de Mendaña and directress of the disastrous voyage of 1595;
Captain Bully Hayes (1829 - 1877), last of the great Pacific buc-
caneers; Louis Becke, Australian trader, adventurer, and author
(1855 - 1913); Will Mariner, the boy chief of Tonga (1791 -1853);
and Edgar Leeteg (1904 - 1953), brawling bohemian of Tahiti whose
paintings on black velvet created a South Sea legend.

The scene of their operations was not only the open ocean but
land areas from Peru to the China coast and from Hawaii to New
Zealand, including episodes in the Marquesas, Tahiti, Samoa, the
Dutch East Indies, Tonga, the Solomons, and Formosa. Endpaper
maps and a thorough index revealed the broad scope of the book,
and extensive bibliographic references revealed the obligations of
scholarship in research areas where materials were often slight or un-

reliable. Intentionally, the differences among the characters were also great. The main basis for final choice was that they were all strong-willed, dramatic, and energetic. Only slowly did it dawn on us that they all had one thing more in common: they all had seemed to dream of setting up some sort of private kingdom on a Pacific isle, which has long been almost the standard romantic symbol of escapism. Taking this cue, Michener wrote his excellent introduction "To All Who Seek a Refuge," directed to the escapists of our own troubled time.

The book that finally resulted from our joint labors stayed on national best-seller lists for ten weeks and was favorably reviewed around the country as well as in the British Commonwealth. It was translated into six languages abroad. I shall refrain from making judgments on its value and instead quote those of others. Darwin Teilhet said in the *Saturday Review*: "Not since Sam Clemens and Robert Louis Stevenson closed up shop in the Pacific has a gallery been opened as richly and satisfyingly mounted as *Rascals in Paradise*. . . . Commodiously informed, rich in detail, wonderfully varied, and a joy to read. One finishes it with the feeling not of surfeit but of wanting yet more, please."[1] "Adventure, glory, danger, riches and relaxation under the tropical sun—it's an illusion not to be trusted, say our old Pacific hands," remarked John K. Hutchens, and went on: "Their warning having been dutifully given and duly received, how soon would you like to start?"[2]

Charles Poore reported: "What stands out, though, is the painstaking way Mr. Michener and Mr. Day have sifted the records, the testimony of highly impeachable witnesses and the cool truths of court reports to find out, so far as may be possible, what really happened, what animated their galleries of scoundrels in landscapes where prospects pleased and men were vile."[3] Said P. J. Searles: "All the stories are excellent, mostly lurid, filled with high adventure, bloodshed and brutality. Messrs. Michener and Day have selected a dozen of the most picturesque characters in almost four centuries and the writing does them justice."[4] John T. McCutcheon, Jr., said: "Professor Day, an authority on the literature of the Pacific, and Mr. Michener, who has helped to create it, have assembled a new series of tales of the South Pacific—all of them true, this time, but still with the intoxicating atmosphere which always seems to result from mixing Michener with the Pacific. . . . These are tales it will be hard to forget."[5]

According to Walter F. Morse, "It deserves a permanent home

among the classics prepared and designed for armchair explorers."[6]
Said William Hogan, "Michener and Day seem to be the most ef-
ficient collaborators since Nordhoff and Hall (or perhaps the
Rodgers and Hammerstein of 'South Pacific'). They have produced
a man-sized book."[7] Richard H. Dillon wrote in the *Library Journal:*
"An excellent volume overall, and highly recommended. It is a
splendid sampler of the curious, colorful characters, most of them escapists, who have peopled—and who still inhabit—the South
Pacific."[8]

Although I here abjure any value judgments on *Rascals in
Paradise*, this chapter does offer a chance to present Michener in the
role of literary collaborator, and to discuss the method he followed in
that role.

Many people wonder how it is possible for two authors to write
one book between them. I had previously collaborated on three
books with friends, and had found such teamwork to be congenial
when the partners, widely different in experience and knowledge,
were agreed on general aims. From the first, I looked forward with
zest to the chance to work side by side with Michener.

Outside of playwright circles, true collaboration is quite rare. Of
course, the sort of "as told to" writing, in which one person has a
story to relate but employs the pen of a trained craftsman to tell it, is
a common thing, whether or not the "ghost" gets credit on the title
page. But a real sharing of the writing task is not common. It is difficult enough for an author to create a work that will satisfy himself,
let alone satisfy a partner who has his own ideas of what words will
be the best. The bark of friendship of even Mark Twain and Bret
Harte splintered on the rock of attempted collaboration.

Yet the Pacific region has somehow been compatible with true
collaboration. Charles Nordhoff and James Norman Hall, neighbors
in Tahiti, turned out no less than eleven books jointly, including the
celebated *Bounty* trilogy and six other volumes with Pacific settings.
Robert Louis Stevenson and his stepson, Lloyd Osbourne, wrote *The
Wrecker* in collaboration. Louis Becke and his journalist friend
Walter Jeffery did several novels together (including *The Mutineer*,
which concerned Bligh, the *Bounty*, and Fletcher Christian). D. H.
Lawrence wrote *The Boy in the Bush* with Mary Louisa Skinner. In
recent years, William Lederer and Eugene Burdick produced *The
Ugly American*.

In all these instances, so far as I can find out, and also in others
such as the better-known collaboration of Joseph Conrad and Ford

Madox Ford (Hueffer) on the novel *Romance*, one writer would do the first draft of a section and the other would revise it. This was true of our own manuscript. The first draft of each was done by a single person. It was then rewritten back and forth until both were satisfied. Sometimes, neither could be quite sure that any particular passage was entirely his own words.[9] However, the chapters on Leeteg the painter and Coxinga the pirate were the two in which my participation was very slight.

II Research on Rascality

Several reviewers assumed that it was my task to supply the facts of research and Michener's to supply the style. Actually, it worked out that a good many pages of my original prose survived without a great deal of rewriting by Michener; and he, working in the Library of Congress and elsewhere, did much digging for historical facts.[10] The facts in the final version of our book, except for one minor slip,[11] have never been controverted. Our interpretations of character, of course, were our own.

The minor difficulties of collaborating from a distance are amusing in retrospect. In my leisure time in Sydney I was able to collect a mass of usable facts in the Mitchell Library, which is probably the most valuable collection of materials in the world on Pacific history. Michener passed through Australia in the fall of 1955 on his honeymoon, but we did not meet because by that time I was working in Melbourne and his route lay at the opposite end of the island continent, through the cattle stations of western Australia and the ports on the Indian Ocean.

In Australia I was able to draft five chapters to carry back to Honolulu, but we did not get together until mid-April, 1956, when Jim and Mari arrived by ship from the Orient. Thereafter until mid-June, with almost daily consultations and much midnight writing and revising, seven chapters were put into nearly final form. I never worked harder in my life, but trying to keep up with Michener was wonderful sport.

Then Michener returned to Pennsylvania, where he did the first draft of the Coxinga chapter; in Honolulu I wrote the two remaining ones. Heavy use was made of air mail for the rest of the work of revision and seeing the book through the press. Our correspondence file is almost as lengthy as the manuscript of this 150,000-word volume.

Further difficulties of collaborating with a world traveler are suggested by this paragraph from a letter Michener wrote me on

August 10, 1956: "I also want to advise you that I am leaving New
York on September 5 for Japan, Indonesia, Thailand, Burma, Rome,
and New York, returning sometime after the election. . . . This
means that I'll be incommunicado during some of the heavy working hours, but proof sent to me in Rome for October 16 arrival could
be worked on."

No disagreements occurred during all the enterprise that were not
amicably settled on the spot. At one time, I urged that Michener use
fewer quotations in the Coxinga story; at another, he and the editors
at Random House asked me to rewrite the chapter on Doña Isabel
Barreto because the tone, spare and sarcastic, was out of keeping
with that in the rest of the book.

The pleasures of watching a master craftsman at work were great.
For example, I handed him the first draft of the story of the *Globe*
mutineers with some trepidation. For years I had wanted to put this
yarn into shape, but the events were so complicated and so many
characters were involved that a unified narrative seemed impossible.
"The trouble," said Michener after he had read it, "is that the main
villain, Comstock, is killed half-way through the story. But the
reader will go along with you if you frankly state that the *Globe*
mutiny was not a single drama but several, and then go on to tell the
amazing sequels." No less than five rewritings of this chapter, back
and forth between us, were necessary. But the result set a definite
pitch and was chosen as the opener for the book. Moreover, before
Rascals in Paradise was published, an abridgment of this gory
chapter appeared in four installments in a Sunday magazine with a
twelve million circulation; of it, one editor wrote: "Our 37
newspapers have shown more enthusiasm for this series than
anything else *This Week* has published in recent years."

Concerning the idea of an introductory section, Michener wrote
me on July 19, 1956: "I think it extremely important that we get a
concise, handsomely written preface. A good many reviewers and
casual bookbuyers are going to look at this for a statement of what
our book is all about. I want to present them with a moving testament and one that will excite their interest. I also want to explain
how the book ties into their lives." The culmination of this attractive
preface was his story, which was reprinted in all editions of the
Reader's Digest, about the man who in the summer of 1939 decided
to hide out during the age of world wars; and, by a process of keen
logic, he finally picked out as the safest spot the Pacific island of
Guadalcanal.

"Avoid using a lot of unnecessary proper nouns," was a Michener dictum drawn from his editor days. "If we don't refer to a man or a place at least three times, let's not trouble the reader by using the name at all." He was also careful to avoid words that verged on the pejorative, words like "Asiatic," Chinaman," "half-caste," or even "native."

Early in the game I suggested that, since some Pacific places have their names spelled in a dozen different ways, we stick slavishly to the form in the printed Index of the National Geographic Society's map of the Pacific. Amused at himself, Michener confessed in a letter to me of August 10, 1956: "I have vacillated on this point several times and came up with a silly compromise that followed the Geographic except where my personal preferences were concerned. This leads only to confusion and I abandon it."

Another reward of close cooperation comes from this warm paragraph, in a letter to me of August 6, 1956: "Your foresight in sending me the Ferrando translation at the same time that I was asking you for it is a fine example of why I have found our collaboration so pleasant."

On the financial side, Michener was generous. He had worked out the main plan of the book and convinced his publisher of its soundness. When the time came to discuss terms of division with me of royalties on the book, he insisted: "Fifty-fifty. I don't want to work with anyone who can't carry half the load, and I would refuse to work with anyone who carried half the load and didn't get half the money." Twenty years after publication of the finished book, modest royalties still accrue to me.

Much better known than I in the market place, Michener rejected an offer to sell the Doña Isabel story, which we had researched together, to a magazine under his name alone. "There is, I find," he wrote me on February 9, 1957, "a temptation to capitalize on my participation in this and to try to leave you out." (This actually happened when, unknown to Michener, several chapters ran in a magazine in Australia with his name as the sole by-line.) "As you well know, I will not be a partner to such deals and have made it very clear to everybody involved that I would not be. So, although I might have done this and then split the money with you under the table, I just thought I ought not to be involved with it in any way."

Michener wrote all but five words of Chapter 10, depicting Edgar Leeteg, the artist of Tahiti. To this lengthy study Michener applied his lifetime expertise in art criticism. It also created the need for

92 JAMES MICHENER

clarification of the author's loyalties to his subject and his readers. After publication, Barney Davis of Honolulu, Leeteg's last sales agent, wrote a lengthy letter objecting strongly to the tone of the presentation of the man he had made celebrated as "the American Gauguin." Michener responded with an equally lengthy, friendly letter in which he said, in part:

> I have been through this several times with other subjects, Barney. People get very angry about not getting the complete puff-job from a writer and then they realize later that because he does *not* do puff-jobs, what he does write is accepted widely around the world and actually does more good in the long run. . . . A good honest story always achieves more of what a subject hopes will be achieved than a second-rate article which merely praises the subject in round and meaningless terms. . . . I always write from the basis of having somebody who knows a lot more about it than I come along twenty years later to review my work. . . . I think that in the case of Leeteg what I have written will last for a long, long time. It is a true account, it is a friendly account, it is in a sense a loyal account of a man whom I knew and liked. . . . As it is, people will be reading about Leeteg long after I am dead and everybody who writes about him will have to go back to what I have written to get the starting point on the facts of this man's life. To have accomplished such a basic statement is a very good thing and I hope that the events of history will bear me out that I have accomplished just that.

This response to Davis is an excellent restatement of Michener's idea that a writer who is insincere will not be read. Once he said to me: "I have been kicked out of seven countries because the government officials disliked my frankness. But each of these seven countries invited me back. They knew that a writer is never worth reading unless he expresses exactly what he honestly believes."

Collaboration does not necessarily save time, and *Rascals in Paradise* was certainly not a rush job. The idea occurred to Michener about ten years before the book appeared, and he had pondered it for a long time before deciding that he could never work on it until he found a person who might share the broad task with him. The actual writing by the two authors extended over a period of almost two years, and revising and polishing efforts extended over five months. And to cap the climax, the volume was already in print when it was decided to hold back the publication date for six months to make way for *The Bridge at Andau*, a more timely Michener book!

III   *Tanks Versus Homemade Bombs*

At Christmas time, 1956, a long letter came to me from Bennett Cerf, breaking the news that Michener had delivered to him a "powerful and revealing book" on the Hungarian rebellion, and raising the question whether the imminent publication of *Rascals in Paradise* should not be delayed to make way for the more opportune volume. "It is so timely and important that it would be unthinkable for us, as publishers, to do otherwise than present it to the public as fast as we can get it in print," Cerf pointed out.

I wired him that Michener should certainly have the chance to make the most of his report on Hungary, and a few days later got a long letter from Michener himself, sent from Vienna, giving me full freedom to express my feelings on this matter as forcefully as I might wish. "They feel that they must publish this book immediately," he said, "and there is no reason why they shouldn't, unless by so doing they kill off sales on the longer book and more expensive one on which you and I have worked together." The result was that *Rascals* was postponed until mid-June, and *The Bridge at Andau* appeared around the end of February.

Michener's speed in reporting the fast-moving events of the Hungarian uprising enabled his book to be the first American volume dealing with this exciting and newsworthy subject. (*Time* magazine's "man-of-the-year" for 1956, it may be noted, was the Hungarian freedom fighter.) The volume was well received. John MacCormac said: "It may be too soon to embalm the Hungarian revolution between the covers of a book. It was, in many ways, a unique event whose cause is not likely to be completely clear until we are further from it. But James A. Michener has made as good a job of it as could be made at this time and it would not be easy to find anyone who could do it better. In so far as he has limited himself to describing actual events, told by actual participants, he has performed a service for which historians may be grateful."[12] Wrote Walter Simmons: "Michener has told this story with his usual magnificent competence in a series of little tales about the little people of the revolt. Some of these people were assisted into Austria by Michener himself, and one even rode on his back."[13] William Hogan praised its strength: "Obviously written in white heat, his book at the same time is more than pamphleteering. It is a dramatic, chilling, and enraged document, made so chiefly by the author's disciplined detachment. Later, perhaps, the Hungarian story will be analyzed more thoroughly, but hardly with anything approaching the emotional wallop of this."[14]

A lengthy review by Emil Lengyel, author of *Americans from Hungary* and *The Danube*, concluded: "On the whole, Mr. Michener concentrates on the bloodiest aspect of the uprising, moving swiftly on the surface of events, paying little attention to the deeper sources at work. He believes that if the revolution had succeeded it would have veered to left socialism—not to capitalism. 'The Hungarian revolution of 1956,' Mr. Michener writes, 'was a turning point in world history.' It unmasked the Russians as brutal butchers; and, in his view, it is bound to have its repercussions not only in the satellite countries but also among Asia's uncommitted nations. Unfortunately, this prophecy has not been borne out by events."[15]

Resting in the fall of 1956 in Amsterdam after a tiring tour of the world while filming television interviews, Michener was not especially responsive when the editors of *Reader's Digest* kept cabling him invitations to cover the Hungarian story. It seemed too big a job; he spoke only English; he had never been in Budapest. But the strength of the growing anti-Russian movement in Europe began to impinge on his mind. One night in Paris he was on his way to the Folies Bergère with his wife when they saw a protest riot in front of the office of a Communist newspaper. "That was when I made up my mind," he said. "I was impressed by the new bitterness and violence of the European revolt against Russia."[16] He agreed to go to Vienna to have a look. Then, "Like other writers, once I reached the Hungarian border and saw refugees, I saw in ten minutes the total dramatic and intellectual situation."[17]

He began work at once, and *The Bridge at Andau* was the fastest thing he had ever written. "I wouldn't like to do it again," he said. "I usually take about two years to do a book."[18] By the end of December he had sent to New York all but one chapter of *The Bridge at Andau*. But his pages were the result of a man-killing routine. He would leave Vienna about ten o'clock each night and arrive at the Hungarian border shortly before midnight, when the refugees would begin slipping across. Several times he himself went through the Iron Curtain to aid exhausted people to flee from the Russian terror. Two interpreters helped him in interviewing hundreds of refugees. "I cross-checked the interviews with two teams of Hungarian experts," he reported.

When any discrepancies showed up I had still a third group look them over. I had detailed maps of Budapest and hundreds of pictures of specific buildings and streets. I made the poeple point out the exact spot where the incidents they related took place, and by comparing one report with another, I was able to weed out the inaccuracies.

Some of it, I admit, was hard to believe. You'd be sitting there in a cafe talking to a mild little man and he'd tell you quite matter-of-factly, "I did this and I did that," and you'd say to yourself, "No, it's impossible; how could this little guy who'd never been in a fight in his life do this kind of thing?" But somebody did it. There lay a great city in ruins and a hundred heavy Russian tanks knocked out with homemade bombs, and somebody did it.[19]

The title finally chosen for the Hungarian book was taken from the central symbol that Michener found to typify his story: "The bridge at Andau was it. It spanned a canal and when you crossed the bridge you were still on Hungarian territory. But it was that lousy little canal that stood between the refugees and salvation."[20] Over it no less than twenty thousand people crossed to freedom. Even when the Red border guards chopped down the timbers and burned them to keep away the hoar frosts of November, desperate Hungarians swam the icy canal if they could evade the bullets of the guardsmen.

IV   *No Gaiety on the Danube*

The first reaction of the reader of *The Bridge at Andau* is to echo Ambrose Bierce: "Can such things be?" The horror, the blood, the tortures, the mass heroism, and the flight of two hundred thousand desperate people from their homes—all this makes the mind boggle. For each group, Michener uses the device of focusing on the adventures of one representative figure or family—a device which intensifies the interest and the pain. For instance, the youthful hero "Joseph Toth" of Chapter 1 is a composite of three eighteen-year-olds who dared not give their own names because they had left relatives behind; they honored two dead comrades by using their names instead. In his final chapter, supporting the authenticity of his reports, Michener reveals the identities of those brave ones who asked that their own names be used to proclaim to the world their hatred of Russian persecutions.

Most of the chapters concentrate on one group, such as the college students, or the Red workers of the island of Csepel which was the factory center manned by the most favored Communist converts, or the family men, or the dead-end kids of Budapest, or even the child patriots who, able any moment to betray their parents into death by a word to the authorities, were taught at night to revere the names of the poet Petofi and of the revolutionary hero Kossuth.

Michener tells with thrilling realism of the first spontaneous outburst of October 23, when aroused crowds hauled down the iron statue of Stalin and eighty thousand Hungarians gathered in Parliament Square to listen to Imry Nagy lead them in their national hymn. He shows how the Hungarian soldiers went over to the side of the crowd and how even Russian tank commanders fired their cannons against the sniping special police of the Allam Vedelmi Osztag, or the AVO. He tells how no less than twenty Russian tanks and eleven armored cars were destroyed by Hungarian boys and girls, using only bottles of gasoline or merely sticks and stones in their bare hands. He shows how, even when the Russians returned on November 4 with Mongol infantry (the Russian regulars were considered too corrupted by human feelings to be able to fire on Hungarian women and children) to crush the new government's program and to "revel in revenge," the might of the Russian armed forces was defied for days by disillusioned Hungarians. Their leaders, Nagy and Pal Meleter, had been kidnapped; but the masses published newspapers, carried on a tight general strike, and fought to the death or fled the country rather than submit.

Communist brainwashing of children had apparently not been entirely successful. "Hungarian boys and girls had been trained by Stalin as intensively as human beings could be to strike the enemies of Communism. . . . Yet when the test came, almost a hundred per cent of Hungarian youth hated Russia and tried to destroy Communism" (176).[21]

Most painful is the chapter on "The AVO Man," in which Michener describes in detail the atrocities of the sadists who were put in charge of suspects and prisoners in the torture chambers of the puppet government. For ten years some thirty thousand of these brutal police and secret agents had terrorized the citizenry unchecked. And most depressing is the realization, as he says, that "Communism requires an AVO to perpetuate its system. From what I have seen of Communist regimes, I am satisfied that each Communist country has its exact equivalent of the AVO," because "it sooner or later runs into such economic and social problems that some strong-arm force is required to keep the civil population under control" (130 - 131).

Michener is always the supporter of the underdogs, even—as in this case—when the underdogs have been good Communists until they came suddenly to a realization of what Russian intentions were. The greatest significance of the Hungarian rebellion, according to him, was the fact that "It was the young men whom Communism had favored most who most savagely turned against it" (17). The people who fled were "the best people in the nation, the most liberal" (202). Furthermore, "It remained for the Communist terror, as administered by the AVO, to debase Hungarian life and at the same time to announce that this was being done as an act of friendship. . . . It remained for Russia to introduce into the terror business a completely new dimension: hypocrisy. . . . For this reason the AVO terror can be termed the worst in Hungarian history, since it did the most damage to the social institutions by which any nation must be governed" (144 - 45).

Characteristically, Michener felt that one good result of the rebellion, even though Americans did not support it by force of arms, was that it would make easier his attempts, in talking to Asians, to unmask Russian propaganda. "And the facts that we must hammer home are these: it was the intellectuals who led the revolution, because they had been defrauded by Communism; and it was the workers from Csepel who supported it, because under Communism they not only made no gains, they lost what they had previously enjoyed; and it was the Russian tanks, crudely interfering in the government of a neighboring nation, that destroyed the city of Budapest." But the simultaneous invasion of Egypt by several Western nations, he felt, overshadowed this lesson in Communism because Russia was able to divert criticism and Asians could only point to Egypt and ask: "Now you see what we mean by imperialism?" (260).

Michener's tone throughout *The Bridge at Andau* is one of factual, grim seriousness. There is no place for brightness or humor; this revolution is too intense for any glint of gaiety. Reading it is not a completely enjoyable experience; but reading and rereading such a document is important if we are to remain aware of the way in which the aspirations of a nation, to modify its Communism toward a less steely socialism, can be stamped out by all the might of a midcentury Russian army.

V　*Campaigning for Kennedy*

The summer and autumn of 1960 were spent by Michener in pursuing his favorite sport—practical politics. The result is embodied in

the volume entitled *Report of the County Chairman,* a personal account of the Presidential campaign that resulted in the close victory
of John F. Kennedy. Michener, who found this election to be "one
of the most exciting of my lifetime" (291), was—as has already been
noted—a strong supporter of the Democratic side.

The press reception of *Report of the County Chairman,* as might
have been expected, was far from nonpartisan. Samuel Lubell in the
New York Times Book Review concluded: "Although Michener tries
to make it something bigger, this book remains mainly a piece of
campaign literature. Its chief appeal comes from sharing the
author's own campaign experiences."[22] G. W. Johnson, in the
liberal-minded *New Republic,* appreciated the anti-Republican
shafts: "Hilarious, but very astute, analysis of the election. . . . It
is Michener at his brightest and best. It is uproariously funny, but it
isn't a joke book. . . . I believe that Michener explains more of
what really happened in 1960 than all the solemn and ponderous
analysts."[23] The *Christian Century* concluded: "His generalizations
about the total effect of religion in the campaign, which are based on
his own experience, are too sweeping and lack adequate sociological
documentation."[24]

Most bitter was a political reporter, Sidney Hyman, in the *Saturday Review,* who felt that Michener should stick to novel writing
rather than turn to political reporting: "There remains the long in-
ventory of embarrassing defects. . . . There is an irritating air of
condescension connected with his own part in the campaign. . . . The impression is sometimes conveyed that he and not
John F. Kennedy was the 1960 Democratic candidate for the
Presidency. . . . Finally, Mr. Michener's experience in the campaign was limited almost exclusively to the geographical areas that
Mr. Kennedy lost."[25] Perhaps the fairest short judgment was that of
R. C. Woodward in *Library Journal:* "As the national issues emerge
from this personal, precinct-level revelation, it becomes apparent
that this is not just the story of what happened in Bucks County; it is
a miniaturization of the campaign presented in an extraordinary
way."[26]

Michener found a list of reasons to convince him that Kennedy
would be nominated and should be supported. He wanted a President who had shown he was friendly to literature and the other arts
(19). He found a number of other good reasons, all of which caused
him to plump for Kennedy before the primaries and later to accept
the post of head of the Citizens for Kennedy Committee formed in his

native Bucks County, Pennsylvania. But his deepest enthusiasm was aroused by the chance to strike another blow for the rights of racial and religious minority groups.

Report of the County Chairman is, then, not a rival of Theodore H. White's *The Making of the President, 1960;* rather it is another testimony to Michener's abiding interest in human brotherhood and in the abolition of inequalities. Again and again he found the controversy over these rights to be all-pervasive in the election. "The religious issue permeated every meeting I conducted. . . . Practically no one I met escaped the pressure of this overriding problem and, in my county at least, both parties were ultimately forced to make their major calculations with the religious question a foremost consideration" (107).

Early in the election he found that the fear of a Catholic president was widespread and shared even by some Catholics (26) as well as by Protestants (61). He felt that the anti-Catholic pamphlets which deluged the mails during the summer "ultimately reacted against the Republicans and helped elect a Catholic President" (95). In traditionally Republican Bucks County, the lines were clearer than in many parts of the nation. Michener's loving delineation of the people of his own region reveals the split. The "Pennsylvania Dutch" in the northern part followed the urgings of their Lutheran pastors to get out a strong anti-Democratic vote. The liberal, pro-union, suburban young people of gigantic Levittown were strongly inclined to support Kennedy.

Michener stated that the main breakthrough on the religious issue came with the Peale-Poling report on the anti-Catholic convention in Washington. He devotes several pages to the support that the unions, blacks, and Jews gave to the Democratic cause; but again and again he returns to the religious problem. On a tour of the Midwest, such intolerance aroused him to a speech he felt was "the best I have ever spoken" (249). And one of the main results of the election, he concluded, was that "Religious bigotry was dealt a crushing blow" (291).

Even the humor, and there is much, centers around such stories as the up-county churchgoing lady who, when asked in which party she wished to register, replied "Lutheran." Michener cleverly uses the device of reporting his dialogues with Miss Omwake and Mrs. Dale, two of his neighbors who with Gallup-like genius always voice the majority opinion on all topics; and both are firmly antagonistic to the shadow of the late Cardinal Dougherty.

Michener suspensefully chronicled his hopes and fears during the campaign. He was fearful when Senator Kennedy came out with the proposal to abandon Quemoy and Matsu—a proposal about which Michener shared Richard Nixon's doubts. Michener felt much better after the television debates between the candidates, but he was horrified on the eve of the election when a news story, later found to be fake, broke which stated that Nikita Krushchev had been arrested, deposed, thrown in jail, and replaced by Gyorgy Malenkov. In a heavily statistical final chapter he concluded: "I do not believe that Senator Kennedy won; I believe that Vice President Nixon lost."

The weakest part of the book is the account of Michener's barnstorming around eight states with a team of stars, stumping for Kennedy. He does not seem at ease in describing this shining company, which included Byron "Whizzer" White, Starlet Angie Dickinson, Jeff Chandler, Stan Musial, Professor Arthur M. Schlesinger, Jr., and various "Kennedy girls." He sounds strangely piqued by the remark of one of a group of Republican ladies at a neighboring table in the Boise, Idaho, Country Club, who pointed out the barnstormers with the words: "They're the ones who are going to take it away from us."

One of the most charming contributions of *Report of the County Chairman* is the delineation of the two Bucks County politicians, Johnny Welsh and Sam Thompson; these real characters outdo the imaginings of even the most skillful novelist. Recollections of his feelings when driving to rallies include not only exhausting labors in stuffy meeting rooms but also the evocation of crisp autumn leaves and a dazzling early Pennsylvania snowfall.

Michener's experience in his grassroots campaigning for Kennedy undoubtedly gave him the further taste for political blood that caused him two years later to wage a campaign for his own candidacy for the United States House of Representatives. The 1960 battles and the volume that records them gave him another chance to voice his liberal credo and his belief in the American freedoms. And, although the number of people whose votes were switched through the efforts of the Citizens Committee was tiny, it is quite possible that, around the nation, the efforts of people like Michener did sway the balance enough to give Senator Kennedy the fraction of one per cent of the total popular vote needed to inaugurate a Democratic administration in Washington.

CHAPTER 6

Passages to the Fiftieth State

H AWAII, after sixty years of territorial status, was granted
statehood on August 21, 1959. In November, as a giant-sized
salute to the fledgling state, Michener's novel *Hawaii* appeared. For
twenty months it remained at or near the top of the national best-
seller lists. All in all, considering even such excellent volumes as
Ruth McKee's *The Lord Anointed*, Marjorie Sinclair's *The Wild
Wind*, Albertine Loomis' *Grapes of Canaan*, and Oswald A.
Bushnell's *The Return of Lono* and *Molokai*, Michener's is the best
novel ever written about Hawaii.

National reviews were laudatory, in the main. Maxwell Geismar
wrote in the *New York Times Book Review:* "A brilliant panoramic
novel about Hawaii from its volcanic origins to its recent statehood.
It is a complex and fascinating subject, and it is rendered here with a
wealth of scholarship, of literary imagination, and of narrative skill,
so that the large and diverse story is continually interesting. . . . As
this large novel draws into the modern period, and particularly in
the World War II episodes, it becomes more uncertain in tone,
thinner in feeling, and hortatory in its message. The writer who has
described the first millennium of Hawaiian history with such elo-
quence becomes himself a kind of 'missionary,' or apologist."[1]

Mary Ross felt that "Mr. Michener has written a saga of the land
that is now his home with the zest and freshness of observation of a
convert, the particularity of a novelist, and insight gained, one
suspects, from laborious exploration of many fields as diverse as
geologic processes, the life of ninth century Polynesians, and the
culture of pineapples. The prevailing quality of this book, like that
of the huge Hawaiian princesses, is that it is enjoyable. . . . Strange
as some of its people seem, they are real; they could have existed.
Moreover, the book has the unusual quality of making concrete,
through the lives of individuals, the impact of ideas and emotions

and situations that are shared by the rest of the nation."[2]

William Hogan was somewhat more exacting. "Michener's characters are prototypes rather than people. As he has adjusted details in Hawaii's history to suit his fiction, the author is forced to adapt characters to fit into the big historical picture. And that is the book's main weakness. Michener sacrifices drama for pageantry, true characterization for literary showmanship."[3] Wrote Fanny Butcher: "One of the most enlightening books ever written, either of fact or fiction, about the integration of divergent peoples into a composite society. That it is also an engrossing story makes its message the more cogent. . . . What makes the novel unforgettable is not only the deep understanding of national dreams and ways of life, not only the exciting panorama of events, but the human beings who were the motivators and the movers in the creation of today's Hawaii."[4]

Horace Sutton in the *Saturday Review* was enthusiastic: "The subject is so well covered that it may be a long time before anyone essays another major work on the islands. . . . A masterful job of research, an absorbing performance of storytelling, and a monumental account of the islands from geologic building to sociological emergence as the newest and perhaps the most interesting of the United States."[5] Paul West stated: "Mr. Michener makes a very fine attempt at putting the primitive mind into modern English. . . . As the book unwinds into the twentieth century, familiar Michener stereotypes emerge, but Mr. Michener goes into them more deeply than usual; and for that reason most of all, this is easily his most impressive, most honest novel by far."[6] Even Riley Hughes in the *Catholic World* concluded: "There are some unpleasant, even repellent, passages in this book, particularly as the author reports the periods of sexual license in Hawaii's history; but the impact of the whole is one of integrity and courage of the Polynesians, New England missionaries, Chinese and Japanese who came in that order to form the major groups of power."[7]

I   *Eight Pages of Ancestries*

Even in Honolulu, where cries arose from a few racial bigots, reviews were generally favorable. Professor William Huntsberry of the University of Hawaii, himself a novelist, wrote of the ordinary reader in the islands: "Whichever one of the racial groups he belongs to, he will be at times incensed, at times pleased; but finally he will grant that the completed portrait is amazingly well done. . . . Everyone in Hawaii should read this book."[8] But some residents of Hawaii, of the *kamaaina* or old-timer group, were horrified at what they feared was skeleton-rattling. They assumed that this novel would be taken by mainland readers as verbatim history, and that the visitors' bureau image of the islands as a carefree Polynesian paradise would be shattered. Actually, thousands of visitors to the new state came because they wished to see the place that Michener had dramatized in his big volume.

Those who had lived in Hawaii for years and had read its history were probably least qualified to judge this book objectively. As they read the novel, they kept finding that it was not history. The book is not even historical fiction under the usual definition. There are almost no historic personages named in the entire volume with the exception of a few rulers; even King Kalakaua is merely referred to as "the last king of Hawaii" (561).[9] According to the records, the first mission in Lahaina, Maui, was opened not by "Abner Hale" but by William Richards and Charles Stewart; and, at annexation, the Hawaiian government was headed not by "Micah Hale" (579) but by Sanford B. Dole. The brig *Thetis* is not the *Thaddeus* that brought the First Company of Congregational missionaries in 1820. Michener's book is a pageant of the coming of the various peoples to the islands, and it is founded on truth but not on fact. As writer of several volumes of Hawaiian history, I feel that the reviewer in the *Library Journal* was in error when he called the book "truly a comprehensive social history of our Fiftieth State."[10] And yet few problems of Hawaiian life over the past century and a half are left untouched.

As Michener states on the flyleaf, "This is a novel. It is true to the spirit and history of Hawaii, but the characters, the families, the institutions and most of the events are imaginary." Disregarding this plain warning, and the clear realization that most of the characters are not modeled, say, on one particular missionary or sea captain but on a composite of several, some readers assumed that here was an exposé of a cherished ancestor. And as one longtime inhabitant of Honolulu once remarked to me, "I've never lived in a place where people were so worried about the reputations of their grandparents."

Criticism in Hawaii itself centered, then, mainly around the identifiability of the characters and the authenticity of the setting. The many other contributions of a good novel were overlooked in favor of these two aspects. Those who would never have troubled, for instance, to try to identify each person in *Sayonara* or to date the episodes in that novel were indignant that some revered Hawaiian personage had apparently been pilloried. As soon as *Hawaii* was published, Mrs. Clarice B. Taylor, Michener's research assistant on the novel, was incessantly telephoned by people who asked her: "Why did you let Michener say that?" The crime of the author was compounded when it often appeared that his presentation was plausible. "Isn't it true?" Mrs. Taylor would counter, and get the reply, "Oh, yes, but we should never talk about it!"[11] ·

Like Jack London half a century before him, Michener was condemned for publicizing nineteenth-century conditions in the leper colony on a peninsula of the island of Molokai. Now that modern medicine has eliminated any need for isolation of cases of what formerly was euphemistically termed Hansen's disease, everyone would like to forget those conditions; but those apologists who would refute Michener's picture of the Kalawao colony before 1870 might have a difficult job. And his references in this novel to other incidents or customs are frequently based solidly on documentary research.

Most of the criticisms voiced in Hawaii were far from displeasing to Michener. As he wrote me on December 12, 1959, he felt that such discussion ought to help accomplish "what I have wanted this novel to accomplish ever since I conceived it some years ago: I wanted people to talk about it in Hawaii in terms of history, sociology, relevancy, politics, vision. Nothing would make me happier than to have the book dissected page by page, for in the doing so perhaps Hawaii will grow up artistically. Then maybe we'll get the great books out of the islands that the islands have a right to expect." He assured me once that he would achieve his aim if his novel were superseded by a dozen better novels, each expressing the spirit of Hawaii as honestly seen by other authors.

That sooner or later some modern novelist would see in Hawaii's story the material for an epic piece of fiction was self-evident. In 1944, while escorting John Dos Passos around Manoa Valley, I suggested that he, as the author of *Manhattan Transfer* and *U.S.A.*, would be qualified to do a panoramic novel about the island territory; but unfortunately he walked into the propeller of a warplane on a Pacific island soon afterward and did not return to Honolulu.

Michener was a much more available candidate for the task. During his first lengthy visit to Hawaii, the longshoreman's strike of 1949 cut off shipping of supplies to Hawaii for one hundred and seventy-eight days and aroused such bitterness in the population that he was then and there inspired to write a novel about social relations in this melting pot of the Pacific. Four or five years later he outlined a plot to his editor and began serious planning on the book.

Michener's interest in Hawaii was combined with another interest—the novel covering several generations in a family. Chatting with me in New York in 1957, he mentioned that he admired the sort of book done by Joseph Pennell in *The History of Rome Hanks* and by Glenway Westcott in *The Grandmothers*. (The latter of these he mentions in *Hawaii* [723], along with Willa Cather's *A Lost Lady* and Kate O'Brien's *Without My Cloak*, as the kind of "family histories" that should be written to help people speculate about their home regions.) The production of Michener's own chronicle novel covering a number of generations in Hawaii necessitated an eight-page series of genealogical tables at the end of the volume, to keep straight the scores of characters mentioned and the some fifty-five generations between Tamatoa IV of Bora Bora and Kelly Kanakoa, Waikiki beach boy born in 1925. The invention of vital statistics of ancestors not even mentioned in the story was only part of Michener's painstaking search for verisimilitude.

II   *Five Hundred and One Sources*

The novel that burst out at such a well-timed moment in 1959 had origins going back for at least a decade, and it required months of factual research. On March 22, 1957, Michener had written me confidentially:

For a good many years I have wanted to do a major, long novel on Hawaii and have had it outlined for the last three. It falls into five parts: (1) the coming of the Polynesians to Hawaii; (2) the coming of the haoles to Maui; (3) the coming of the Chinese to Oahu; (4) the coming of the Japanese to Kauai; (5) the coming of the Filipinos generally. . . . I would hope that we would see, through the successive intrusions of new characters and new peoples, the full range of Hawaiian history. The time of the novel would range from about 1050 A.D. to 1954. It would be as strong as the events which it covers.

Now obviously to accomplish such a novel I must enlist the aid of some good researcher, not because I could not do the basic research required but because I have neither the eyesight to do so nor the time. I therefore propose to employ, if I can find, someone solidly based in Hawaiian history and culture.

I proposed the name of Mrs. Clarice B. Taylor, who for years had written a daily newspaper column that roved through the many mazes of Hawaiiana. According to Michener's remarks in an article, "Writing a Book in Hawaii," her contribution as a research assistant was eminently successful. He found that she was "not only extremely wise but hilariously funny." Together they launched into a full year of study, and he lugged home with him some five hundred books on various aspects of his story material. Her collection of clippings was also invaluable. But perhaps the greatest inspiration came from long hours of conversation. "For this quiet little woman has an absolutely unquenchable love of the ridiculous, the absurd, the pompous-deflating yarn," Michener commented. "If I had dared to use half the riotous stuff she told me, both I and my book would have been banned in Boston."

Mrs. Taylor has published several accounts of her own adventures in working with a popular author. In "A Preface to a Novel," she tells of her first meeting and her skepticism about the idea of doing a novel in which the lives of the four main racial stocks in Hawaiian history would be intermingled. "His terseness was deafening. For a month we sparred. Finally I said to him: 'The things you want are not to be found in books. You are breaking new ground. . . . All this material you want has to come out of my head.' . . . Each time I said to him, 'You are the first,' . . . his determination seemed to say, 'I am going to do it!' " In the end, he also depended upon Mrs. Taylor for help in getting some idea of the Puritan doctrines of the missionaries, and he even argued with her when she swore that a marriage between a Punti Cantonese man and a Hakka woman was completely inconceivable. And perhaps the rollicking humor of the brown-skinned Pacific voyagers as revealed in *Hawaii* is directly traceable to Mrs. Taylor's imitations of the name-calling chants of Polynesian enemies.

Michener's method of getting into a story is shown in Mrs. Taylor's piece on "Michener and Names." She says: "His first request was for a list of about two hundred Hawaiian names, and a five-generation genealogy. . . . The name he liked best was I-liki, meaning the salt spray pelting a chief's face during a storm at sea. . . . He found 'Jerusha' among one of the aunties of a missionary wife. He knew at once that Jerusha was to be his favorite character. . . . Just where he found the name of his sea captain, Rafer Hoxworth, I do not know."

Among the five hundred books consulted, Michener got great

help for his opening section on the geology of the islands from a multivolume scientific work, *Insects of Hawaii*, by Elwood P. Zimmerman. He discovered much fascinating Polynesian lore in the publications of the world-famous Bernice P. Bishop Museum in Honolulu, especially *Ancient Tahiti* by Teura Henry, granddaughter of an English missionary; she had reworked her grandfather's copious notes, which were later mysteriously lost. The indomitable spirit of the missionary wives of Hawaii he found embodied in the courage under the surgeon's knife of Mrs. Lucy G. Thurston, whose memoirs are a permanent part of Hawaiiana. The heartbreaking efforts of the New Englanders to negotiate the Strait of Magellan were modeled in part upon the 1826 journal of Captain James Hunnewell of the small sailing craft *Missionary Packet*. Valuable illustrations came from *Dr. Baldwin of Lahaina* by Mary Charlotte Alexander and from *Historical Missionary Album* by Lyle Alexander Dickey.

Among the many pleasures of writing in Hawaii a novel about Hawaii, Michener appreciated the advice and assistance of the librarians of the many libraries of the territory; of the staff of the Bishop Museum; of the University of Hawaii professors of many departments; of the community leaders of Oriental as well as Caucasian ancestries; and of the people of Polynesian descent such as Mrs. Mary Kawena Pukui and Liliuokalani Morris.

Much of the background of the novel was drawn as well from Michener's own observations—not only in Hawaii but in Japan, China, New England, and the South Pacific. In order to refresh his recollection of the islands from which he assumed the first Hawaiians to have emigrated, he made another trip to Bora Bora. There he renewed his acquaintance with World War II friends, first met when he had viewed those islands under the tutelage of the greatest of Polynesian scholars, Sir Peter Buck.

However, it should be emphasized again that, although based on a wealth of background investigation, *Hawaii* is still a story of what could have happened rather than a documented chronicle. That the first arrivals in the empty volcanic chain of Hawaii came from Bora Bora is speculation only, and that they came because they were forced to flee from religious persecution is even more speculative. Nobody is sure whether the Hawaiian Columbus came from Bora Bora or Tahiti or the Marquesas, or from another Polynesian settlement. But the story is plausible, and that the Polynesians were skilled navigators of their hundred-foot double sailing canoes is beyond cavil. And Hawaii was settled by such Polynesians, quite possibly in the way that Michener so painstakingly describes.

III   *A Difficult Man to Love*

Hawaii is a big book. It runs to half a million words—a length that seems even greater if one reads it, as I did, in gangling galley proofs. Its bulk impelled an Australian reviewer to term it "a relentless flood of a book that seems poised ready to engulf the reading public with the literary equivalent of a Pacific tidal wave."[12] Moreover, the novel begins in a way that any textbook of fiction writing would denounce as absolutely fatal: it opens with no mention of human beings, but with twelve solid pages of description. These cover the geological formation of the Hawaiian chain rising through aeons from a volcanic crack in the profound floor of the Pacific. Yet Michener again applies the principles of exposition in such a dramatic way that this section of the book remains a *tour de force* of popular science and was printed as a separate feature article in *Life* magazine.

The stage is set, after the lapse of millions of years of almost imperceptible evolution. But only plants and a few birds inhabit it. The empty archipelago awaits the coming of the various races which are to be depicted in the next four books of the novel (the narrative on the coming of the Filipino group was regretfully jettisoned by Michener when the book was already well along and its bulk was becoming too great to be contained in a single volume). Erecting this empty stage is a basic part of Michener's plan, for one strand of his theme is that the "Paradise of the Pacific" was never originally an Eden but merely a place where one could possibly be built by human hands. "For these islands," he says, "were a crucible of exploration and development" (15). Again, he apostrophizes: "Therefore, men of Polynesia and Boston and China and Mount Fuji and the barrios of the Philippines, do not come to these islands empty-handed, or craven in spirit, or afraid to starve. . . . Bring your own food, your own gods, your own flowers and fruits and concepts" (16). And in a sense the first-comers of all races were a band of misfits. "No man leaves where he is and seeks a distant place unless he is in some respect a failure," he remarks (70); but he adds that they did at least have courage.

Another and even stronger main theme, however, is the one Michener had used in his novels ever since *Tales of the South Pacific*. It is the preachment once more against race or class prejudice, xenophobia, pigheaded biases, and undemocratic reaction. Stated more positively by Michener himself, his theme is "the enviable manner in which Hawaii had been able to assimilate men and women from many different races."[13] The meaning of *Hawaii* is the triumph of Americanization.

To retell the story of *Hawaii* would require a volume the size of *The Bridges at Toko-Ri*, and I shall not here try to do more than outline the main sections and mention a few of the many special qualities that this big novel offers to its perceptive reader. The best thing to do with *Hawaii* is not to read about it but to read it, for the story moves deftly and clearly and requires little explication.

The opening section, setting the scene, is followed by four novelette-sized portions, each dealing with the coming of founding families to the Hawaiian isles. The first of these four sections is "From the Sun-Swept Lagoon," which tells of the emigration from the South Pacific island of Bora Bora of a great canoe-load of explorers led by the king of that island and his younger brother, Teroro, "The Intelligent One," a priest who cannot accept the bloody new cult of the god Oro. Filled with descriptions of ancient Polynesian customs and of the preparations for the voyage to a region that might well contain no land whatever, the narrative continues with a description of the daring navigation of Teroro on the five-thousand-mile journey until the distant view of a snow-capped, smoking volcano brings hope of a landing.

The discoverers name the new island after their legendary Paradise of "Hawaiki" and transplant to it their material culture, as well as their reverence for the guiding principles of mana and tabu. But Teroro soon leads a return voyage to Bora Bora, to bring back his unpretty but wise second wife, Marama, along with the goddess-stone Pere who presides over volcanoes, and a canoe full of children and flowers—all things that were further needed to ensure happiness in the newly settled archipelago. Slaves, of course, had been brought in the first canoe, but, mercifully, only one of them was sacrificed when the first temple was erected on Hawaii's shores. In a few pages, the earliest occupation of village sites is sketched. And then for nine centuries the curtain falls.

"From the Farm of Bitterness" comes Abner Hale, sallow-faced, puny, fanatical son of New England who, after hearing a talk by an exiled Hawaiian lad named Keoki Kanakoa, gets a call to missionize those distant pagan islands. Abner and his new bride, Jerusha Bromley, make the voyage in the bark *Thetis*, jammed into a tiny cabin with three other missionary couples, whose miseries, sailing in two oceans and through the terrifying Strait of Magellan, are not minimized.

At last, on page 206 of *Hawaii*, we finally begin to observe people living in those islands, mainly in the beautiful port of Lahaina, Maui, where the Hales settle and try to erect a firm church. The beauty of the location is lost upon Abner, whose ingrained Calvinism is at war daily with the polytheistic nature worship of his flock. For example, Abraham Hewlett, one of his fellow missionaries who is stationed at Hana, loses his wife in childbirth because he and Abner refuse to avail themselves of the aid of Hawaiian midwives. When Hewlett is forced to resign from the mission because he has committed the "abomination" of marrying a Hawaiian girl, he condemns Abner and the others in these words: "You love the Hawaiians as potential Christians, but you despise them as people" (290).

Teroro and Marama, of the ninth-century discovery party, have been more or less reincarnated in Kelolo and Malama, high chiefs of Lahaina and parents of Keoki Kanakoa, who has returned there with the *Thetis* company. Their dignity is shocked when Abner embraces and welcomes into the church congregation a slave of the untouchable class, but they strive to understand and to enforce the strange tabus brought to them by the New England *kahuna* in the tall beaver hat. Keoki, their son (who seems to have been suggested by such historic Hawaiians as Henry Opukahaia, George P. Kaumualii, and David Malo), although a sincere Christian, is denied a pastorate; and he backslides so far as to marry his sister, the beauteous Noelani, but soon he dies (as did historic Kamehameha II) of the measles. Noelani then marries Captain Rafer Hoxworth, whaling captain and former suitor of Jerusha Hale.

Most of the missionaries, for one or another reason, leave the mission, which of course was not designed to be a permanent church enterprise. Scientifically minded Dr. John Whipple becomes a partner of Captain Retire Janders of the *Thetis*. Second-generation Americans, growing up in Hawaii, have to find professions if they wish to stay in their native islands. Intermarriage among Hales, Whipples, Hewletts, and Janderses creates a ruling class that will dominate the islands for a century. Micah, eldest and most brilliant of the Hale children, marries Malama, daughter of Hoxworth and Noelani, thus joining the blood of Bora Bora with that of the rising haole (Caucasian) elite. Micah becomes the partner of his father-in-law. Growing commerce based on sandalwood, whaling, and sugar planting creates stable fortunes for concerns like Janders & Whipple and Hoxworth & Hale.

The most interesting character in this section, though, is recalcitrant, scrawny Abner Hale, slightly mad from a kick in the head by Rafer Hoxworth, but even more mad through fundamentalist zeal that is doomed again and again to be confronted by the seeming victories of paganism, as when Noelani's prayers to the goddess Pele halt a devastating lava flow. Yet in the depths of dejection at his failures, even Abner can experience an authentic conversion, when his untiring, devoted wife Jerusha inspires him to preach a sermon which he based not upon the brimstone of Calvin but upon the compassion of Jesus Christ. Again Michener stresses that what we all need is an open mind and a change of heart.

Jerusha, indeed, is answer enough to any reader who might feel that Michener expresses "antimissionary" sentiments (see the tribute to her on page 353). And Abner, extremist that he is, often wrings our admiration, especially when he defies the belaying pins and cannonballs of mariners like Hoxworth, who demand that the Hawaiian mission maidens continue to prostitute themselves in the forecastles of the whale ships.

Michener's attitude toward Abner Hale—although this figure, like most others, is a composite—probably reflects what he has said elsewhere concerning Hiram Bingham, vigorous leader of the First Company who battled personally against seafaring men bent on continuing the corruption of the islands that had gone on since Cook's crews had introduced venereal disease forty years earlier. Bingham's "self-righteous, unyielding rectitude," says Michener in his Introduction to *A Hawaiian Reader*, "gave Hawaii its formative character. . . . Hiram Bingham is one of the most difficult great men in history to love, but everyone looking at either Hawaii or the Pacific in general is required either to stand for Bingham, the bigoted Old Testament figure, or for those other Americans who almost destroyed the islands. I have always been for Bingham."

IV *Americans from Asia*

The native Hawaiian race has been reduced to a tenth of its number since Cook's day, and labor is required to maintain the domains of the planters and merchants. Importation of Orientals is the answer. Thus the next two books of Michener's saga are concerned with the troubles and triumphs of the Chinese and the

112   JAMES MICHENER

Japanese elements that were added to Hawaii's polyracial crucible.

"From the Starving Village" goes back to 817 A.D., but soon brings the story up to 1865, when Kee Chun Fat, successful in California, returns to his Punti village in South China and encourages his people to emigrate to Hawaii. His nephew, Mun Ki, Macao gambler, makes the hellish passage on the *Carthaginian* under Captain Hoxworth. On arrival, Mun Ki marries a shipmate, a Hakka girl, Char Nyuk Tsin, who was consigned to a Honolulu brothel. They become house servants of Dr. John Whipple, who gives the hardworking woman a patch of boggy ground on which she can raise vegetables. This land is the basis of the Kee fortune, destined to become one of the largest in Honolulu a century later. As Dr. Whipple prophetically reflects: "In fifty years my descendants here in Hawaii will be working for the Chinese!" (456).

The Kee family beget five sons, all named for continents of the earth. The last one is born in the terrible leper colony on a peninsula of Molokai, for Mun Ki has been sent there as a medical case, and devoted Nyuk Tsin has voluntarily gone along as a healthy *kokua* or helper to dwell in the houseless plain where gruesome creatures brawl unchecked and kill for food. Things improve somewhat after the Chinese couple murder with sharp sticks the ringleader of the faceless band of terrorists on the barren peninsula, and a primitive rule of order is established. The fifth son, Australia, is sent as a baby to Honolulu; and, after the death of Mun Ki, the faithful wife returns to that town, just as a priest named Father Damien arrives in the settlement of sufferers.

The fifth son disappears for some years, and turns up as the adopted child of the Hawaiian governor of Oahu. This lad, under his name of Keoki Kanakoa, is given some pineapple land that will stay in the family. All the boys become community leaders—Africa, for example, shows an aptitude for law and gets a degree at Michigan. Through practice of all the old Yankee virtues of thrift, family solidarity, piety, scholarliness, efficiency, common sense, and getting along with people, the Chinese community thrives and adds its customs and characteristics to the bubbling racial pot.

The predominance of haole prestige continues through the nineteenth century, however; and, among the proliferating Hawaiian-American families, two leaders stand out—Micah Hale, political sage, and "Wild" Whipple Hoxworth, rakish grandson of Rafer and Noelani. Initiated by Rafer at the age of thirteen into the delights of the bordellos of Iwilei, Whip comes to be a cabin boy on a whaler, a world adventurer, a scientist, a land developer, and a leader in irrigation, sugar planting, pineapple culture, importation of immigrant labor, and revolutionary gunrunning. He is also a connoisseur of women of all shades. As his grandfather had remarked: "Anybody can be brave enough to love a girl of his own color." Whip is no coward.

His attitude toward the males of other racial groups, however, is far from affectionate. He enforces fully the Masters and Servants Law of the kingdom, and he is the real enemy of Queen Liliuokalani when she is dethroned. Whip's interpretation of the complicated Blount investigation is simple: "We may be in deep trouble. Since Cleveland's investigator comes from Georgia, he probably despises niggers. . . . As a sensible human being he'll try to compensate and prove that he doesn't hate other people with dark skins" (569). And the forcible reenthronement of Liliuokalani by American gunboats is prevented because of her insistence that sixty American leaders of the Provisional Government should all be beheaded. The description of the bubonic plague episode of 1899, however, is a retelling of history much closer to actuality. It is this end-of-the-century event that gives the biggest opportunity for the Kee family, led by aging Nyuk Tsin, to use their syndicate or *hui* for further economic triumph.

Annexation by the United States, the not-so-manifest destiny of Hawaii, is accomplished through the wisdom of Micah Hale. But he recalls how close was the chance that the island kingdom of Japan might have swallowed the island kingdom of Hawaii (561). And the next section of the novel deals with the coming of the Japanese component, which arrived later than the Chinese and had an even harder time establishing itself under the patterns of Hawaiian and American social mobility.

This section is handled with warm enthusiasm and special knowledge, for Michener's fondness for the Japanese in Asia is easily translated to a championship of the acculturation of the Japanese in Hawaii. If the author plays favorites among any of the four groups he shows making their various passages to the Paradise of the Pacific, it is toward the Japanese.

"From the Inland Sea" and the concluding book, "The Golden Men," cover many of the developments in Hawaii during the twentieth century, among the haoles as well as the Orientals; but primarily the story deals with the decline of haole prestige and the rise of the Chinese and Japanese clans. Specifically, it tells of the family of

Kamejiro Sakagawa, peasant of Hiroshima, who comes to Kauai in
1902 to labor in the sugar fields of Wild Whip Hoxworth in order to
earn enough money to go back to Hiroshima. Stocky and
courageous, for fifteen years he becomes successively hot-bath
operator, pineapple cultivator, and tunnel-drilling dynamiter. He
marries a picture bride, but not the one he had sent.for, because on
the pier he impulsively swaps his pretty, lazy choice for the sturdy
bride of his superpatriotic friend Mr. Ishii. The Sakagawas rear four
boys and a girl. Suspected of trying to help organize labor on the
plantation, Sakagawa takes his family to a slum in Honolulu and survives as a privy cleaner, wartime barbershop operator, and grocer.

He demands that his children make progress through the
American school system that is the best path open to them, and they
try hard. Pretty daughter Reiko is rejected by the best of the public
schools through the device of the "English-standard" system, but by
athletic prowess the boys overcome their environment. Tadao is
even offered a football scholarship at swanky Punahou, where
"there aren't many Japanese" (713); but Australia Kee, Chinese,
had crashed that admissions barrier twenty-five years before.

After Japanese war planes bomb Japanese people in Honolulu on
December 7, 1941, Reiko falls in love with an American navy lieutenant, but her father complains to the commodore and she winds
up marrying Mr. Ishii, thirty-five years older than she and still crazi-
ly peddling Shintoism and the banzai spirit. Her brothers, loyal to
Hawaii, battle for the privilege of enlisting in the American army.
All four of them serve through World War II, led by Colonel Mark
Whipple, and two of them die because they have to fight harder
than any other soldiers to prove their right to be called Americans.

World War II is a time of opportunity for the Kee family; they
buy out the properties of frightened inhabitants of the islands who
are fleeing to the American mainland. Still under the tutelage of old
Wu Chow's Auntie, the Chinese reap a growing financial
predominance. The war is, however, the beginning of the collapse of
the tidy paternalistic barony of the old haole dynasties that have
ruled by the interlocking of marital and economic ties. Hoxworth
Hale—leader of the latest generation and head of "The Fort," the
figurative stronghold of these dynasties—is a scholarly sort who did
a bit of research at Yale on such personages in Hawaiian history as
James J. Jarves, and he has by no means the completely closed mind
of his cousin Hewie Janders. On military business, Hoxworth visits
some of the other island communities in the Pacific; gets a chance to

compare the problems of Fiji, Samoa, and Tahiti with those in American Hawaii; and also tastes the simple delights of Bora Bora, from which one of his distant ancestors had come. But he fails to understand his son Brom, a promising writer who is later killed flying a B-29, or to foresee the power that the Chinese and Japanese will have in controlling Hawaii at midcentury.

V *Golden Men and Waikiki Women*

"The Golden Men," final section of the novel, has been considered the weakest. The author, after eight hundred concentrated pages, is beginning to flag, and the statehood deadline is approaching. He often substitutes synopsis for scene development because he wants to cover so many more aspects of the events. The number of postwar conditions of life in Hawaii that are dealt with is amazing. These include the genetic perils of interbreeding of old families (809), tidal waves (838), need for land reform through taxation (843), the "modenne" girl of Japan (847), unhappiness of Japanese war brides of American Japanese (872), the incursion of mainland chain stores through the cleverness of a Boston Irish lawyer aided by Hong Kong Kee as a local "blockbuster" (856), the rise of the Democratic Party (867), union organization (860), terrifying shipping and sugar strikes (862), antistatehood shenanigans of all kinds (887ff.), the McCarran-Walter Act (899, 905), the rise of Waikiki tourism (818), the "Cousins Society" (836), lack of intellectual stimulus among descendants of peasant immigrants (921), the Smith Act trials (924), the legend of the beastly whip-wielding plantation overseer (929), the survival of "spendthrift trusts" to protect inheritors of Hawaiian lands (910), and the further financial conquest of Hawaii by the Kees. The schizophrenia of the Japanese group in the islands is well demonstrated, not only by Mr. Ishii, who persists for years in believing that Japan won World War II, but by the elder Sakagawa, who finally returns to his native province in Japan but sneaks back to Honolulu because he is too old to use the primitive Japanese privies.

The "Golden Men" of the subtitle are defined as the present population of Hawaii, which might or might not be a product of interracial marriage but would at least be a "product of the mind" (807). Such a man might be "influenced by both the west and the east, a man at home in either the business councils of New York or the philosophical retreats of Kyoto." Each might pride himself on a high ancestry, real or invented. Hoxworth Hale might boast of being "pure haole"; Hong Kong Kee, a "pure Chinese"; Shigeo Sakagawa, a "pure Japanese"; and Kelly Kanakoa, loafing beach boy, a "pure Polynesian" whose lineage could be traced in the Mission Children's Library as far back as one hundred and thirty-four generations (820). But they are all of mixed ancestries, and that is a good thing, for civilizations always accelerate at racial crossroads.

Throughout the book, ancestor worship by *all* the racial groups and the fear of contamination of the "purity" of the tribe or clan through outmarriage are stressed again and again. Teroro of Bora Bora, a thousand years ago, should not wed a girl from neighboring Hawaiki; and, in the final pages of the book, both sides of each family are ashamed when Judy Kee marries Kelolo Kanakoa or when Senator Shigeo Sakagawa marries Noelani Hale. The older generation always fights against this dilution of the blood, but the young ones go merrily on their way swapping genes. And the result is usually a more vigorous admixture that will some day make little Hawaii one of the greatest American states.

But as the final page of the novel points out, "in an age of Golden Men it is not required that their bloodstreams mingle, but only that their ideas clash on equal footing and remain free to cross-fertilize and bear new fruit" (937). Paradise is what men bring to it; and, in Michener's awkward metaphor of pineapples blighted because of a lack of zinc in the fields, the slightest trace of an element added to or subtracted from the sociological soil might make all the difference. "No man could say out of hand what contribution the Filipino or the Korean or the Norwegian had made, but if anyone stole from Hawaii those things which the tiniest component added to the society, perhaps the human pineapples would begin to perish" (908).

The weakest part of the book, in the opinion of many readers—at least Republican ones—is the "election of 1954" in which "Black Jim McLafferty's team of brilliant young Japanese war veterans" (935) sweep into commanding power. Actually, the Democratic landslide did not come until the autumn of 1962. Michener at that later time was able to crow: "A novelist is a man who looks ahead to the true depth of things. I was writing about 1962."[14] And certainly the young "Americans of Japanese Ancestry," as they call themselves, have more than made their mark in Hawaii. Two of them are in the United States Congress in Washington today, voicing their special knowledge of American interests in the Pacific.

One of the high points in the final section comes when Congressman Carter of Texas, investigating Hawaii's claims to statehood, refuses to shake hands with "slant-eyed" young lawyer Shigeo Sakagawa. He is told that Shigeo is really one of Carter's constituents; for when a bunch of Japanese-American soldiers in France sacrificed eight hundred of their men to rescue three hundred Texans of the "Lost Battalion," Shigeo and the other survivors were given honorary citizenship in the State of Texas.

Yes, the "Golden Men" of Michener's coinage do represent the neo-Hawaiian sociological type that is emerging today through an amalgam of seven or eight racial stocks in the Fiftieth State. It is indeed a land where a Punti Cantonese and a Hakka could found a family or the offspring of a samurai marry an Okinawan girl at a Congregational church. The one-hundred-percent harmony that Michener desires is still a few years in the future, but already the lowly sons of immigrants have won supremacy in the economic life of the islands. The reviewer in *Time* acidly described the outcome of the novel as the triumph of the two-party system when "the barons and their one-time vassals all lie happily together on the same interlocking directorates."[15] The pendulum has certainly swung far from the days when one drunken German plantation foreman (665) aroused resentment leading to labor solidarity. (Today the Big Five has been replaced by the Big Two—the bosses of the powerful leading unions—and the even more dominant public-employee unions.)

On the final page of his big novel, Michener attempts a surprise ending more suitable to an O. Henry short story. The teller of the entire tale turns out to be Hoxworth Hale, who throughout has embodied the spirit of reaction. The idea is to point up dramatically the realization that even the Hales are among the golden men "who see both the West and the East, who cherish the glowing past and who apprehend the obscure future" (937). Most readers, however, feel that the effort to accept retroactively all the previous pages as the narrative of one of the later characters is not worth the readjustment. Such a hefty volume gains nothing by the addition of a whirligig ending.[16]

Although the scope of the novel leaves little place for Michener's powers of descriptive writing, the spell of the Pacific setting is still fresh for him, and he even finds space to catalog the loveliest scenic views in the islands (688). However, the action of the book is so extensive and covers such a broad period that characterization suffers. The one million people who have lived in Hawaii since Captain Cook's day cannot be represented even by Michener's large cast.

And with his cast of dozens, it is impossible to develop any one of
them in the round. Several, as has been mentioned, are com-
binations of three of four historical figures or composite photos of
types of persons. Sometimes plausibility goes by the board. Wild
Whipple Hoxworth, for instance, is a grotesque. He stands for all the
American enterprisers of the latter nineteenth century in the islands.
He single-handledly develops irrigation, sugar planting, the pineapple industry, and even the importation of the succulent mango. He
combines all this with world adventure, sexual athleticism, and the
leadership of the revolution resulting in annexation. Uliassutai
Karakoram Blake, the only character in the entire book who—according to the author—is not imaginary but "is founded upon a
historical person who accomplished much in Hawaii,"[17] is the least
believable of all.

On the other hand, such women characters as Aunt Lucinda
Whipple or Malama Kanakoa of The Swamp do almost seem to be
drawn from life. And Char Nyuk Tsin, known as "Wu Chow's Auntie," the Hakka woman who served as a *kokua* on Molokai, seems
quite a believable sample of the Chinese matriarchs that helped to
make that group the wealthiest element in Hawaiian society today.
Endearing is her habit, developed on Molokai, of examining her skin
nightly for signs of approaching leprosy—a habit she continues even
to the day when she obtains American citizenship and dies at the age
of one hundred and six.

Some readers have felt the outcome of *Hawaii* to be a libel on the
noble Polynesian voyagers who first found and possessed our newest
state. Elinor Henderson calls Kelly Kanakoa the "dispossessed," but
he responds (830) that "I got everything I want" and that maybe the
descendants of the Congregationalist missionaries are really the dispossessed because they have lost the God they had brought to
Hawaii (837).

When discussing the scenario of the proposed film of *Hawaii* with
one of the writers faced with completing that tremendous task, I
found that he shared the idea that the ending is unfair to the
Hawaiians. "Here you have everybody else winning what he
wants," he said, "but Kelly Kanakoa, descendant of generations of
kings, remains sitting in a loincloth on the beach, strumming a
ukulele." I tried to point out that Kelly not only was marrying a
beautiful heiress to a Chinese fortune, but that he also was a golden-
voiced idol among residents and tourists alike, and nobody could
desire more than that. Elinor Henderson is not the only one who

feels that Kelly is "the best thing in Hawaii" (821). Reminiscent of
Alfred Apaka, whose death in 1960 caused universal mourning
throughout the state, Kelly is supreme at doing all the things the
Polynesian group has contributed to Hawaii. As Michener says, "the
people loved Hawaii because of the Polynesians" (917). Kelly
Kanakoa makes music and fun, he offers love and welcome, he
voices the spirit that most of all makes Hawaii a paradise—the spirit
of aloha. This spirit of unprejudiced welcome should long survive,
for the Hawaiians and part-Hawaiians are the fastest growing seg-
ment of the present population of the Fiftieth State.

CHAPTER 7

Israel, Japan, Spain,
Pennsylvania . . .

A QUITE different part of the world is unfolded in the giant novel *The Source* (1965),[1] for the setting is the Holy Land, the racial melting pot from which sprang three of the world's greatest religions: Judaism, Christianity, and Islam. The genesis of *The Source* tells much about the ironic working of a writer's mind:

> In 1963 I was at the end of a ten-year period of extensive work on the Muslim world. I had lived in a score of different Muslim communities, all the way from Spain in the west to Indonesia in the east, and I was prepared to settle in Istanbul for two years to write a long, impassioned novel about Constantinople. . . . And then, by sheerest chance, I accepted an invitation to visit the Jewish city of Haifa. . . . I studied Acre dispassionately and judged that it would fit nicely into my Constantinople novel. The trip had been precisely as fruitful as I had anticipated. And then, on the last day, an Israeli archaeologist invited me to see a much different Crusade site, a castle near at hand, and as I stood alone in the dungeon of that ancient fortress, with the shadowy forms of warriors long dead moving in the dust, I suddenly conceived my entire novel *The Source*. Feverishly, in a small notebook I always carry, I outlined the seventeen chapters, taking no more than minutes to do so, and they remained just as I wrote them down, and in their exact order. . . .
> Such flashes of inspiration can happen. They come, of course, only when someone has been preparing himself for a long time; for an undedicated man to hope that the lightning will strike him, if he has done nothing by way of preparation to invite it, is self-delusion. I had spent ten years studying Islam, and without being aware of the fact, I was at the same time educating myself in its sister religion, Judaism.[2]

I *Life is Meant to be Life*

Michener's discovery that the long years he had spent planning a novel about Islam had become his training for a novel about Judaism caused him two regrets. First, he could never write both the novel on Islam and the one on Judaism; and, second, since he had the bad luck to work in an era when a good word spoken in behalf of Israel was interpreted as two bad words spoken against the Arab states, his work "was interpreted as being pro-Jewish and therefore anti-Arab. . . . It was not intended to be that way."³

The setting of *The Source* is an imaginary archaeological site in the modern state of Israel in 1964, almost twenty years after its founding by insurgent Zionists. A group comes together to begin excavating a "tell," or mound, that had been inhabited for some twelve thousand years by people of different stocks and cultures—the residue of one abandoned settlement after another, each resting upon the ruins of its predecessor. Lying between Acre and Damascus, Makor (meaning "the source"), near an enduring wellspring, is to be examined by a scientific team financed by Paul Zodman, a wealthy Jew of Detroit, who is invited to visit the diggings to see a dramatic "find" that a journalist has labeled "The Candlestick of Death." In the opening chapter, fourteen other objects from different historic levels are excavated; and each find forms the basis of a lengthy piece of fiction about the particular period. To remind the reader of this "frame," continuing events among the team members at the site are interspersed between stories. At the end of the book, the labor is concluded for the year, and the people of various backgrounds who have come together during this effort must separate, having enjoyed an unforgettable experience under the Palestinian sky.

Structure has often been of high importance to Michener, who sometimes could not begin a book until he had a tight scheme of development in mind. It is especially important in *The Source*. The series of fifteen stories begins in reverse order, for Michener presents in flashbacks what has happened to mankind on this site from the earliest time.

The flashbacks look at society in terms of profound problems, built upon incidents that are implied by what the archaeologists uncover. Thus we have a novel somewhat in the form of a César Franck symphony—a theme at the beginning, a return to the theme at the end, and discursions and excursions during the body, with the theme repeated. This is what gives the book its character, and will either allure or repel the individual reader. It's a complicated and sometimes beautiful and sometimes difficult ebb and flow of

122   JAMES MICHENER

time and history; my gamble is in being able to make it interesting enough
so that the reader will try to stay with it to the very end.⁴

About half of the contemporary account is given at the beginning of
the novel; fourteen interchapters are scattered among the stories;
about a third of the contemporary account appears in the
penultimate chapter; and the conclusion appears in the last chapter.
"This sounds unacceptably complex," Michener agrees, "and I certainly would not recommend it to another novelist, nor would I have
the courage to use it again myself, but in *The Source* it worked."⁵

The main focus of narration is upon forty-year-old Dr. John
Cullinane, the enlightened Irish-Catholic scholar from the University of Chicago who becomes more and more attracted to lovely,
petite Dr. Vered Bar-El, a thirty-three-year-old widow and Israel's
top expert in dating pottery sherds. Jemail Tabari is an Arab; but, as
the son of a trusted statesman, he has remained in the Jewish state to
carry on archeological work of the highest standard. Another scientist, Dr. Ilan Eliav, whose other capacities have caused him to be
drafted by the government, is a tall Jew who is two years older than
Cullinane; and between Eliav, a contemplative administrator, and
charming Vered an engagement is celebrated that Dr. Cullinane
hopes will not result in a marriage. The excavation work is done by
enthusiastic young students from many countries who vie for the
chance to work at Makor during the summer. Meals are
served at the nearby kibbutz or pioneer village, where Jews from
various countries—such as the brusque secretary Schwartz and the
stocky waitress Aviva—have built a thriving agricultural colony in
the desert. In the kitchen sometimes works one-armed General Ted-
dy Reich, hero of the War of Independence and now a cabinet
member, to show the younger kibbutzniks "that work, productive
work, is the salvation of man, and especially of the Jew" (53).

The last of the artifacts uncovered in the opening chapter is a
series of four serrated flints that once formed the cutting edge of a
sickle that dates from about 10,000 B.C.E. (before the common era).
This object, which betokens the beginning of the period when early
man was forsaking his cave in favor of a shelter alongside the field of
grain that he (or his woman) had domesticated and planted near the
well of Makor, introduces the first of the separate stories, "The Bee
Eater," at level XV. Although mastering the wild grain opened the
way for an intricate, interlocking society, Ur and his family were
then vulnerble to inimical natural effects—wind, rain, wild

beasts—which they sought to placate by erecting a monolith on the sheet of granite that would be the base of future cities. The seeds of religion were sown, and the anguish of Ur—"the mystery of death, the triumph of evil, the terrible loneliness of being alone, the discovery that self of itself is not sufficient"—is the anxiety that torments his human successors to this day (96).

"Of Death and Life," set around 2200 B.C.E., tells of Urbaal, a descendant of Ur, who is the leading man of Makor, now a walled town of Canaan, a land that is both a crossroads and a battleground of peoples between Mesopotamia and Egypt. The townsfolk are polytheists who worship many gods, among whom Melak (god of war and death) and Astarte (goddess of love and life) are the most potent. Out of the desert that lies east of the River Jordan comes a nomad clan of "'Habiru" or Hebrew herdsmen who are allowed by Urbaal to settle in vacant lands near the town. Mad because of his desire for a lovely slave girl, Urbaal is destroyed by the goddess of life; he kills his best friend and finds sanctuary at the altar of the One God of the Hebrews. Joktan, the patriarch of the nomads, is slowly corrupted by the life of the town and by the temple rites of Astarte, as Urbaal had been; but Urbaal's faithful wife Timna learns to pray to the One God and begins the conversion to monotheism.

"An Old Man and His God" tells of Zadok "the righteous," the leader of a Hebrew nomad clan in biblical times; to him his god, El-Shaddai, speaks from a burning bush and directs him to enter the Canaanite territories to find a dwelling place. Uriel, headman of Makor and descendant of Urbaal, permits the group to settle near the town. The Hebrews are drawn from their monotheistic worship by the "abominations" of Baal, and a religious conflict begins that will run for a thousand years, tempting them to whore after false gods. The warlike spirit of Zadok's son Epher triumphs; the town is razed by a holocaust in 1419 B.C.E. when the Hebrews capture it by a stratagem, and of all the Canaanite men only ten—including Zibeon, son of Uriel—are left alive to carry on the line.

"Psalm of the Hoopoe Bird" tells of an engineer, Jabaal, descendant of Uriel, who is charged in 966 B.C.E. with rebuilding the town walls during the reign of the powerful Jewish king David. People of many other sects—Canaanites, Hittites, Moabites, islanders of Cyprus, Babylonian refugees, Egyptians, dark-skinned Africans, and red-headed Edomites—accept the religion of the Hebrews and marry their daughters. Gershom the harpist plays before David and writes down the Psalms that bring needed emotional warmth to the harsh creed of Zadok; but Jabaal is found to have created an engineering epic in the shaft and tunnel that protected Makor's water supply.

Space does not allow more than a brief mention of the remaining dozen chapters that are based upon the later levels of the excavation of Makor. The pattern is followed of giving a date and a corresponding artifact, but the setting is usually the site of Makor, inhabited or rebuilt by successive groups from many ancestral stocks.

"The Voice of Gomer" deals with a heroic woman, prophetess of the will of Yahweh in 605 B.C.E., at the time the Hebrews were forced into captivity in Babylon. In "In the Gymnasium," Makor has succumbed to the pagan Greek culture with its Hellenistic emphasis on physical prowess; and Antiochus IV persecutes the Jews, who respond in 167 B.C.E. with the guerrilla battles of the Maccabees. "King of the Jews" is the usurper Herod, Roman governor of Judaea, who murders tens of thousands of his subjects but dies horribly in 4 B.C.E. in fear of the rumor that a messiah will be born at Bethlehem.

In "Yigal and His Three Generals," 40 - 67 C.E. (the common era), Michener tells of the siege and destruction of Makor, gateway to the sacred city of Jerusalem, by the Roman generals Vespasian, Titus, and Trajan. "The Law" (326 - 351 C.E.) chronicles the hammering out of the Talmud, the establishment of the Byzantine Christian church in the rebuilt town, and the beginning of the Diaspora, the scattering of the Jews around the earth. "A Day in the Life of a Desert Rider" (635 C.E.) describes the flaming assault of Islamites, the scourge of Christians and Jews alike, who are gathering up the pieces of an empire. "Volkmar" (1096 - 1105) and "The Fires of Ma Coeur" (1289 - 1291) depict the beginning and end of the Crusader occupation of the Holy Land; and the events are represented by a family of German knights who intermarried with other groups in a country devoid of Jews for almost two hundred years. At the end of that time, the towering castle of Makor (spelled in French as "Ma Coeur") is leveled by the Mameluke besiegers; and anyone looking at the mound would not guess that it had once been the home of human beings.

But the spirit of Makor spreads to nearby Safed and Tiberias. The Jews begin once more to foregather in the Galilee in "The Saintly Men of Safed" (1521 - 1559); and they arrive from such regions of persecution as Italy, Spain, and Germany. In the mountain town of Safed (modern name, Zefat), the third book of Jewry, the esoteric

Kabbala, is explicated; but the emphasis on present or future rewards results in separation of the sects—Ashkenazi legality versus Sephardi mysticism. "Twilight of an Empire" (1855 - 1880) shows that Turkish custodianship of the Galilee will eventually fail because it is based on materialistic exploitation and that Jewish custodianship is justified because it is based on moral concern for people. The long chapter "Rebbe Itzik and the Sabra," detailing the stirring events of the siege of Safed in April, 1948, during the Israeli War of Independence, describes the triumph of the heavily outnumbered guerrilla fighters over the Arab occupiers of the Galilee. Some of the characters in this section are persons involved in the 1964 excavation of Makor, and the final pages of the book relate not only the decisions of Cullinane and the others but also the outcome of the first year of work at that site, when even more startling discoveries are made at the base of the historic mound.

The Source is one of the longest books by Michener, and it is his best in the opinion of many readers. It covers in highly readable style a number of crucial periods in the history of mankind in the Mediterranean region, but Michener sticks quite closely to the main theme—which, of course, is connected with religion. Michener's plunge into theology is deep; and if it seems that he more strongly favors that of the Jews, it is because he gives in extensive detail the reasons this sect has survived and thrived. The long and persistent challenge of the "Family of Ur"—the original occupants of the land—brought forth energetic response in the mode described by Arnold Toynbee in his *A Study of History.* As Michener says early in *The Source:* "This maturing of Yahweh is another instance in which a challenge had produced an illumination which an easy acceptance could not have. The complaisant town of Makor with its amiable gods could never have produced Yahweh; that transformation required the captivity in Egypt, the conflict with the Pharaohs, the exodus, the years of hunger and thirst in the desert, the longing for a settled home and the spiritual yearning for a known god . . . these were the things required for the forging of Yahweh" (215). And at the end of the novel, Eliav, future premier of Israel, realizes that the secret of Jewish survival lay in their responsible adherence to life as well as to law: "Life isn't meant to be easy, it's meant to be life. And no religion defended so tenaciously the ordinary dignity of living. Judaism stressed neither an after-life, an after-punishment, nor heaven; what was worthy and good was here, on this day, in Zefat. We seek God so earnestly, Eliav reflected, not to find Him but to discover ourselves" (909). Life is meant to be life.

II   *Christianity versus Islam in Spain*

Other books that derive from Michener's experience of Asia deal with his lifelong interest in art, and the student of literature can find much to enjoy in his books about Japanese prints. *The Floating World* (1954), on which Michener labored for two years, is the most "literary" of the group, and in it he often uses rhetorical devices to make graphic and dramatic his treatment of another form of art. This book attempts to show the life and death of a particular sort of picture, the *ukiyo-e,* representing the "floating," evanescent, temporal world, which soon focused on the representation of the passing scene, especially that of the city, the Yoshiwara, and the theater. The rise and decline of this form in the period 1660 - 1860 he found to be a better example of the growth of regional art than the Sienese school he had gone to study on his first trip abroad.

He states in his preface strong reasons why his fellow Americans should be interested in Japanese prints. But again, as in almost all his books, Michener's main reason for writing seems to be his attempt to remove prejudice and his championship of popular rights. The *ukiyo-e,* he says, was "ever a child of freedom and perpetually a thorn in the rump of authoritarianism . . . irreverent, disrespectful and an incitement to riot" (245), and reflected social change: "the irresistible upthrust of great masses of people from what used to be called the lower social orders" (vi). He defends the crude Otsu-e, religious paintings preceding the woodcuts, as the "gaudy poor man's art" (8), lively, colorful, dramatic, and immensely decorative. And probably his main motive in expending his energies on this scholarly book—complete with historical background, biographical details, bibliographies, and other apparatus—is to put in the hands of his American readers at a reasonable price a collection of charmingly displayed examples of a popular art, and to share with them his enthusiasm for it.

The Hokusai Sketchbooks: Selections from the Manga, an outgrowth of the earlier book, was published in Japan in 1958 in a style resembling that of a Japanese volume. It is an anthology of the best of the woodblocks issued by Katsushika Hokusai (1760 - 1849), popular artist who died reluctantly at the age of eighty-nine, having published some five hundred volumes of art. Michener has selected the best surviving examples of 187 plates from the fifteen-volume series of the *manga,* or sketchbooks, issued over a space of sixty-five years. Hokusai's books were printed until the blocks wore out and had to be replaced; moreover, they were read to pieces by the citizen and his children. Hence the task of finding clean copies and of restoring their appearance was an exacting one. To the prints Michener adds an exhaustive commentary, even retelling legends forming the subjects of the sketches or commenting on the connection between a detail and some Japanese custom.

Michener expresses confidence that in the years to come the best Hokusai drawings will be "generally recognized as the equal of those of Rembrandt, Goya, and Van Gogh" (43), and elsewhere he includes comparisons between the Japanese artist and Breughel, Hieronymus Bosch, and Leonardo da Vinci. The author's devotion to his self-assigned task of recovering the best Hokusai drawing-books was intensified when he had to abandon the original manuscript during an airplane ditching off Iwo Jima, losing a number of irreplaceable quotations. But the rewritten manuscript again bespeaks his admiration for popular art. The *Manga* was "the victory of the common citizen who saw in Hokusai a rugged, peasant-type artist who created an art that he, the commoner, could comprehend and enjoy" (39). The efforts of the Tokugawa dictatorship to preserve the social status quo were thwarted by Hokusai's crowded pages, which to the man of the middle or lower class were his "history book, his newspaper, his scientific summary, and his treatise on moral principles" (40).

A third labor of love was *Japanese Prints: From the Early Masters to the Modern* (1959), likewise sumptuously printed in Japan. Most of the 256 pictures are in full color and carry the history of art over three centuries, including samples through 1957. Michener's ample commentary is supplemented by authoritative notes by Dr. Richard Lane. All the prints were taken from Michener's collection, valued at more than one hundred thousand dollars, which was later permanently donated to the Honolulu Academy of Arts. An expensive, limited-edition volume, *The Modern Japanese Print*, appeared in 1962.

As a young man, Michener spent an adventurous week in Spain, and thereafter it became one of his favorite countries for visits. As a result, a big book appeared in 1968 entitled *Iberia: Spanish Travels and Reflections*, with many vibrant photographs by Robert Vavra. Michener's "didactic frame of mind" led him to write a book which, in his opinion, "tells you more about Spain than you want to know." He summarized it in the same interview: "I would describe it as a nineteenth-century travel book in the classic tradition, filled with very personal reactions and the imprint of the history and culture and economics of the land. It's told in a very leisurely and, I hope, evocative manner."[6] Surprised when the book achieved a wide popularity, even though it was about one of the principal tourist meccas of Europe, he stated that he " . . . had thought, when writing a group of articles on Spain for the *Digest*, that this country was a private thing, savored by odd types like me but not appreciated by the general public. How wrong I was."[7]

Michener had first landed in Spain in 1932 around the age of twenty-five when he was serving as a "chart boy" on a Scottish collier. While the return cargo, which consisted of barrels of orange peel for marmalade, was loaded offshore from the Mediterranean village of Burriana in the province of Valencia, the captain allowed the young man to wander ashore for a few days. There Michener attended a festival at Castellon de la Plana; mingled among poor peasants; took a long third-class train trip to Teruel; saw the fiery fiesta of *fallas* in the ancient city of Valencia; listened to the haunting music of the flamenco; and even exchanged a few words with the president of the Spanish Republic. When he attended his first bullfight on April 3 in Valencia, he witnessed a performance by Domingo Ortega, a torero with whose entourage Michener later spent some time while observing the art of tauromachy that later engaged him in much serious study.

In the early 1960s Michener began his methodical observation of the regions of Spain with the intention of compiling the series of sketches to be published under the title of *Iberia* (a title somewhat misleading, since Portugal is comprised in the peninsula but is barely mentioned in the book). He chose ten cities in which to make lengthy stays and from which he could also explore the surrounding countryside. Additional chapters deal with Las Marismas, the marshy wildlife reserve at the mouth of the Guadalquivir River, and with "The Bulls"—the animals bred for an ancient sport that is nowadays being replaced, even in its homeland, by championship soccer.

Michener had usually made more than one visit to a particular city, but in each chapter he combines his observations. The first place described is Badajoz on the Portuguese border, a "nothing city" of bougeois contentment. From there, however, he made excursions into the arid region of Extremadura to the birthplaces from which conquerors of the New World like Cortés, the Pizarros, and Nuñez de Balboa emigrated to find fortunes denied them at home. Toledo he found overrun with tourists and plagued by noise and bad meals, but he thought it a paradise for lovers of art. Cordova—even more than neighboring, glamorous Granada—he found most typical of the Muslim culture of the Moors that had begun taking over most of Spain in 711 A.D. and that had survived until the last rulers were dislodged from Granada in 1492 by Ferdinand and Isabella, who are appropriately buried in that Arab fortress. Michener discourses on four famed men of Cordova: Seneca, "perfect Roman and ideal Spaniard" and tutor of Nero; Bishop Osio, fighting enemy of Arianism; Moses Maimonides, Jewish doctor and sage; and the contemporary and fellow philosopher of Maimonides, the Arab Averroës. Michener debates the relative contributions of Christianity and Islam in Spanish history, discusses the flamenco and other music, and analyzes the appeal of "romance" to lovers of Spain.

III   *Why Not Enroll at Electoral?*

After a digressive chapter on the wildlife wonders of the marshes of Coto Doñana, Michener concludes his survey of the southern region, Andalusia, with a chapter on Seville. He avers that no festival in the world can top the *feria* that follows Holy Week in that ancient city, that is the scene of *Carmen* and *Don Juan*, the center of colonial administration, and the realm of the nobility that is still prominent in national politics. In Seville he met John Fulton, American torero, and his friend Robert Vavra, whose photographic impressions so well complement the text of *Iberia*.

The chapter on Madrid is one of the less satisfying in the book. The capital, it is true, is the least Spanish of the ten cities visited; however, its attractions as an international metropolis cannot be treated even in the longest chapter, for they would require an entire book and an extended residence. When Michener contrasts, with nostalgia, the Madrids of 1950 and 1966, he does so to the discredit of the later year. He gives space to some glories of the Prado but omits mention of a dozen almost equally rich museums. From the many diversions he selects the *zarzuela* variety of musical show, *frontón* ball, soccer, and the *tertulia* or conversation group. He goes outside the city to describe El Escorial, giant tomb of the Hapsburgs built at the order of Philip II; to recall at Alcalá de Henares the achievements of Cardinal Cisneros; and to talk about modern Spanish painting at Cuenca, village of hanging houses.

The chapter on Salamanca, site of the famed university known to admirers of Fray Luis de León and Miguel de Unamuno, is filled with tales about the royal families of Spain and Portugal—in particular, about Isabella of Castile and Ferdinand of Aragón, "the Catholic monarchs," and their offspring. Michener visited towns associated with Isabella, such as her birthplace at Madrigal de las Altas Torres; her girlhood in the castle of Arévalo; the battleground of Toro, where Ferdinand of Aragón insured the safety of Isabella's realm; the old commercial town of Medina del Campo where she died; and Tordesillas, last home of her wandering, mad daughter Juana. Tours of the shrine of Guadalupe, mother church of all Hispanic countries, and the walled city of Avila, home of St. Teresa and St. John of the Cross, provided material for a debate about the effect of the Inquisition on the lack of cultural and economic progress in Spain.

The section on Pamplona gives much space, of course, to the fair of San Fermín and the running of the bulls—an event later given a chapter in *The Drifters*. It also contains a round-table discussion on Ernest Hemingway, descriptions of the town of Santillana del Mar and the neighboring painted caves of Altamira, and an account of a picnic in Roland's valley of Roncesvalles. As for Barcelona, which Michener first approached in 1964 driving up from Granada with his wife—who had previously visited this major city of Cataluña— this great city is, like Madrid, worthy of an entire book. The chapter mentions Spanish music, the publishing business, Catalan nationalism, museums (Michener visited eighteen major museums in Barcelona and the only second-rate one was the newly opened Picasso Museum), the *sardana* folk dance, the monastery of Montserrat, the architecture of Antonio Gaudí, and student riots. On a visit to the resort island of Mallorca, Michener became involved in the respective achievements of the Catalan philosopher Ramon Lull, or Lully, and Father Junípero Serra, builder of California missions—both sons of Mallorca.

After the expansive chapter "The Bulls," Michener makes a nostalgic return to Teruel, which a few years after his first visit to Spain was the scene of a crucial siege during the Civil War (1936 - 1939) that was a dress rehearsal for World War II. The final chapter of *Iberia* comprises some scenes in the northwest province of Galicia and a retracing of the eleven-century-old pilgrim trail from France through the Pyrenees to the cathedral city of Santiago de Compostela, shrine of St. James, cousin and disciple of Jesus. The long book ends during the national celebration of pilgrimage when, behind the main altar, the author puts his arm about the stone shoulder of the jewel-encrusted statue of St. James, patron of Spain and of James Michener.

When *Iberia* was first published, Michener remarked in an interview: "Spain, you know, is a unique area. It's always attracted fellows like me—people with an appreciation of the authentic statement. There's not much phoniness in Spain. It's a rugged, to-hell-with-you country—a first-rate country that makes little concession to the artist. I think that's why the artist had always liked it."[8] Michener's Spain may not be the Spain of everyone, for that country does challenge its admirers, and each province is so different that anyone should be able to find himself somewhere in the country. Nevertheless, as one who has lived and traveled in Spain for several years, going back to the reign of Alfonso XIII, and who has read all the books of travel about that land, I believe that *Iberia* is the best such volume available if the reader is able to read only one. It does not, of course, replace a good standard guidebook, but it has maps and an index and is useful for reference after one has followed the story.

Michener filled out the decade of the 1960s with two nonfiction volumes—*Presidential Lottery* and *The Quality of Life*—that reflect his interest in politics and in the environment. Over the years, he has spent much time, money, and energy in practical politics—efforts which, channeled into writing novels or travel books, would have made him even more prominent among contemporary authors. As has been said, he served in 1960 as county chairman for John F. Kennedy and campaigned for him across the nation. He ran unsuccessfully as a Democrat in 1962 for the House of Representatives, but he made heavy inroads into the supporters of a long-term incumbent in a predominantly Republican district. He campaigned in 1964 for Lyndon B. Johnson, and in 1968 he worked vigorously for Hubert H. Humphrey and even wrote the candidate's official campaign biography. On the state level, Michener served in 1967 as secretary of the Pennsylvania Constitutional Convention—the only body to achieve a complete reform of a state constitution in recent years.

Late in August, 1968—a presidential year—Michener was asked to be a member of the Electoral College, the group of people who under our Constitution cast the final ballots by which a president is chosen. Upon the members of the Electoral College, not upon popular majority, falls the duty of officially naming our presidents and vice-presidents unless the electors lack a majority, in which case the election is the task of the members of the new Congress. Few Americans, according to Michener, are aware of the deadly danger this system offers if, as in 1968, the leader of a third party such as George Wallace might be able to dictate the choice of a Republican or Democrat by swinging his electoral votes in return for major-party concessions.

Presidential Lottery, the book Michener published in April, 1969, is based upon his adventures in 1968 when he served in November as the man chosen as president of the Electoral College of the State of Pennsylvania. His conclusions, based on his wide study, are clear: Americans preserve a system of electing a president which contains so many built-in pitfalls that sooner or later it is bound to destroy us. The system has three major weaknesses. First, this system places the legal responsibility for choosing a president in the hands of an Electoral College whose members no one knows and who are not bound to vote the way their state votes. Second, if the Electoral College does not produce a majority vote for some candidate, the election is thrown into the House of Representatives, where anything can happen. Thus, since it is quite possible that the man who wins the largest popular vote across the nation will not be chosen President, turmoil could result. Third, the potent functions of the Electoral College are almost unknown to most citizens; a poll resulted in such silly responses as: "Every boy and girl should go to college and if they can't afford Yale or Harvard, why, Electoral is just as good, if you work" (43).

IV   The Pragmatic Thrust of America

Leaving home in a November blizzard that almost prevented Michener from reaching the capitol at Harrisburg, he found on arrival that a number of the required twenty-nine authorized electors were absent, and on short notice he had to round up ten Democrats to be sworn in as substitutes. His problems in conforming to the many rules of the state and to sending six copies of the electors' decisions to various official places are amusingly told in Chapter II, "The Forty-nine Steps." Almost everyone in the nation presumed that Richard M. Nixon would be the next president; but, until such rituals were performed in the capitals of fifty states, there was no guarantee that the "faceless men" of the Electoral College would vote for their party candidate or that the lack of a majority there would not throw the election into the houses of Congress, where the opportunity for making deals would be even more tempting.

Michener's scholarly study of "the reckless gamble in our electoral system," based on his consideration of the problem and possible reforms of that system, includes lengthy appendixes that concern the Constitution and the election results of 1968. He concludes that, unless a reform is accomplished, a similar election year could wreck the United States. As he reported in a special note in the paperback edition of *Presidential Lottery* published in November, 1969, his book and the proposals of other worried writers caused President Nixon to announce, early in his administration, that, even though he personally favored election by direct vote, he would support the "proportional" plan as the one most likely to win nationwide acceptance. Since 1969, the time-bomb aspect of the current, unreformed system has not been a clear and present danger; but there is still no assurance that another third-party election year could not cause all the turmoil and recrimination that occurred in the Jefferson-Burr tie of 1801 and in the chaotic events of the centennial year of 1876. Of Michener's involvement in creating *Presidential Lottery*, he wrote in 1973: "I have never written on a public matter with more driving force than I did this time. I wanted Congress to produce a simpler system of electing the President, a system which would avoid the dreadful dangers inherent in the one we now use. I tried to muster support for a constitutional amendment. I failed."[9]

One of the great banks of the world, the Girard Company of Philadelphia, commissioned Michener in 1969 to write a companion piece for their annual report. The result was *The Quality of Life*, a small volume beautifully illustrated by James B. Wyeth, a third-generation Pennsylvania artist; and thousands of copies were sent free to the bank's customers in February, 1970. Michener had been given complete freedom to express his views. If he did not invent the phrase "the quality of life," this book—which was soon issued for mass distribution by a Philadelphia publisher—certainly spread the use of the phrase; for these words became a commonplace expression to sum up the various aspects of life that make it worth living.

These aspects of life are included in chapters dealing with "Saving the City," "Adjusting to Race," "Education," "Youth," "Communications," and "Preserving Our Environment." The commercial edition added a chapter, "The Population Cancer," on the explosion of world birthrates that the author considered to be the main threat to ameliorating all the earlier problems. The title of his final chapter was changed from "The Challenge" to "What We Must Do."

Considering Michener's background and rooted attitudes, the most revealing of the chapters is "Adjusting to Race." His lifetime residence on the outskirts of Philadelphia—one of the most heavily black cities in America—combined with his familiarity with Asia, Hawaii, and the South Pacific enabled him to have a broad view of power movements by ethnic groups. His attitude toward "black power" is to encourage a dignified, nonviolent progress toward aspirations so that one-eighth of the population of the United States can lead the most productive and satisfying lives and the others can avail themselves of this economic asset.

One reviewer of *The Quality of Life* has remarked that "The author disarms the reader in his introduction by confessing that he is not a philosopher, not an historian, not a sociologist or political scientist. He then briskly begins drawing conclusions which ought to be the products of the methodologies of these several crafts. He is really not very good at defining terms, removing ambiguities, lining up evidence, and the other tools of scholarship."[10] Certainly, Michener's brief treatments of America's hazards in the 1970s could have been excelled by monographs written by professional philosophers or sociologists; but since his essays informally and interestingly state the main problems of the future for a wide readership that would not seek the writings of the experts, these essays are still worth reading. His conclusions concerning the preservation of the good life required that the United States leave Vietnam; that it evolve a new spiritual agreement that would maintain democracy, an accepted morality, a new patriotism, and a more equitable distribution of the benefits of society; and that it continue to maintain control over subversion and civil violence. "To handle these problems," he concluded, "we will need new thinking, tough decisions and gutsy administration. Above all we must have courageous leadership, and this we deserve" (127).

Michener's general outlook was optimistic, and few readers in America's bicentennial year would quarrel with his expectation of our country's survival: "I find no evidence in American history that we are so stupid. We are often tardy in our decisions and grudging in their implementation, but in our fumbling, stumbling way we do grope for right solutions and adopt them when their efficacy has been demonstrated. To deny this is to deny the pragmatic thrust of American history" (107).

CHAPTER 8

Rambling Around in the Seventies

MICHENER had two big books—*The Drifters* and *Kent State*—on the best-seller lists in the spring of 1971. Both are set in recent years, and both are filled with immediate reactions to the violence of the latter 1960s.

He had written in 1969, about the minority of young Americans who would not seek the normal life: "As to the others, those real drifters who will never succeed in stabilizing their lives or utilizing their capacities, I am afraid they must be written off as total losses, tragic but irredeemable. There are probably more of these today than there used to be, and I see no likelihood that their numbers will be diminished in the decades ahead. They are the hippies, the yippies, the acid-heads, the drug addicts and the totally alienated. They have always been a part of society; today they seem to be starting their downward plunge sooner" (68).[1] The key word in this passage appears in the title of *The Drifters: A Novel*. Michener was to encounter more of the "totally alienated" when he spent several months in the autumn of 1970 researching a book on the outbreak during the previous May at Kent State University. Such insights enabled him to produce a nonfiction report like *Kent State: What Happened and Why*—which is reviewed later in this chapter—as well as a fictionized chronicle of uprooted youth in *The Drifters*.

I *Six Characters in Search*

The first six of the dozen chapters of *The Drifters* introduce in depth the six characters—all of college age, and all with varied pasts that have caused them to rebel against their home situations—who form the group that comes together by chance in the spring of 1969 at the southern Spanish enclave of Torremolinos. The narrator of the story is a sixty-one-year-old financier, George Fairbanks, whose occupation has previously enabled him to become acquainted with

four of the group and who, as an adopted uncle, speedily becomes
informed about the remaining two. On his authority we take as fact
the events that have caused each individual to relapse into an
aimless detachment from his society.

Joe is a bearded, shaggy-haired dropout from a California college
who has rejected the draft and the Vietnam conflict and has landed
in Spain. Britta is a Viking beauty who has fled from the cold
darkness of her native town of Tromsø, Norway. Monica, a dark-
haired vixen, is the daughter of widower Sir Charles Braham, dis-
missed diplomatic adviser to the Congolese republic of Vwarda; but
she is determined to shock at all times the British stiffness of her
social heritage. Cato is a handsome, bright black from the
Philadelphia ghetto who has become an outlaw because he made
armed revolutionary demands in a white church. Yigal, who because
of his parentage holds three passports—American, British, and
Israeli—is a teenage veteran of the Six Day War in the Sinai; and he
is vacationing before he must decide which country will hold his
allegiance. Gretchen is the wholesome, ballad-singing daughter of a
staid Boston family who was revolted by an incident in a police station when she was returning from the Democratic National Convention in Chicago in 1968.

When Michener was collecting material for his Spanish sketches
in *Iberia*, he had been told about the delights of Torremolinos and
the "goings-on in the marijuana belt"; but he had judged at that
time that Torremolinos was a town that "merited a younger man
than I to record its frivolity" (548).[2] He returned to observe this
"Lourdes of LSD," however, and his spokesman in *The Drifters* is
Uncle George Fairbanks, whose work requires him to spend some
time in this sybaritic, polyglot resort. He tries to join in the frivolity
of the six and to open his mind to their values and casual sleeping
arrangements, and he even begins to appreciate some qualities of
the mind-blowing "mod" recordings brought to them from London
by a peripatetic British dandy named Clive. When the tourist season
opens, the Spanish police evict from Torremolinos the bearded,
longhaired aliens like Joe until autumn comes. The six, on the
recommendation of Fairbanks, crowd into the yellow pop-top
Volkswagen camper that Gretchen has bought with an inheritance
and drive to the low-priced paradise of the Algarve in southern Portugal for an idyllic interlude.

Midway in the novel a character is introduced who is midway in
age between the six drifters and the sixtyish Fairbanks. He is forty-

four-year-old Harvey Holt, ex-Marine and "tech rep"—the
technical representative of an American firm, one of those invaluable experts who keep equipment running in one or another of
the far reaches of the world. At home in jungles and on deserts,
where Holt can usually find a local beauty to do his cooking, he is a
devotee of old films that feature Humphrey Bogart and Spencer
Tracy and of tape-recorded dance-band gems of the 1930s. As has
been his annual custom for sixteen years, Holt is taking a vacation
from his radar-maintenance work to attend the fair at Pamplona in
northern Spain, where Fairbanks often joins him to run with the
bulls during the ten-day festival of San Fermín. The two men seek in
this way to prove themselves at the game; and, when asked why a
man would expose himself to being gored by a bull's horn, they
would suggest a more pertinent question: "If any man finds such joy
in a given act, why would he do anything else?" (467). Michener had
given only a page or two to this sport in *Iberia;* but in *The Drifters*
he devotes a chapter to the Pamplona festival, the main scene of
Ernest Hemingway's first important novel, *The Sun Also Rises.*[3]

During the lurid days at Pamplona, when the celebrants sleep six
in a room when they sleep at all, Yigal is taken away to Detroit by his
grandfather, who will challenge the lad with life in America. Holt, as
a member of the earlier generation who expects men to be manly,
serves as a foil for the outspoken ideas of the remaining five; and,
through daily association and conversation, he surrenders some of
his hard-hat prejudices. He is, however, unable to deter the three
young men of the party from running with the bulls on the climactic
morning of June 14, Bastille Day. Holt is gored during a heroic
stand, protecting Cato from injury, and Britta stays behind the party
to console his convalescence. The remaining four, at the suggestion
of Fairbanks—who feels that these young people now need to get
close to nature—embark at Barcelona and land, along with the
Volkswagen, at Lourenço Marques in the Portuguese East African
colony of Moçambique.

The culmination of their safari comes at Zambela Game Refuge,
where, under the guidance of Fairbanks, they come close to the
ecological problems of East Africa. Next they take passage to Moroc-
co; and, after Joe is given the government haircut reserved for hippies, they drive to Marrakech, the haven of drug addicts and the
sinkhole of Arab vice. Here the young people, after their European
and African *wanderyahr*, decide their future careers and separate.
Monica, however—the only one born with a spirit of unredeemable

evil—succumbs to the heroin habit and ironically dies of an infected hypodermic needle. Penniless Britta is happiest of all, for she will go with millionaire Holt to Ceylon, the dream Eden of her Nordic father.

The main theme of *The Drifters* emerges early and is repeated again and again. Most young people have always been rebels, but nowadays the rebellion is more obvious and possibly more effective. As Fairbanks reflects, ". . . every age produces its drop-outs, every nation. The percentage remains constant; it is only the manifestation that varies" (329). Most of those worthy of survival will eventually rejoin society and perhaps produce more greatly than those who live the safe life. For who, actually, are a nation's dropouts? As Fairbanks continues to ponder,

Of a hundred average young people I had grown up with, a good forty had dropped out from all reasonable competition by the time they were twenty-five. . . . It was not these inevitable drop-outs that I referred to in my estimate of forty per cent; it was, rather, that constant group of Americans who avoid difficult tasks and grab onto the first job offered, clinging to it like frightened leeches for the remainder of their unproductive lives. It was the girls who marry the first man who asks them, building families without meaning or inspiration, producing the next cycle of drop-outs. It was the adults who surrender young and make a virtue of their unproductivity, the miserable teachers who learn one book and recite it for the next forty years, the pathetic ministers who build a lifetime of futility on one moment of inspiration entertained at the age of nineteen. These were the drop-outs that concerned me most. (330)

As Gretchen's father is told by the wise old professor at the institute at Besançon, the "amiable drifters" from various countries are "searching . . . exploring . . . rejecting"; and twenty years later they are "going to run this world" (274). Who else would there be to do so? Gretchen herself realizes that "the essence of life" is "to serve at the source of power, to do what had to be done, and . . . above all else, to participate, to be at the center of life as a participant" (283). Life is for living, and when one is young it is to be lived to the full. If this creed might descend to crass hedonism, so be it!

The main objection of Fairbanks to the life-style of his young friends is, however, their arrogance: "The new generation was so convinced of its values that it judged us older poeple not by our standards but by their own" (322). And "They insisted upon being kids—the gang, the mob, the girls, the boys—as if growing up were an ugly thing and responsibility something to be deferred as long as possible" (323).

When *The Drifters* first appeared, many of Michener's readers felt that he had created a menagerie of monsters; for his characters seemed to resemble no young people with whom one might be acquainted. But even the most sheltered American of the 1960s could not avoid seeing in newspapers and on television screens the screaming objectors to the society they condemned. In Europe even more than America, *The Drifters* was widely read with approval; for the alienation of youth was not merely a national problem. The temptations to revolution were thereafter to be found unavoidably in such events as the attempted assassinations of President Ford and the celebrated Patty Hearst trial.

The structure of this novel is loose. The type might be classed as the picaresque that dates back at least to the *Don Quixote* of Miguel Cervantes, which was imitated by Henry Fielding and Tobias Smollett in England. The characters in this type of novel are usually drawn from lower- or middle-class life; there is little plot—merely a series of interesting episodes along the road. There is likewise little development of character, but change may occur through accident, as when Britta's love makes her a Cinderella. The tone is unromantic, the language is free and even vulgar, and the detail has the vividness allowed only to the realist. The ending is seldom a culmination; the characters, often unscarred and unredeemed, vanish into the dust of the next road. Satire, often an important element, is found in *The Drifters*, especially in the two-page collection of epigraphs that precedes each chapter. Some are familiar quotations, but a number of them are sardonic reflections that could have come from Michener's notebook: "I am a serious student. Please do not spindle, fold or staple me." "The President is going on a twelve-day tour to visit some friendly nations. What will he do on the other eleven days?" "Support mental health or I'll kill you." And, first and last, "Youth is truth."

Even if the reader tires of the raffish company in which he finds himself immersed in this long novel, he can enjoy some special contributions. When Michener gives much attention to the early backgrounds of his six searching characters, he uses his knowledge of conditions in several countries. Fairbanks recalls historical events to his unhistoried young friends; and their adventures in Spain, Portugal, and Africa have many elements of a travelogue. Michener's early interest in folk ballads finds a vent in the characterization of

Gretchen Cole, who has been reared in the neighborhood where
lived Harvard professor Francis J. Child, compiler of the ten-volume
anthology *The English and Scottish Popular Ballads*. At suitable in-
tervals throughout the novel, Gretchen tunes her guitar and sings a
suitable ballad, always prefacing it with a "Child number" garnered
from the volumes presented to her by Fairbanks when she was little.
But it is still hard to believe that Michener, who could appreciate the
pathos of the ancient ballads and the richness of the classical eras of
music, could find, as elsewhere he claims to find, justification for the
earsplitting, repetitive beat sounds of the rock generation.

II   *Mother Could Die in Peace*

Through Michener's writing years, he has published about one
hundred articles that testify to his skill as a freelance journalist of
note. Although these items range in value from competent reporting of ephemeral topics to a number of pieces that have enduring
worth, he works on all of them with concentrated zeal. He is almost
equally eager to complain about Manhattan fire laws that deny
painters a comfortable studio ("Should Artists Boycott New York?")
as he is to pay tribute to Frances Sabin, a busy Waikiki bookseller, or
to risk ostracism by calling American housewives "The Hardest-
Working Women in the World."

Michener's continuing interest in the Pacific region is shown in
several articles on Hawaii and its progress to statehood, as well as
such essays as "Sea of the Talented Travelers" and "People of the
Pacific." Nowhere is Michener's genial sense of humor expressed
better than in the short piece called "My Other Books." Frequently
complimented for writing volumes on the Pacific that were actually
the work of other authors, he has become used to being asked: "Tell
me, how did you have the energy to write *From Here to Eternity?*";
and, as a result, he has come to think of that book as one of his more
successful efforts. When asked how he thought of those hilarious
scenes in *Mr. Roberts*, he explains that he once knew a captain who
actually carried a rubber plant about with him. On the more serious
side, Michener has become persuaded that *The Ugly American* is his
best effort. His most successful work continues, however, to be *Kon-
Tiki*, even though he has now outgrown some of the theories expressed therein but still held by Thor Heyerdahl. Michener has also
become accustomed to being introduced as the author of *Teahouse
of the August Moon* and of *The Naked and the Dead*, but he is
proud that some of his admirers are still amazed at the versatility

that could enable him to write both the *Bounty* trilogy and the music for *South Pacific*.

During the interim between *The Drifters* (1971) and *Centennial* (1974), a collection of articles that had appeared between 1947 and 1970 in the monthly *Reader's Digest* was published, as has been noted, under the title of *A Michener Miscellany* (1973). These twenty-five articles were printed in the original versions submitted by the author rather than in the "digested" form after their editing; in fact, they were largely revised where necessary to suit the readers of 1973. The essays were "selected and edited by Ben Hibbs," but it is clear that Michener had more than a hand in choosing the items to appear in book form. Before each of more than a dozen selections, he appended, moreover, personal notes that give an insight into what it is like to contribute to a magazine printed in twenty foreign countries, in thirteen different languages, and in an edition of twenty-nine million copies.

Michener recounts in his introduction to this collection the beginning of an extraordinary friendship. He got a call in 1951 from DeWitt Wallace, who with his wife has developed the superpopular *Reader's Digest* and guided it for more than half a century. Invited to lunch with Wallace and some of his staff at their headquarters at Pleasantville, New York, Michener was subjected to a barrage of questions that were based on knowledge of his work and his interests. Soon thereafter a junior editor, Hobart Lewis, sent him a list of seven topics on which he might wish to write articles. After meeting with Lewis he was made acquainted with the system by which a freelance author could submit lengthy essays which would be heavily rewritten and cut in the office of the publication. However, he felt that this sort of collaboration was not demeaning. "On only one occasion did an article suffer conspicuously from heavy cutting; more often the brilliant researchers who fine-tooth-comb every sentence helped me to avoid error" (9).

Almost all the articles were written on topics assigned by an editor at Pleasantville. Only once did Michener propose an idea that found acceptance ("Presidential Lottery"); and he submitted a good deal that was never printed in the *Digest*. "If an editor conceives the idea for an article," he reasoned, "and if he assigns it to a specific writer whom he trusts, when the manuscript comes in, the editor is already predisposed to like it, for it reflects his judgment" (378). The first selection by Michener to appear in the *Digest* was "The Milk Run," a sketch that the editors had sought out in *Tales of the South Pacific*.

The first story he ever sold to a recognized magazine, however was "Remittance Man,"—also a chapter from *Tales*—which first appeared in the *Saturday Evening Post* of December 14, 1946. The publishing of this story, as Michener tells it in the *Miscellany*, allowed his mother to "die in peace." As a solid citizen in a solid Pennsylvania Dutch community, she felt that no good would come of embracing a career as fickle as writing, and even the winning of a Pulitzer Prize did not appease her. "But when she saw a story of mine actually in print in the most permanent of all journals, Ben Franklin's *Post*, which our family had subscribed to for decades, she felt that I might one day make it. I heard her telling a neighbor, 'Well, he did sell a story to the *Saturday Evening Post*, and they don't fool around' " (368).

III   A Very Tough-minded Guy

Never did Michener cover an area with the thought in mind that it would make a good subject for a book. However, not seldom an assigned article provided background material that years after would materialize as lengthy segments of a novel or travel volume. "A writer is a man condemned to work his way through an enormous mass of experience: organizing it, rejecting it, filing portions of it away. He cannot possibly know at any given moment what will be of crucial value a decade hence. . . . Of the twenty-five essays in this anthology, ten provided basic research on which, sometimes years later, I built books" (87).

One two-part *Digest* article that was not reprinted in *A Michener Miscellany* concerns the outbreak of violence on the campus of Kent State University in Ohio early in May, 1970. The article that appeared in March and April, 1971, was a condensation of a big volume, *Kent State: What Happened and Why*, published just a year after the event as a "Reader's Digest Press Book." The work was a sample of cooperative journalism, for a number of researchers collected the material that Michener used for the final manuscript. The plan originated in Pleasantville. A senior editor of the *Digest* went to the Ohio scene soon after the shootings of May 4 to see whether a good book might result from in-depth reporting. Michener arrived early in August, spent an anonymous week surveying the situation, and thereafter made himself available for many interviews. He was aided by a dozen other reporters and photographers, several of them students. He spent several subsequent months in the town, and the "Afterword" is dated "Kent,

Ohio, July-December, 1970." His role was to collect all available information from any source; to put it into highly readable form by arranging suspenseful sequences of reports; and to editorialize, upon the basis of the apparent facts, about a highly emotional conflict. Some of the incidents provide springboards for generalizations about the state of the world, and a number of conclusions and admonitions are far afield from the chosen topic.

Based on interviews by team members who talked to eyewitnesses and to others involved in the events of the early May, 1970, weekend that culminated in the killing of four students by National Guardsmen, *Kent State* is an attempt to chronicle events—sometimes minute by minute—and to extract the lessons that might be learned from this very recent event. Michener and others carried on conversations that sometimes lasted for hours with students, faculty, and administrators of the university, as well as with radical leaders, policemen, National Guardsmen, citizens and officials of the city and county, black liberals, and revolutionaries sought by the Federal Bureau of Investigation. A number of responses are given in apparently verbatim form.

Michener's main attitude might have been anticipated in a paragraph in his recently published *The Quality of Life:* ". . . controlling student revolutionaries does not mean muzzling them. They have a right to question authoritarian boards or outmoded procedures, but to do so through assaults on professors or the burning of buildings is so provocative that, if persisted in, it must provoke harsh countermeasures. What we require is a balance between protest and stability" (126). He rejected violence as an answer to anything, but in *Kent State* he had to deal with acts of violence on several sides—the university, the community, the students. He tried throughout the massive study to be objective in reporting, but obviously his sympathies lay with the young idealists and with open-minded faculty members—such as Glenn Frank—who attempted to exert restraint in a charged atmosphere.

Since the riots at Kent were not so violent as those at such universities as Columbia, Berkeley, or Wisconsin, Michener's treating them at extreme length might be considered an act of journalistic overkill. The four days in May were hardly Armageddon. Indeed, at the end of 558 pages, the author refers to his book as "as true a picture of one small aspect of a great state university as we could construct." The killing of four students by National Guard gunfire, however, seemed to many like a dramatic epitome of a hundred national conflicts, and public imagination was inflamed by photographs such as that of "the girl with the Delacroix face" who was screaming beside the body of a student (Michener devotes his final chapter to this fourteen-year-old runaway from Florida). The author emphasizes the role of outside agitators on campus, the small fraction of the students and faculty who were indicted (only twenty-five in all), and the local and state political situation that mobilized public opinion. He asks that older people exert twice as much effort as the young in the mutual need to attain understanding, for the elders, having lived longer, should be more experienced at such efforts (508). He insists that professors whose researches are recondite or too advanced for the public should be protected from being summarily fired (489), but he wants to abolish the protections of tenure except for those with thirty years of satisfactory service. He points out that "even if all the SDS [Students for a Democratic Society] demands had been accepted at the moment of issuance, others would have been quickly forthcoming" (517); but he then says "the problem is one of conciliation" (519), although no conciliation—as in Israel or in Ireland—seemed possible.

Did the shootings at Kent State have to happen? Throughout the book, Michener implies that matters came to a bloodstained climax because of a dismal chain of mischances, "a series of unfortunate events" (181). There was death but not murder; the skirmish "was an accident, deplorable and tragic" (410). Two pages later, however, Michener states that "The hard-core revolutionary leadership across the nation was so determined to force a confrontation—which would result in gunfire and the radicalization of the young—that some kind of major incident had become inevitable. . . . That it happened at Kent State was pure accident, but the confrontation itself was not" (412).

Six years after the event, many of the judgments made about the conflict that temporarily closed a fine university are already moot. None of the three direful scenarios (484 - 86) of future disasters—an October revolutionary war, an igniting of a national student rebellion, or a mobilization of students versus vigilantes—eventuated. Sobered by the excesses of the protestors of the 1960s, most of America's campuses are again the scene of quiet study. The protest era was not another 1848; it was an international wave of student unrest that was exacerbated by political and economic events but that was in many ways an enlargement of the normal nihilism of youth. Since the violence and the arson that began the tragic four days at Kent started on the first evening of spring, the youths involved may have been expressing age-old urges. Michener's energies and talents could well have been devoted in the latter half of 1970 to covering some scene of real rather than transient revolution.

One aspect of the episode that shocked Michener and his aides extremely was the militant behavior of girls and women. Mothers are quoted as saying: "It would have been a good thing if all those students had been shot" (454). Pretty coeds flashed their nudity before Guardsmen, threatened their wives, and screamed obscenities that would make a lumberjack blush. As a writer, in fact, Michener feels that resort to obscenity as a weapon is inexcusable, for it immediately murders communication. To the defense that "young people are devising a language which older people cannot steal from them," Michener retorts that the white leaders who complain that their terse and colorful lingo has been filched from them by Madison Avenue "admen" forget, ironically, that they stole it from the blacks.

The large number of persons mentioned in this big book and the confusion surrounding just what part each was playing result in a lack of reader concern for most of those mentioned and usually presented only in thumbnail portraits. Even the five main victims are not clearly kept in mind unless one keeps checking back. The lack of an index makes it difficult to check the movements of all the characters. In such a lengthy case study as *Kent State*, the large cast—some of whom have had their identities concealed for legal reasons—can easily stray from the mind of even the scrupulous reader, although many fine photographs do something to help him.

In an illuminating interview that appeared at the time *Kent State* was published, Michener spoke freely about his concerns. "I find myself fairly completely on the side of the young people," he stated. "Where we part company is where they see these freedoms and these attitudes justifying violence. I am inherently frightened of civil violence because it leads to fascism. . . . I think that social change can be obtained through orderly channels, but would add finally that in orderly channels I would include protest." In the same interview he refers to having been under Federal Bureau of Investigation surveillance for a quarter of a century as an "occupational hazard." "I think maybe fellows like me ought to be under surveillance. . . . It must be a constant question as to whether or not I am loyal. . . . I have been through this all my life and I do have self-defense. I am worried about the person who doesn't."[4] In the

course of ranging and reporting the world, Michener has had to
become "a very tough-minded guy."

IV   *Challenge-and-Response in the Sports World*

Returning to *A Michener Miscellany*, one may note that the topics
therein vary greatly; but the subjects are grouped into sections with
such titles as "The Puritan Ethic," "The Spirit of the Age," and
"Doing Research." A number of the items fall into the class of travel
essays. Perhaps not surprisingly, almost a third of them deal with art.
As a boy, Michener collected stamps and post cards—a hobby that
not only inspired in him a love of world travel but also gave him a
delight in the forms and colors of pictures. In this anthology his essay "Why I Collect Art" is an excellent prelude to an understanding
by the reader of the impulses that resulted in the donation by the
Micheners of a three-million-dollar collection of twentieth-century
American painting to the University of Texas.

In the *Miscellany* the author regrets that he did not find an opportunity to write as much about sports as he would have liked. Only
one essay of this sort, "Soccer: The World Cup," is included, but
Michener amended this lack of reporting on the sports scene by
publishing in 1976 a big volume of personal essays entitled *Sports in
America*.

One strong aspect of many-sided Michener is his lifelong interest
in a variety of sports and games. Indeed, he claims that his life was
twice eminently affected by sports. As a boy of the streets, he was
saved from a probable career as a delinquent by becoming involved
in playing basketball under the volunteer guidance of a local roofer.
He was proud about playing on a championship high-school team,
and he also engaged in several other sports at Swarthmore. Later in
life, in the autumn of 1965, he was stricken by a massive coronary attack; and, aided by advice from Dr. Paul Dudley White, the
specialist who treated President Eisenhower, he learned how to
avoid becoming a cardiac cripple by continuing to engage in
planned exercise.

"As a boy," Michener writes, "I could recite the batting order and
batting averages of every team in the two leagues" (315); and "I
started my writing career as a fourteen-year-old sportswriter for our
local newspaper, and one of the saddest days of my life came when I
failed to land a job with the *Detroit Free Press*" (318). This early interest and his flypaper memory enabled Michener to keep track of
achievements on the sports scene and to encourage him not only to

serve as spectator at various meets but to hike, to take fishing trips, and to play fast tennis even at the age of seventy. He feels that without steady exercise he is not fit to work at his desk with any profit.

But the justification for Michener's big book on American sports "goes far beyond anything personal. Sports have become a major force in American life. We devote more money and time to them than we realize. They consume a major portion of our television programming, and our newspapers allocate tremendous space to their coverage. They dominate the dreams of ghetto children, who see them as their tradiitonal way of escape; they have become a fetish to our black community, distracting it from more serious solutions to problems. Their effect upon our schools and colleges is oftentimes deplorable, and they have been accused of generating at least some of the violence that assaults us" (9). Yet the critical analysis of school and university sports has been grossly neglected by qualified writers.

A baker's dozen of chapters presents a number of facets of the main topic of *Sports in America*. He debates the mutual relationships of sports and health, delineates the "jungle world" of juvenile participation in which ambitious parents drive children to violent competition, pleads for a greater share of attention to the participation of women in athletics, explodes the myth of black social mobility through sports, offers advice to college and university administrators about the handling of the demands of victory hunters, and states "the inescapable problem" of teaching younger athletes how to make the transition from stardom to a lifelong program of healthy physical activity. He offers opinions concerning the roles of the media, financing agencies, and government in the area of sports. He deals with the charge that competition creates an atmosphere of ugly violence, and he recurs in an epilogue to the values that sports have brought him through the years: fun, revelation, beauty, solitude, power, exquisite grace.

Much research went into this study by Michener of the sports scene:

While working on this book I enjoyed opportunities that would rarely be accorded the average fan, and I was always mindful of that fact. I was allowed to work out with a professional football team. I was invited into the inner sanctum of another NFL team and watched many inside operations. I met with our leading coaches, attended seminars of college presidents concerned with sports, followed baseball teams closely, and watched private practices in college basketball. I was able to travel, too, and experience big-game fishing in Hawaii, the Super Bowl in New Orleans, a rodeo in a little town in Montana, auto races everywhere, trotting races at a beautiful rural track in upper New York, and soccer's World Cup in Munich.

He lived for some weeks with a small band of professional racetrack gamblers, and he recalled conversations he had held with some sixty outstanding athletes. He benefitted by the aid of a research associate, the sportswriter Joseph Avenick. Acknowledgment of quoted sources takes up four pages, and arguments are bolstered by many more pages of tables of figures. Throughout the statistics and barroom tales, however, the reader hears the voice of a novelist who has been fascinated all his life with the achievements of men and women who have stood above the ruck and achieved records that thousands of others could admire.

Perhaps the most interesting chapter is "The Athlete," for in it Michener is not talking about money or facilities but about breathing people who have striven greatly. The author points out that the literary image of the athlete is that of an early stardom—complete with fame, fortune, and pretty girls—that is followed by collapse around the age of thirty and by a despairing life of poverty that is enlightened only by recollections of the days of fame. Such accounts, he implies, are probably written by cloistered men who envied the glorious ones and who compensated by continuing the myth of skyrocketing success and failure. To the contrary, as Michener points out, most former athletes—who are probably superior to their fellows in intelligence, stability, and social poise—have adjusted well to the needs of later life. And most of life, as Michener has found, is "a falling-away, a gradual surrender of the dream. The reason sports provide such dramatic material is that the climax comes so early in a man's life, the decline so swiftly. For a truly great athlete like Jimmy Foxx to enter the downward slide in his mid-thirties is tragic. But his story merely intensifies the story of us all. What a book I could write about the young authors of promise I have known whose descent to oblivion was as swift as Foxx's but less well publicized" (253). A special section is presented concerning coaches, who are the quintessential athletes that must continue to produce or perish.

In discussing financial aspects, Michener surprises with the statement that "A recent study has shown that we spend about one hun-

dred billion dollars a year on sports and recreation, considerably
more than we spend for national defense"; and he would justify using such a portion of the gross national product if it went for the improvement of nationwide health. "But if a great deal of this investment is merely subtracted from the creative processes of the nation,"
he continues, "and siphoned into the hands of a few essentially
brash young men and women, the consequences can only be
destructive" (372). Concerning the charge that sports encourages a
too-competitive and a too-violent attitude for modern living, he concludes: "But for life to be meaningful, there must be competition,
either external or internal; I therefore reject all recent philosophies
based upon a theory of non-competition, because such theories run
counter to the experience of nature, of the individual and of society.
Destructive competition carried to neurotic levels, I cannot condone.
Creative competition, which encourages the human being to be
better than he or she might otherwise have been, I applaud" (427).
Michener approves the challenge-and-response theory of the rise
and fall of civilizations championed by the historian Arnold
Toynbee, with whom he once shared a platform (425 - 26).

V *"The Best Remainin' Spot on Earth"*

Challenge-and-response is strongly evident in *Centennial*, the
gigantic novel that appeared in 1974, and one which embodies
Michener's most exhaustive effort in research. The book acknowl-
edges the advice and assistance of more than a hundred persons,
and it is dedicated to three men who were his major informants
and who inspired him to narrate this authentic story of a small
Colorado town that typifies the macrocosm of the American West.

Before the publication of each book, Michener suffers qualms that
his work will be a fearful flop in the marketplace. Recalling the great
expenditure of time and talent upon this project and the amount of
editorial labor that went into the enterprise—and underestimating
the vast audience of his faithful readers—Michener was more ap-
prehensive than ever in the summer of 1974. He readily agreed with
his publisher that a special effort would aid in the launching of
Centennial. He need not have worried, for the hardbound volume
was to sell nearly a million copies in the United States before the
paperback edition was issued. But Michener's extra effort resulted in
another title for his bibliography, a small volume called *About
"Centennial": Some Notes on the Novel.*

This sixty-four-page work, limited to only thirty-two hundred copies and distributed free to "those who are concerned with the making and dissemination of books," was sent to librarians, booksellers, and reviewers in the United States previous to the publication of *Centennial*. No copies were for sale; and, since the small book is already a collector's item, a few facts from it are recorded here, because they reveal much about the creation of what some reviewers have considered to be Michener's most ambitious novel.

As *About "Centennial"* recalls, Michener in the late summer of 1936 began a three-year period as a history professor at the Colorado State College of Education at Greeley, a town on a tributary of the South Platte River—a drab stream usually empty of water, "too thick to drink, too thin to plow." There Michener fell under the wing of Floyd Merrill, an erudite newspaper editor who revealed to him the often hidden natural attractions of Colorado and who preached a gospel of what was much later to be termed "ecology." At the urging of Merrill, Michener began writing in 1950 a novel about Colorado; but, since he was at that time occupied with other projects, he was not free to commit himself to returning to the West and to spending several years of additional research there. But something happened two decades later to spur Michener to engage in this strenuous labor of writing a novel with deep roots in America.

Depressed by the failure of his efforts, as mentioned in Chapter 1, to involve Congress in a noble celebration of the then forthcoming bicentennial of the signing of the Declaration of Independence, Michener concluded that "the best we could hope for would be for each citizen in our country to assume responsibility for his or her own centennial celebration." His responsibility, he decided, was to write about the spiritual condition of his nation and to create the book whose inspiration went back to 1936.

In the spring of 1970, then, Michener spent some weeks on the plains to refresh his memories and to interview men whose knowledge of the land was wide and deep. A prediction that the gasoline shortage would cramp his explorative efforts caused him in August, 1972, to speed up his field work. He packed a station wagon with books, maps, and other reference materials and then traced each mile of the famed Oregon Trail, and also visited other regions of his chosen territory. Then he established headquarters for prolonged labors in the city of Denver—which, he claims, has "a higher rate of highly educated men and women than any other city in America." Here he was aided by the availability of experts on Western technology and the possibility of driving out in any direction to seek further advice on hundreds of background details. He worked each morning in his apartment, seven days a week, without rest breaks. Late in 1973, after more than a year of research and writing in the field, he headed home to Bucks County to write the final chapters of *Centennial*—a blockbusting tome that from its publication in September, 1974, would be listed at or near the top of the monthly best-seller lists during the following year.

The title of the book comes from the fact that Colorado joined the Union in the year 1876 and is therefore known as the Centennial State. Michener's imaginary village, to celebrate that historic year, changed its pioneer name of "Zendt's Farm" to "Centennial." The author, of course, was not unaware that such a title would appeal to a readership that even earlier than 1974 was looking forward to the celebration of the American Bicentennial in 1976.

The book planned over the years would include no less than seventy named characters and cover a period from the creation of the earth to 1974. The main periods of Western development would be represented by prehistoric animals, Indians, trappers and mountain men, covered-wagon emigrants, army officers of the plains, cowboys and cattle drivers, buffalo hunters, ranchers, sheepmen, homesteaders, irrigation experts and dust-bowl farmers, and a sampling of Colorado residents of today. Since structure is always important to Michener, the problem of lending some unity to this disparate collection of materials was solved to his satisfaction by finding a narrative device to serve this end. "I found it," he wrote, "by basing my story on a learned man from the state of Georgia who is sent to Colorado by a magazine to report on the scene as he sees it in 1974, against his own rich background in American history. The first chapter would establish this gentleman; chapters two through thirteen would consist of his reports back to his employers in New York, and the final chapter would represent the impact of all this material on both him and the last major character in his report" (47). This choice of a narrator would not only lend unity but would be congenial to Michener, himself a former young history professor. To remind the reader in each chapter that it was the work of Dr. Lewis Vernor, informal comments are attached that give his personal remarks to the editors concerning minor items in the report.

Chapter 1, then, as told by Dr. Vernor, carries him to New York and then to the village of Centennial; and he is accompanied by the clever young lady who has already written the feature article for *US Magazine* that Vernor will spend some months in authenticating. He meets a number of the principal local characters who appear in later chapters, and he surveys the geography of the region (which is shown on the book's endpapers and on other maps for each chapter). The crux of Chapter 11 is even hinted when Vernor observes in Chapter 1 a strange action by Morgan Wendell, the leading realtor of Centennial.

Michener then puts the reader through an ordeal that is designed to deter the casual person from the pleasures of the chapters of fiction to follow. In the parlance of a poker game, he wants to "weed out the ribbon clerks."[5] He presents eighty solid pages of nonfiction essays that cover geology and archeology through some thousands of millenia. The composition of the earth between its center and the boundaries of the State of Colorado is charted and described until the present contours finally emerge. Chapter 3 is devoted to the creatures that finally began to crawl on this surface. Loving depiction of the dinosaur race that survived for a hundred and thirty-five million years shows Michener as the foremost modern champion of these giant reptiles; his wife once remarked: "You know, Mitch, I think that diplodocus is the best character you've ever drawn!" The eohippus, ancestor of the modern horse, also appears, as well as the bison, the beaver, the rattlesnake, and the prairie dog—all well-adjusted inhabitants of this broad range before the appearance of the first arrowhead-makers from across the land bridge to Asia.

Michener's habit of setting the geographical stage in long novels such as *Hawaii* and *The Source* is given such free rein in *Centennial* that the impatient fiction lover would lose little by starting the book on page 118. However, Michener has discovered that his chosen audience looks upon one of his books as "a home in which someone reading it can live intellectually for a long period of time."[6] He can afford nowadays to select those who find his novels—even one that runs to more than half a million words—as all too short. But he did agree at lunch one day with a prominent reviewer that an unknown author probably would not be able to find a publisher for a manuscript like *Centennial*.

All the remaining chapters of this novel, except for the personal postscripts by Vernor, tell stories with Michener's usual skill. The Indians are presented through the Arapaho warrior Lame Beaver. The period of the mountain men centers around the roving French *coureur de bois* known simply as Pasquinel, who had one family among the Indians and another in St. Louis. The period of settlement and of diminishing Indian power through army action is handled in Chapters 6 and 7. The hegira of Levi Zendt and the brave hired girl Elly from Lancaster County, Pennsylvania, to the town site known for years as "Zendt's Farm" is based on a serious study of similar emigrations. Authentic likewise are the stories of Colonel John Skimmerhorn, who blazed the cattle trail from Jacksborough, Texas, to the Venneford Ranch north of Zendt's Farm; of Potato Brumbaugh, pioneer in using the Platte, the "nothing river," for irrigating the land; and of the Venneford Ranch, a baronial cattle range covering no less than five million acres and supported by English investment capital.

An episode that could be extracted from the rest of the epic is Chapter 11, "The Crime," that is based on the visualization of a comment by Floyd Merrill in 1937: "One couple made it big in our country by working the badger game." Morgan Wendell comes as close to being the villain of the book as can be found. He is the true son of the man who enticed the hopeful farmers into the region after 1889 to cultivate the dry lands that, lacking the lifeblood of irrigation, were doomed to be stripped of grass and to invite the dust storms that raged in the 1930s.

The racial interminglings that have fascinated Michener from childhood are prominent in this book that was his birthday gift to America. In the final chapter of *Centennial*, Dr. Vernor devotes the month of November, 1973, to the daily trailing of Paul Garrett, the man he considers the person whose life best epitomizes the history of the American West. Preceding the final chapter is Garrett's "stud book"—his pedigree for five generations. The thirty ancestors, it is revealed, are all persons who have appeared as characters in earlier chapters—including his great-grandfather Levi Zendt, his Arapaho Indian grandmother Pale Star, his great-grandfather John Skimmerhorn, and his European forebears. "Garrett, Messmore and Buckland were of English stock," he tells Vernor. "The Lloyds were a Welsh family that emigrated to Tennessee and Texas. Patrick Beeley was a hard-drinking Irishman, Pasquinel and Mercy were French. . . . Zendt, Skimmerhorn, Staller and Bockweiss were Germans. Deal was Dutch. . . . Red Wolf and Pale Star were full-blooded Indians." Garrett is married to Flor Marquez, daughter of an ambitious Mexican couple from bandit-ridden Chihuahua. And other prominent characters in the heartland of America are Nate Person, grandson of a valiant black cowboy; Potato Brumbaugh, from Czarist Russia; and the Takemoto clan from Japan, prominent in the sugar-beet industry that today is the most obvious occupation of the people around the South Platte River. Paul Garrett, apex of the genealogical pyramid, is content to live and work in Centennial—a settlement that after a hundred years is in danger of becoming a ghost town—because, he agrees, "it's maybe the best spot in America . . . could even be the best remainin' spot on earth."

CHAPTER 9

Area of Assessment

MICHENER says, "I have only one bit of advice to the beginning writer: be sure your novel is read by Rodgers and Hammerstein." Actually, James Michener has scattered through his works and his interviews and conversations a multitude of highly valuable bits of advice about writing. His opinions range all the way from breaking into print to the function of literature in our modern society. A brief selection of these scattered comments should prove valuable to the student of the art of writing and should reveal as well the mainsprings of Michener's own achievement in the art.

Once I was present when he answered a drumroll of questions from an advanced writing class in Honolulu. For more than two hours at a stretch, without pulling any punches, he replied, frankly and unhesitatingly, to the most personal, probing inquiries. His opinions are eagerly sought wherever he goes, and he is generous in taking time to give them to aspiring authors, believing as he does that "art can prevent moral downfall; the totality of art, the whole body of literature, constructs a core of belief, of decency."[1]

Himself a late starter, since he published his first novel at the age of forty, Michener advises a much earlier blossoming, if possible. His years as a professor, as a writer of educational articles, and as a textbook editor did, however, serve to train him in what Dr. Strunk calls "the elements of style."

I *Millions of Words with Two Fingers*

Michener does not believe it is easy to tell anyone "How to Succeed in the Writing Business without Really Trying." He has warned in his valuable essay "The Chances Against the Beginning Writer" that "There are few harder ways to make a living; there are few fields of endeavor which can consume so much of one's energy in return for so little spiritual reward." Then he adds: "But everyone is convinced he can write, and those who would shudder at the prospect of submitting an amateurish daub to the Metropolitan Museum have no compunction about thrusting their verbal daubs at the editors of the *Atlantic Monthly* or the *Saturday Evening Post.*"[2]

In another valuable source, a tape recording of a lengthy interview before a college group, Michener stated his belief that no aspirant can avoid an apprenticeship to his literary craft. "I *did* serve an apprenticeship," he affirms, "and a very intense one, and I learned what a great many people never learn. I learned how to write a sentence and how to write a paragraph. . . . The English language is so complex, so magnificent in its structure that I have very little patience with people who won't put themselves through an apprenticeship."[3]

Despite his picture of the pulp-writing business in *The Fires of Spring*, Michener never worked on a newspaper or a magazine staff. He feels that a future writer should avoid a vocation in which the compulsion to write would be diminished—jobs such as newspaper reporter, advertising copy man, or publicity, radio, or television writer. He believes that university teaching is legitimate but dangerous because it encourages preciosity, delay, and faddism.[4] His apprenticeship came, however, from academic writing. But he feels that the art of character creation is something that requires an insight that is seldom taught in a college English department. "It would seem to me," he says, "that the one course in the English field that might be of inestimable value would be a course in contemporary literature under a professor who really bored into what the men were trying to do. I have had to give myself that course, and in doing so I found out a few things."[5]

To those who are "too busy" to write, he replies that finding time to work haunts every creative person, and that very few novelists in the United States make a living writing novels. "Think of the number of women who have written books getting up at four o'clock in the morning before their families rise. If you want to write a book, that's what you do."[6]

What are the chief aptitudes for success in writing?

Vague longings, the praise of one's family, and an apartment in New York have practically nothing to do with success in writing. A study of what can be accomplished in words, an above-average mental capacity, vivid feeling, intelligent analysis of one's own potentialities, and very hard work are the best paths to a career in writing. Nine young people out of ten are too lazy or too little gifted ever to complete the arduous training period. Never in a thousand years will nine out of ten who, in their twenties, vaguely 'want to write' ever do so. The chances are all against them. And yet, if I must denounce the idle, day-dreaming attachment to writing that is so prevalent, I must also report the magnificent opportunities that await the young writer with a true talent and the energy to perfect it.[7]

The main reason Michener is one of the world's great reporters is that he listens. Almost nobody in this world pays real attention to what anybody else says. Michener has trained himself to interview people casually, without a notebook or a candid microphone; he *listens*. Two years after I had made a random remark, he repeated it to me in my own words. When he sits down to write, he can recall almost everything he has heard anyone say on his subject. In fact, he prefers to get aural information when he can. "I found he was like a Hawaiian," reported Mrs. Taylor, his research assistant for *Hawaii;* "he didn't want to read typewritten dissertations on a subject. He wanted the story told."[8]

He is, however, meticulous about checking all details, and pores for hours over large-scale maps of his locale. To assure the authenticity of *The Bridges at Toko-Ri,* he lived for about five weeks on one aircraft carrier and nine days on another; and his experience of the Korean War also included time with the army, air force, and marines. To check the multifarious details of Polynesian, Chinese, and Japanese life, as well as of New England missionary life for his big novel *Hawaii,* he employed Mrs. Taylor, who later wrote in "Preface to a Novel" and elsewhere about his almost fanatical efforts to get every factual touch exactly right.

Although Michener has written much about foreign lands and has traveled more than almost any other modern writer, he feels that wide experience is not required for good writing. "I speak with a certain harshness on this point because people say, 'Well, it's easy for you to write because you have traveled.' I never heard a worse *non sequitur* in my life. . . . Writing is not dependent upon a vivid experience; writing is dependent upon a vivid imagination. . . . Most of what Dostoevski wrote about he never experienced. Most of what I've written about I've never experienced. But what you can do is have an experience trigger your imagination; then you're off."[9]

"When it comes easy, the stuff is lousy," is Michener's version of R. B. Sheridan's "Easy writing's curst hard reading." He adds: "You write the first draft really to see how it's going to come out." The first draft is a "miserable experience" to Michener: "My connectives, my clauses, my subsidiary phrases don't come naturally to me and I'm very prone to repetition of words; so I never even write an important letter in the first draft. I can never recall anything of mine that's ever been printed in less than three drafts. I've never even released a book review in first draft."[10]

His first drafts are put down in as finished a form as possible, but without worrying where the verbal chips might fall. Nor does he believe that it is good to start a book by writing the easiest parts first, or skipping around back and forth. He does not usually rewrite chapters as he goes along, or read his previous pages before starting to work each morning. He may write an entire novel without ever reading the first draft, or the second or the third. But at every point he remembers what he must do to improve a chapter.

Like most writers, Michener has several book ideas simmering all the time at the back of his mental stove. When he gets into production, though, he concentrates on one book at a time. He refuses to be distracted by trying to drive two horses in different directions.

Michener also feels that writers should never wait for "inspiration" to strike. His businesslike attitude toward his program is exemplified by a remark he made to me in New York in June, 1957: "I have three different books in mind, on which I could start work tomorrow. And I have no strong preference among them for the one I would begin on."

Michener gets up and works each morning from about 7:30 until about 12:30. Afternoons he keeps free. He never actually writes in the evenings, but he may do rewriting, correcting, or drafting. While on a writing task, he works every day of the week and allows nothing to interrupt. He does not aim to turn out a set number of words each day but rather to finish a particular subject. The best he expects to produce in a day is about twenty-five hundred words. Typing skill may be dangerous, he feels; authors who are speed typists can write so fast that their words outrun their thoughts and their sentences outrun their style. Instead of writing in longhand, he uses two fingers on the typewriter and just about keeps up with the pace of his thought.

II   *The Function of Fiction*

"When I started to write, often under incredibly difficult circumstances," Michener recalled in 1973, "I sought only a large flat space on which to arrange my papers. One of the best working surfaces I ever used was an unfinished door propped up on cement blocks. This provided a big solid expanse on which to spread papers. I have written three of my best novels on such doors. I have written in the tropics, in the arctic, with noise on every side, and in various paradises like Samoa and Ceylon, but the places I remember with most affection were the quiet bare rooms without much view."[11]

Concerning the basic problem of choosing a structure for the novel, Michener has suggested that an aspiring young writer should know the English language, should have some familiarity with world literature and psychology, and should also engage in an activity like pottery or eurhythmic dancing to experience the sense of changing form. "I am never impressed when a would-be writer tells me, 'I got A in English at Vassar,'" Michener remarks in a scarce booklet. "Anyone should be able to get an A in English, and doing so has precious little to do with writing. But if someone were to tell me, 'I took this course in architecture and I learned how to achieve emphasis by moving some elements forward and others back, how to subdue mass or make a virtue of it, how to emphasize line, how to avoid unnecessary adornment,' I could get very excited about the prospects of this person as a writer, because the man or woman who seeks to write a book must always solve the problem of structure."[12]

Aside from planning the structure of his novels, Michener is always concerned with research. Michener luckily has a sharp memory when research is needed to supplement his previous knowledge. "I really have a prodigious memory about things I'm working on," he once remarked. "I would suppose that I retain 500 or 600 books verbatim almost. I remember where a certain sentence is on the page and how far into the book it is. But this is only if I know when I read something that I'm going to be interested in it later on. I don't read fast, but with terrific purpose. Of course, when my research is done, because I'm a prudent man, I try to find someone knowledgeable on the subject I've been writing about to check it. I am by no means arrogant about my scholarship."[13]

Aspiring writers who are envious of the financial rewards of a book like *Hawaii* might consider the physical effort required to produce a major novel. "Five years of research, months of character development, extensive work on plot and setting, endless speculation on psychology and concentrated work on historical backgrounds" are only the beginning, according to Michener. All morning for seven days a week for eighteen months he sat at his old typewriter and, using only two fingers, put down some three million words—for everything he writes in first draft must be revised at least once, and some passages may be rewritten half a dozen times. On the Hawaii novel he consulted several thousand books and conducted about two hundred interviews, all of them two or three hours long.[14] Many a yearning author would hardly be willing merely to type out three million words for any amount of money, let alone create the prose that made Hawaii a masterpiece of evocative narration.

The importance of having an income from his work derives from the fact that Michener is one of the few American authors who supports himself solely by his writing. "Shortly after I wrote *Tales of the South Pacific*," he told an interviewer in 1972, "I made the decision that I wanted to be a writer. And now I'm one of the very few writers who has always been completely self-employed. I've never had any guarantees, never a salary, and there just aren't very many people who can do this."[15]

Some of the animosity displayed in Honolulu after the publication of *Hawaii* may have arisen from a feeling that Michener was profiting by the national interest in the birth of a new state. He felt that the success of his novel was harming no one, and in a letter to me on December 12, 1959, he remarked: "I have recently been reading the life of Mozart, and when one studies the indignities he suffered I sometimes wonder why so many people are so incensed when an artist gets his fair pay. If Mozart had earned a little of what I have earned—all after an age when he was dead—we would now have fifteen or twenty great symphonies, half a dozen operas, and God knows how many string quartets. Who is happy that he died of poverty? It all perplexes me, yet quite a few of the critics seem to have been infuriated because my book was a best seller even before publication. I hope that the Mozart of this day is getting a little income, indeed I do."

As to which is more important, talent or hard work, Michener thinks that "it comes down to this: I have always felt talent is common. There is much more of it around than we suspect. But disciplined talent, organized talent, apparently is pretty rare," he concludes. "It's a valuable commodity. I think that anybody could write a book, anybody can write as well as I write, but very few do."[16]

What advice does Michener give to young writers? "They ought to find two or three authors in the last century who make them feel they knew what it was all about. And then try to figure out how they did it. Where style is concerned I would go to as many movies and plays as I could, and read the works of people who are experimenting. Don't bother with Bellow, Michener, or Roth; these are the old timers. Look at the new people to figure out what they are into and then decide values of your own and go to work. But I would certainly look at revolutionary and experimental forms in all fields; poetry, drama, painting, architecture, and then I'd move into the twenty-first century twenty years early."[17]

Finally, what does this novelist believe to be the function of the novel? As early as 1949, Michener expressed his idea that it should have a purpose: "In a complex and wandering society the symbols of art form a cohesive bloc. The arts keep a society pure, cleaned up. They are fresheners. They are a carbon through which society is filtered. Perhaps because I was brought up a Quaker, I feel keenly that literature must be looked at from the point of view of utility. For myself, I cannot see literature without a purpose. . . . The hope exists in this minute building up of fresh and humane opinion that is the function of art."[18] James Michener feels, in brief, that the function of a novelist in our era is to report and at the same time relate events to the emotions of people. He is sad that, in his lifetime, poetry has fallen into the hands of purely esoteric writers; and he fears this tragedy might happen to prose.

III *Naturalist, Muckraker, or Reporter?*

Since his first book in 1947, James A. Michener has published in thirty years a hundred·magazine articles and more than a score of books—most of which have enjoyed extended stays on best-seller lists. More than four million words from his typewriter have appeared, many of them in a dozen different languages around the world. After rereading all this prose, after studying his manuscripts and letters, and after recalling many conversations with him, it should certainly be possible for me to make more than a tentative assay of his achievements.

His main quality is a deep belief in a simple credo in which he was brought up in Bucks County, Pennsylvania, where he is still a member of the Society of Friends (Quakers). He stated this credo in 1954: "I really believe that every man on this earth is my brother. He has a soul like mine, the ability to understand friendship, the capacity to create beauty. . . . I believe it was only fortunate experience that enabled me to travel among my brothers and to live with them. Therefore I do not believe it is my duty to preach to other people and insist that they also accept all men as their true and immediate brothers. These things come slow. Sometimes it takes lucky breaks to open our eyes. I had to learn gradually, as I believe the world will one day learn."[19] As he says, "People are important." If the world does learn universal brotherhood, part of the credit should go to the "friendly persuasion" found throughout James Michener's writings.

Michener's idea of his function, in summary, is to report the world, factually or imaginatively, but also emotionally and even poetically. And the act of writing implies the taking of some moral stand as well, even though "morality" is today an unmodish word. He fought to keep the song "You Have to be Taught" in the musical show *South Pacific*. He labeled himself a coward because he was persuaded to omit a chapter called "Lobeck, the Asiatic," from *Tales of the South Pacific*. His powers of characterization and description save him from selling his author's birthright for a pot of message, but there is no doubt that usually his themes are strong.

Primarily, Michener is not a born writer but a teacher or even a preacher. He did not publish a book until he was forty, and it is possible that his volumes, impressive and popular as they are, serve merely as an extension of his teaching activities. He is the professor *malgre lui*. In print, his classroom is the world.

His scholarliness often endangers his popular appeal, and there is a strong didactic strain throughout his work. His theme again and again is a variation on the Quaker belief in the literal brotherhood of man. Even in his fiction, from *Tales of the South Pacific* through *Centennial*, the main intention of the author is the exposure of unbrotherly prejudices—social, political, racial, religious. In book after book—even on such abstruse subjects as Japanese engravings—his interest seems to center on freeing mankind from illiberal attitudes. He is the friend always of the underdog; he is the foe of snobbishness, segregation, reaction, and bigotry.

Born with a keen intelligence, a retentive memory, and an urge to travel, Michener was early inculcated with a friendly religion that has served to shield him from deep doubt and to urge him to an almost missionary zeal. A deep-seated drive came from his orphan birth and heritage of hunger, which kept him from slackening on any job he undertook. He is clearly of the inner-directed generation. He was early the recipient of scholarships that aroused in him a feeling of indebtedness to the world and of a need to repay bountifully the help that had been offered him. His spirit of obligation to society is shown by his generous donations of time, money, energy, and intellect to a dozen worthy institutions. He showed the volunteer spirit not only in wartime but in that time when it seemed he should devote all his efforts to winning a seat in the United States Congress.

Michener's mind would qualify him for success in several fields other than authorship. He enjoys the art of writing, but has mastered the craft by intense application, and his effects are achieved by calculated art, much rewriting, and a study of reader interests. His works are also popular because, when he is not in too much of a hurry, his aim is high and his achievement is great. But he early revealed other talents which, given the same development, would have brought him success in other careers. He won recognition as a teacher, and he was slated for an eminent position in the editorial world. Strong enthusiasms with him are the study of mathematics and the practice of art criticism. He has always been an amateur of practical politics, and has sharpened an uncanny talent for anticipating world events. As he wrote in 1955 for *Twentieth-Century Authors:* "In 1940 I lectured that we would be at war in the Pacific shortly. In 1945 I wrote that Asia must become our major problem and that we would probably be at war with China one day. And in 1950 I pointed out that all the turmoil in Asia would shortly be repeated in Africa. (My wrong guesses, which would fill the remainder of this volume, I have conveniently forgot.)" More than once he has been called upon by the American government to carry on confidential negotiations with other national groups.

Michener's trained memory, power of observation, and itching foot have qualified him to be one of the finest world reporters of our time—a time when travel has become America's favorite hobby and when no corner of the world can escape the journalist. Several of his books, such as *The Voice of Asia, The Bridge at Andau, Report of the County Chairman,* and *Kent State,* derive from sought or unsought reportorial coups. He has been called "Mr. Pacific" and even "Mr. World," but his broad sense of humor keeps him from becoming pompous about his travels. "If I ever write my autobiography," he once told me beside his swimming pool at his Bucks County home, "I'm going to call it *On a Clear Day.* During all my visits to other lands, I never got to one of them at just the right time. The inhabitants always said, 'On a clear day you can see so-and-so from here.' But somehow I have always missed the most impressive view!"

Accidental assignment in World War II took Michener to the South Pacific, but it was not chance that he was useful in a task that required energy, mobility, and the power to get along with a variety of people from all walks of South Pacific life. And he was able as well to share with readers his knowledge of those lives. As Congressman Daniel K. Inouye stated in the United States House of Representatives on September 17, 1962, concerning Michener: "He is literally Mr. Pacific, a man who has brought the attention of the world to this glamorous, lovely area. In vivid prose, that has been translated into dozens of languages, Michener has told the story of romantic places, of powerful struggles, and of history that envelops us all."

But the author's exploration of the Pacific was extended beyond it to Asia and Russia. He is probably the person who has done most to make his fellow Americans aware of the dangers and challenges that the United States must face as the course of empire, taking its westward way, has come full circle and is now eyeball to eyeball with the East. Again to quote the speech of Daniel Inouye, who is still serving as America's first United States Senator of Japanese ancestry: "When I travelled through Asia on matters affecting our Government I found that in many capitals in that part of the world, James A. Michener was one of the best known Americans. He had worked for many years explaining America to Asia and Asia to Americans. His books were loved by people who wanted closer ties between that vast part of the world and the United States. The popular motion pictures that showed Asia to the rest of the world were enjoyed in these capitals. But most of all I found men and women of Asia knew Michener for the large number of books and articles he had written about the serious problems in this continent."

Michener's amazing versatility in type of publication has been mentioned in Chapter 1. From the start he resisted the temptation to follow up a former success. His name is almost as well known on stage, film, and television announcements as it is in the columns of *Publisher's Weekly*. But he himself feels that his main achievement has been in the short story, and even more in the novel.

Aside from a handful of masterly short stories, such as "A Boar's Tooth," "Our Heroine," "Fo' Dolla'," "The Cave," "Mutiny," "Wine for the Mess at Segi," "Mr. Morgan," and "Povenaaa's Daughter"—a list impressive enough to make a reputation for anyone—Michener's greatest contribution so far has been in the genre of the novel. *Tales of the South Pacific* is, all things considered, the best novel to come out of the World War II conflict in the Pacific. *Hawaii* is, all things considered, the best novel yet written about the genesis of America's newest state. *The Source* probes deeply into the origins of religion and the millenia-old history of the Holy Land. *The Drifters* best dramatizes the international alienation of the young people of the 1960s. *Centennial* tells more about one of America's Western states than any other novelist has told before.

A final query comes to mind: Can we classify this novelist among the usual critical categories? Although Michener has studied and admired the great European novelists, it is clear that he himself is deep in the American tradition. He speaks respectfully of such early twentieth-century American naturalists as Theodore Dreiser and Frank Norris; and he is aware of the current of naturalism that descended to them from Emile Zola and Gustave Flaubert. Is Michener a naturalist?

If we apply the usual Parringtonian criteria of objectivity, frankness, amorality, determinism, pessimism, and a resultant bias in character selection, it seems obvious that the label will not fit. Michener in his author stance is closer to the soap box than to the laboratory of the social scientist. He is highly moral and confessedly optimistic, and is committed to a faith in progress and the rational improvability of man. His characters are often chosen or molded to enact his theme, but seldom does he offer for our admiration a "hairy ape" with strong back and weak mind, or a Strindbergian neurotic, or an alcoholic, dope-riddled, epicene antihero, or a flabby victim of "circumstance" or "society" in a world he never even tried to make. Michener is frank to the point of horrifying some of his otherwise adoring readers, but frankness is expected nowadays in any novel that does not wish to be damned as Victorian.

No, Michener is perhaps less close to the naturalists than to the "muckrakers" of the early period—those crusaders like Jack London and Upton Sinclair who found in fiction a broader extension of their revelatory reportage. And perhaps he is most of all the contemporary reporter, in fiction as well as fact—one of the noble, articulate band of rovers that keep showing our generation what we are really like. After all, John Steinbeck and John Hersey have made literature of suffering and injustice and prejudice and courage; and all of his life Ernest Hemingway never disdained the proud title of reporter. So long as modern Americans need to know who they are, so long will Michener's books be read.

Notes and References

Chapter One

1. "VII. Edwin Joseph Michener was born 2 - 20 - 1876. He married 7 - 7 - 1900 Mabel Haddock. She was a daughter of Robert and Kate Haddock. He died 3 - 17 - 1902. She died 3 - 22 - 1946. *Children:* Robert Ezra, born 10 - 23 - 1901. James Albert (adopted), 2 - 3 - 1907."—Anna E. Shaddinger, *The Micheners in America* (Tokyo, 1958).

2. *Report of the County Chairman* (New York, 1961), p. 244.

3. *New York Times,* February 3, 1947, p. 17.

4. Ibid., December 24, 1956, p. 4.

5. *Report of the County Chairman,* p. 9.

6. *Honolulu Star-Bulletin,* November 17, 1959, p. 1B.

7. *Saturday Evening Post* 235 (May 5, 1962), p. 8; reprinted by special permission,©1962, the Curtis Publishing Co.

8. *Honolulu Sunday Star-Bulletin and Advertiser,* September 23, 1962.

9. "The Mature Social Studies Teacher," *Social Education* 34 (November, 1970), p. 760.

Chapter Two

1. Bob Krauss, "Success Story of a Story," *Paradise of the Pacific* (Honolulu), 71 (November, 1959), 157.

2. February 2, 1947, VII, 5.

3. 36 (Spring, 1947), 576.

4. Krauss.

5. May 16, 1948, VII, 8.

6. The narrator appears in thirteen of the nineteen sections. Tony Fry appears in nine; Bus Adams, in six; Harbison, in five; Billis and Dr. Benoway, in four each; and Joe Cable, in two. Of the women, Latouche De Becque appears in three and Nellie Forbush in two. Admiral Kester is often onstage or in the wings.

7. The officer-narrator tells thirteen of the tales. Bus Adams tells "The Milk Run" and "Those Who Fraternize." An omniscient narrator gives us "An Officer and a Gentleman," "Our Heroine," "Dry Rot," and "Passion."

8. A model of short-story commentary is "History and Setting in Michener's Story of Norfolk Island, 'Mutiny,' " by Amos P. Leib (*Australian Literary Studies* 4 [October, 1970], 349 - 59).

9. Page numbers in parentheses in this chapter refer to pagination in the

hardbound first edition of *Tales of the South Pacific* (New York, 1947).

10. This incident is used as a climactic one in the musical play *South Pacific*—in it, however, the "big dealer" Luther Billis causes the navy tremendous trouble.

11. Prophetically, a decade before Little Rock became synonymous around the world with racial prejudice, the region was selected by Michener as the place of Nellie's origin.

12. "Happy Talk," *New York Times,* July 3, 1949, II, 1.

13. *New York Times,* September 23, 1956, II, 1.

14. "Happy Talk."

15. *New York Times,* May 16, VII, 8.

16. "Biographical Note," *Saturday Review of Literature,* 34 (April 28, 1951), 10. Appreciation of Norman Mailer's book is greatly tarnished by the revelation that it is a Marxist allegory hewing to the party line (see Robert Lee Scott, "*The Naked and the Dead:* A Tour de Force," [M.A. thesis, University of Hawaii, 1953]).

Chapter Three

1. *Return to Paradise* (New York, 1951), p. 3.

2. "I Would Not Minimize That Apprenticeship . . ." *Northwest Review,* 4 (Spring, 1961), 7.

3. *Report of the County Chairman* (New York, 1961), p. 4.

4. *Yale Review,* ns, 38 (Spring, 1949), 574.

5. *Library Journal,* 74 (January 1, 1949), 60.

6. *New York Times,* February 6, 1949, p. 7.

7. *Christian Science Monitor,* February 15, 1949, p. 12.

8. Page numbers in parentheses in this chapter refer to pagination in the hardbound first edition of *The Fires of Spring* (New York, 1949).

9. 173 (August, 1951), 390.

10. May 6, 1951, p. 3.

11. *Commonweal,* 54 (April 27, 1951), 67.

12. *Saturday Review of Literature,* 34 (April 28, 1951), 10.

13. See, for example, his introduction to *The Spell of the Pacific,* edited by Carl Stroven and A. Grove Day (New York, 1949), and his essay, "Sea of the Talented Traveler," *Saturday Review,* 37 (October 23, 1954), 47 - 48.

14. Any resemblance to Harry Brunner, pilot hero of Wolfert's *Act of Love,* is probably coincidental. The main character of Michener's *The Bridges at Toko-Ri* is a flyer named Harry Brubaker.

15. A fairly good estimate: in 1963 the best population figures for the Crown Colony showed about 213,000 Indians, 178,000 Fijians, and 37,000 others. During a speech Michener gave at the University of the South Pacific at Suva, Fiji, in 1976, he and his wife were crudely heckled by an organized group of East Indians who were incensed about a few selections from the essay he had written more than a quarter of a century earlier.

Chapter Four

1. *Library Journal,* 76 (November 15, 1951), 1932.
2. *New York Herald-Tribune Book Review,* October 28, 1951, p. 5.
3. *New York Times,* October 28, 1951, p. 6.
4. *Selected Writings* (New York, 1957), p. x.
5. "Talk with Mr. Michener," *New York Times Book Review,* July 12, 1953, VII, 16.
6. *Catholic World,* 178 (October, 1953), 71.
7. *New York Herald-Tribune Book Review,* July 12, 1953, p. 1.
8. 36 (July 11, 1953), 22.
9. *New Republic,* 124 (August 17, 1953), 20.
10. *New York Times Book Review,* July 12, 1953, p. 5.
11. *New York Times,* July 2, 1953, p. 21.
12. Page numbers in parentheses in this chapter refer to pagination in the hardbound first editions of *The Voice of Asia* (New York, 1951); *The Bridges at Toko-Ri* (New York, 1953); *Sayonara* (New York, 1954); and *Caravans* (New York, 1963).
13. *New York Herald-Tribune Book Review,* January 24, 1954, p. 4.
14. *Spectator* (June 25, 1954).
15. *Saturday Review,* 37 (February 6, 1954), 11.
16. *Chicago Sunday Tribune,* January 31, 1954, p. 3.
17. Prints of Hana-ogi by the artist Utamaro are to be found in Plate 53 of Michener's *The Floating World* (New York, 1955) and Plate 163 of his *Japanese Prints* (Tokyo, 1959). In the latter book he remarks: "It was from my account of this haunting woman that I was able to afford most of the prints shown here, so in a very real sense she can be called the patron saint of this collection, except that the word saint is one which hardly applies to this remarkable woman" (142).
18. "I intended the theory in my writings of having the central character more bland than peripheral characters and I've been severely criticized for this and I think justly so. But still, I like the device, I use it, and if I were doing it again I would still use it. I don't know why."—John P. Hayes, "James Michener," *Writer's Digest* 52 (May, 1972), 23.
19. *Newsweek* 62 (August 12, 1963), 82.

Chapter Five

1. 40 (June 8, 1957), 33.
2. *New York Herald-Tribune,* June 10, 1957, p. 15.
3. *New York Times,* June 22, 1957, p. 13.
4. *New York Herald-Tribune Book Review,* June 16, 1957, p. 1.
5. *Chicago Sunday Tribune,* June 23, 1957, p. 3.
6. *Chicago Sun Times,* June 9, 1957.
7. *San Francisco Chronicle,* June 11, 1957, p. 21.
8. 82 (June 15, 1957), 1672.

9. Our method was not too different from that used by Nordhoff and Hall while writing *Mutiny on the "Bounty,"* as described in a letter from Hall to Dr. Chilson H. Leonard of The Phillips Exeter Academy, Exeter, New Hampshire, January 5, 1935: "When we had done our preliminary reading, we of course talked the story over, from every possible point of view, and decided what our method of telling it should be. . . . When it came to the task of writing, we divided the story into chapters, each of us taking those which most appealed to him. Then, the first draft completed, we exchanged work, each man criticising and making suggestions before we did our revising. Throughout the trilogy each chapter is largely the work of one or the other of us, although there are certain paragraphs, sentences, and fragments of sentences written in collaboration."

10. The various versions of the *Rascals in Paradise* manuscript, along with our correspondence on the writing of it, are housed in the Hawaiian Collection of the University of Hawaii and may be examined by researchers.

11. Captain Joshua Slocum's visit to Manila (243) was not made in the yacht *Spray* but in another vessel.

12. *New York Times*, March 3, 1957, p. 1.

13. *Chicago Sunday Tribune*, March 3, 1957, p. 1.

14. *San Francisco Chronicle*, February 28, 1957, p. 23.

15. *Saturday Review*, 40 (March 2, 1957), 13.

16. "An Author Explains," *Newsweek*, March 4, 1957, 104 - 5.

17. Ibid.

18. Robert Clurman, "Talk with Mr. Michener," *New York Times Book Review*, March 3, 1957, VII, 18.

19. Ibid.

20. Ibid.

21. Page numbers in parentheses in the latter part of this chapter refer to pagination in the hardbound first editions of *The Bridge at Andau* (New York, 1957) and *Report of the County Chairman* (New York, 1961).

22. June 18, 1961, p. 12.

23. 144 (May 29, 1961), 144.

24. 78 (June 28, 1961).

25. 44 (June 10, 1961), 42.

26. 86 (June 1, 1961), 2112.

Chapter Six

1. November 22, 1959, p. 4.

2. *New York Herald-Tribune Book Review*, November 22, 1959, p. 3.

3. *San Francisco Chronicle*, November 24, 1959, p. 39.

4. *Chicago Sunday Tribune*, November 22, 1959, p. 1.

5. 42 (November 21, 1959), 40.

6. *New Statesman*, 59 (June 25, 1960), 95.

7. 191 (June, 1960), 185.

8. *Honolulu Advertiser,* October 25, 1959, p. A23.

9. Page numbers in parentheses in this chapter refer to pagination in the hardbound first edition of *Hawaii* (New York, 1959).

10. 84 (December 15, 1959), 3870.

11. *Honolulu Star-Bulletin,* July 28, 1961, p. 18.

12. Terry Chapman in *Sydney Morning Herald,* September 17, 1960, p. 15.

13. *Report of the County Chairman* (New York, 1960), p. 9.

14. Letter in *Honolulu Star-Bulletin,* November 13, 1962.

15. 74 (November 23, 1959), p. 107.

16. However, a student at an Eastern college who had just read *Hawaii* became so convinced of its historicity that he decided to write a speech of tribute to "one of the last of the great Hales of Hawaii." When he could not reach Hoxworth Hale, the narrator of the novel, on the long-distance telephone, he sent a letter of inquiry in January, 1966, to the Honolulu Chamber of Commerce.

17. See flyleaf of novel. The name recalls that of Alatau Tamchiboulac Atkinson, newspaper editor, political satirist, and Minister of Public Education.

Chapter Seven

1. Page numbers in parentheses in this chapter refer to pagination in the hardbound first editions of *The Source* (New York, 1965); *The Floating World* (New York, 1954); *Iberia* (New York, 1968); *Presidential Lottery* (New York, 1969); and *The Quality of Life* (Philadelphia, 1970).

2. *About Centennial* (New York, 1974), pp. 20 - 21.

3. *A Michener Miscellany* (New York, 1973), pp. 231 - 32.

4. Roy Newquist, "An Interview with James Michener," *Writer's Digest* 48 (August, 1958), 42.

5. *About Centennial,* p. 46. At least one other novelist used a quite comparable structure; John Masters in *The Rock* (New York, 1970) gives an account of the periods in the history of Gibraltar in a series of stories going back to earliest times.

6. "A Desire to Inform," *Saturday Review* 51 (May 4, 1968), 29.

7. *A Michener Miscellany,* p. 100.

8. "A Desire to Inform," p. 29.

9. *A Michener Miscellany,* p. 388. The "complete breakdown of our electoral system" forms the major plot line in *1876,* a novel by Gore Vidal (New York, 1976).

10. R.B. Nordberg, *Best Sellers* 30 (December 15, 1970), 398.

Chapter Eight

1. *The Quality of Life* (Philadelphia, 1970), 68.

2. *Iberia* (New York, 1968) Other page numbers in parentheses in this

chapter refer to paginations in the hardbound first editions of *The Drifters* (New York, 1971); *Kent State* (New York, 1971); *A Michener Miscellany* (New York, 1973); *Sports in America* (New York, 1976); *About Centennial* (New York, 1974); and *Centennial* (New York, 1974).

3. A factual account of Michener's participation in the running of the bulls, illustrated with photographs by Robert Vavra, can be found in "Can a Sixty-two-year-old with a History of Heart Trouble Find Fulfillment Running with the Bulls in the Streets of Pamplona?" *Esquire* 74 (December, 1970), 177 - 83. The theory of Michener—who spent four festivals in Pamplona—concerning reasons for participation is therein stated: "Throughout history a certain kind of man has wanted to test himself against the most demanding experiences of his culture. Such a motive is idiotic, jejune, unrewarding, and senseless, but frequently you find it is the best men who insist upon taking the risks. In our age you can climb Mount Everest, fly to the moon, or run with the bulls at Pamplona. The last is the cheapest, most available, and you can do it with the most exhilarating companions" (182 - 83).

4. "Jim Michener Speaks Out," *Publisher's Weekly* 199 (May 10, 1971), 18.

5. "James Michener Puts His Birthday Gift in Writing," *People*, (September 16, 1974, p. 56.

6. Ibid., p. 54.

Chapter Nine

1. J. K. Hutchins, "On an Author," *New York Herald-Tribune Books*, May 20, 1951, p. 3.

2. "The Chances Against the Beginning Writer," in *The Writer's Book* (New York, 1950), p. 103.

3. "I Would Not Minimize That Apprenticeship . . ." *Northwest Review* 4 (Spring, 1961), 8; hereinafter cited as "Apprenticeship."

4. "Apprenticeship," pp. 19 - 20.

5. Ibid., p. 5.

6. Ibid., p. 6.

7. "Chances," p. 109.

8. "A Preface to a Novel," *Honolulu Star-Bulletin*, June 5, 1960, Hawaiian Life supplement, p. 3.

9. "Apprenticeship," p. 14.

10. Ibid., pp. 8 - 9.

11. *A Michener Miscellany* (New York, 1973), p. 163.

12. *About Centennial* (New York, 1974), p. 44.

13. "A Desire to Inform," *Saturday Review* 51 (May 4, 1968), 29.

14. *A Michener Miscellany*, p. 49.

15. John P. Hayes, "James Michener," *Writer's Digest* 52 (May, 1972), 21.

16. Wayne Warga, "Tales of the Rocky Mountains," *San Francisco Chronicle*, November 8, 1974, 23.

17. Hayes, p. 54.

18. Harvey Breit, "Talk With Mr. Michener," *New York Times*, May 22, 1949, p. 26.

19. "This I Believe," *A Michener Miscellany*, pp. 13 - 14.

Selected Bibliography

PRIMARY SOURCES

1. Collections

Selected Writings, with a preface by the author. New York: Random House, Modern Library, 1957. Includes Foreword; "Our Heroine," "A Boar's Tooth" (from *Tales of the South Pacific*); "Mr. Morgan," "Povenaaa's Daughter," "The Mynah Birds," "The Fossickers" (from *Return to Paradise*); 13 selections (from *The Voice of Asia*); *The Bridges at Toko-Ri* (complete).

A Michener Miscellany, 1950 - 1970. Selected and edited by Ben Hibbs. New York: Random House, 1973; Crest (paperbound), 1975. Includes twenty-five selections from the *Reader's Digest* between 1954 and 1970, here largely revised, with various introductory essays.

2. Books

Tales of the South Pacific. New York: Macmillan, 1947. Bantam Books (paperbound, abridged), 1948; (unabridged), 1957. Crest (paperbound), 1973. Serial publication: "Best Man in de Navy," *Saturday Evening Post* 219 (January 18, 1947), 18-19; "Remittance Man," *Saturday Evening Post* 219 (December 14, 1946), 16-17. Collected: "Airstrip at Konora," in C. A. Fenton, *Best Short Stories of World War II,* New York: Viking, 1957; "A Boar's Tooth, in C. Stead, *Great Stories of the South Sea Islands,* New York: Saunders, 1956; "The Cave," in Orville Prescott, *Mid-Century,* New York: Pocket Books, 1959; "Landing on Kuralei," in G. C. Aymar, *Treasury of Sea Stories,* New York: Barnes, 1948; "Milk Run," in P. Jensen, *Fireside Book of Flying Stories,* New York: Simon & Schuster, 1951, also in *Reader's Digest* 56 (June, 1950), 57-60; "Mutiny," in A. Grove Day and Carl Stroven, *Best South Sea Stories,* New York: Appleton-Century, 1964.

South Pacific, a Musical Play (music by Richard Rodgers; lyrics by Oscar Hammerstein II; adapted from *Tales of the South Pacific*). New York: Random House, 1949.

The Fires of Spring. New York: Random House, 1949. Bantam Books (paperbound), 1951. Crest (paperbound), 1973.

Return to Paradise. New York: Random House, 1951. Bantam Books (paperbound), 1952. Crest (paperbound), 1974. Serial publication:
  "Australia," *Holiday* 8 (November, 1950), 98-109; "Circles in the
  Sea," *Holiday* 7 (May, 1950), 68-71; "Fiji," *Holiday* 7 (June, 1950),
  60-63; "Guadalcanal," *Holiday* 8 (August, 1950), 66; "Guadalcanal
  Today," *Reader's Digest,* 58 (June, 1951), 105-8; "Mr. Morgan,"
  Ladies' Home Journal 63 (May, 1951), 58-59; "Myna Birds," *Holiday*
  8 (July, 1950), 26-29; "New Guinea," *Holiday* 8 (December, 1950),
  73; "New Zealand," *Holiday* 9 (January, 1951), 44-47. Collected:
  "Mr. Morgan," in Bennett Cerf, *Reading for Pleasure*, New York:
  Harper, 1957.
The Voice of Asia. New York: Random House, 1951. Bantam Books (paperbound), 1952. Crest (paperbound), 1973.
The Bridges at Toko-Ri. New York: Random House, 1953. Bantam Books
  (paperbound), 1955. Crest (paperbound), 1973. Originally complete
  in *Life* 35 (July 6, 1953), 58 - 62.
Sayonara. New York: Random House, 1954. Bantam Books (paperbound),
  1955. Crest (paperbound), 1974. Originally "Sayonara Means Good-
  bye," *McCalls* 81 (October, November, December, 1953), 30 - 31,
  30 - 31, 38 - 39.
The Floating World. New York: Random House, 1955. Excerpt, "Magic
  Hand of Hokusai," *Reader's Digest* 74 (June, 1959), 236 - 38.
The Bridge at Andau. New York: Random House, 1957. Bantam Books
  (paperbound), 1957. Crest (paperbound), 1973. Condensation,
  Reader's Digest 70 (March, 1957), 23 - 30; (May, 1957), 93 - 98.
Rascals in Paradise (with A. Grove Day). New York: Random House, 1957.
  Bantam Books (paperbound), 1958. Crest (paperbound), 1974.
  Chapter I, abridged, in *This Week* (May 5, 12, 19, 26, 1957); see also
  June 2, 1957, p. 26. Chapter X, abridged, in *True* (February, 1958),
  36 - 39.
The Hokusai Sketchbooks: Selections from the Manga. Tokyo: Charles E.
  Tuttle Co., 1958.
Japanese Prints: From the Early Masters to the Modern. Tokyo: Charles E.
  Tuttle Co., 1959.
Hawaii. New York: Random House, 1959. Bantam Books (paperbound),
  1961. Crest (paperbound), 1973. Excerpt, "Birth of Hawaii," *Life* 47
  (October 26, 1959), 154 - 56. Excerpt, "Some Americans from
  Hawaii," *Reader's Digest* 74 (December, 1959), 82 - 89.
Report of the County Chairman. New York: Random House, 1961. Bantam
  Books (paperbound), 1961. Excerpt, "Inside Kennedy's Election,"
  Look 25 (May 9, 1961), 56 - 60.
The Modern Japanese Print. Tokyo: Charles E. Tuttle Co., 1962.
Caravans. New York: Random House, 1963. Crest (paperbound), 1974.
  Condensed in *Ladies' Home Journal* 80 (July - August, 1963),
  79 - 86.

The Source. New York: Random House, 1965. Crest (paperbound), 1973.

Iberia: Spanish Travels and Reflections. Photographs by Robert Vavra. New York: Random House, 1968. Crest (paperbound), 1973. Excerpt, *Saturday Evening Post* 241 (February 24, 1968), 34 - 38. "Spain's Secret Wilderness," *Holiday* 43 (April, 1968), 40 - 45.

Presidential Lottery: The Reckless Gamble in Our Electoral System. New York: Random House, 1969. Fawcett (paperbound), 1972. Condensed in *Reader's Digest* 94 (May, 1969), 247 - 50.

The Quality of Life. Philadelphia: Girard Bank, 1970. Paintings by James B. Wyeth. Distributed free. Reprint (lacking illustrations) Philadelphia: J. B. Lippincott, 1970, somewhat revised. Crest (paperbound), 1971.

Kent State: What Happened and Why. New York: Random House, 1971. Crest (paperbound), 1972. Condensed in *Reader's Digest* 98 (March, 1971), 57 - 63; (April, 1971), 217 - 20.

The Drifters. New York: Random House, 1971. Crest (paperbound), 1972. Story in *Ladies' Home Journal* 87 (November, 1970), 161 - 68.

About "Centennial": Some Notes on the Novel. New York: Random House, 1974. A 64-page bound volume sent to selected individuals previous to publication of the big novel. "Only 3200 copies of this book have been made and no more will be printed. No copies are for sale."

Centennial. New York: Random House, 1974. Crest (paperbound), 1976. "Lame Beaver: The Life of a Plains Indian," *Reader's Digest* 104 (April, 1974), 206 - 7. "The Crime," story, *Ladies' Home Journal* 91 (September, 1974), 100 - 101. "Life and Death of the Dinosaur," *Reader's Digest* 105 (November, 1974), 219 - 23.

Sports in America. New York: Random House, 1976. "The Jungle World of Juvenile Sports," *Reader's Digest,* 107 (December, 1975), 109 - 12.

Firstfruits: A Harvest of Twenty-five Years of Israeli Writing (ed.). New York: Fawcett, 1974.

3. Serial and Miscellaneous Publications

"A Christmas Present." *Reader's Digest* 91 (December, 1967), 60 - 63.

"A Present for Aunt Bessie." *Vogue* 131 (March 15, 1958), 107.

"An Eastern Art Goes Western." *Horizon* 2 (May, 1960), 102 - 14.

"Afghanistan: Domain of the Fierce and the Free." *Reader's Digest* 67 (November, 1955), 161 - 72.

"All for One: A Story from Korea." *Reader's Digest* 61 (July, 1952), 1 - 2.

"Aloha for the Fiftieth State." *New York Times Magazine*, April 19, 1959, pp. 14 - 15.

"American in Tahiti." *Paradise of the Pacific* (Honolulu) 65 (January, 1953), 28 - 29. Review of autobiography of James Norman Hall.

"Battle for Burma." *Reader's Digest* 72 (April, 1958), 107 - 13.

"Blunt Truths About Asia." *Life* 30 (June 4, 1951), 96 - 100; excerpt in *Reader's Digest* 59 (September, 1951), 73 - 78.

"Can a Sixty-two-year-old with a History of Heart Trouble Find Fulfillment

Running with the Bulls in the Streets of Pamplona?" *Esquire* 74 (December, 1970), 177 - 83.

"Chances Against the Beginning Writer." in *The Writer's Book,* ed. Helen R. Hull, pp. 102 - 10. New York: Harper, 1950.

"China Diary." *Reader's Digest* 100 (May, 1972), 241 - 44.

"Chinese Success Story." *Life* 31 (December 31, 1951), 76 - 81.

"Collector, The: An Informal Memoir." *Texas Quarterly* 13 (Spring, 1970), 6 - 25. The entire issue is devoted to the Michener Collection at the University of Texas.

"The Conscience of the Contemporary Novel." in *The Arts in Renewal,* ed. Sculley Bradley, pp. 107 - 40. Philadelphia, University of Pennsylvania Press, 1951.

"Don't Knock the Rock." *Reader's Digest* 88 (February, 1966), 157 - 60.

"Facts About the GI Babies." *Reader's Digest* 64 (March, 1954), 5 - 10.

"Five Warring Tribes of South Africa." *New York Times Magazine,* January 22, 1972, pp. 6 - 7.

Foreword to *Kishi and Japan: The Search for the Sun* by Dan Kurzman. New York: Obolensky, 1960.

Foreword to *The Lost Eden* by José Rizal. Bloomington: University of Indiana Press, 1961. Translation by León Maria Guerrero of *Noli Me Tangere.*

"Forgotten Heroes of Korea." *Saturday Evening Post* 224 (May 10, 1952), 19 - 21.

"4,100 Miles on a Raft." *Saturday Review of Literature* 33 (September 23, 1950), 12 - 13. Review of *Kon-Tiki* by Thor Heyerdahl.

"Four Miracles, and a Masterpiece." *Reader's Digest* 89 (November, 1966), 158 - 65.

"Frances Sabin Gets People to Buy Books They Didn't Know They Wanted." *Publisher's Weekly* 179 (January 9, 1961), 31 - 34.

"GMRX: An Alternative to Movie Censorship." *Reader's Digest* 94 (January, 1969), 87 - 93.

"Happy Talk: Tribute to the Writers of 'South Pacific.' " *New York Times,* July 3, 1949, part II, p. 1.

"Hardest-Working Women in the World." *Reader's Digest* 74 (March, 1959), 42 - 46.

"Hawaii." *Holiday* 13 (May, 1953), 34 - 35; excerpts in *Reader's Digest* 63 (August, 1953), 102 - 7.

"Hawaii: The Case for Our Fiftieth State." *Reader's Digest* 73 (December, 1958), 158 - 60.

"Hawaii the Fiftieth State." *New York Times Magazine,* April 19, 1961, p. 14; also editorial note, May 10, 1961, p. 4.

"Hawaii Politics." *Honolulu Star-Bulletin,* 1958 (series of five articles): "Governor Quinn's Great Start," November 1, II, 2; "Ben Dillingham Called Hero of Election," November 8, II, 2; "How to Lose an Election," November 15, II, 2; "Four Smart Girls of the First State Election," November 22, II, 2; " 'How Things Now Look' to Michener," November 21, II, 2.

Hawaiian Airlines, Ltd. A special report to the stockholders. Testimony of J. A. Michener, October 28, 1959. University of Hawaii Library.

"Hawaiian Holidays." *Look* 24 (December 20, 1960), 31 - 32.

"Hawaii's Statehood Urged." *New York Times*, January 1, 1959, p. 30; letter dated from Honolulu, December 14, 1958.

"Hermitage: Russia's Fabulous Art Palace." *Reader's Digest* 86 (March, 1965), 133 - 41.

"Historic Meeting in Indonesia." *Reader's Digest* 67 (August, 1955), 75 - 79.

"Homesick for Hawaii." *Ladies' Home Journal* 89 (May, 1972), 58.

"I Would Not Minimize That Apprenticeship." *Northwest Review* 4 (Spring, 1961), 5 - 27. Tape-recorded interview before writing classes of Sylvan Karchmer and Ralph J. Salisbury at University of Oregon. Excerpts, "Thoughts on Writing," *Writer* 75 (May, 1962), 12 - 13; "Two-Finger Exercise," *Beacon* (Honolulu) 1 (May, 1961), 8 - 9.

"Indonesia, Islands of Beauty and Turmoil." *Reader's Digest* 67 (September, 1955), 30 - 38.

"International Maturity: A Report on Asia." *Vital Speeches* 22 (December 15, 1955), 147 - 51. Speech as president of Fund for Asia, Inc., New York, October 5, 1955.

Introduction to *Tokyo and Points East*. by Keyes Beech. New York: Doubleday, 1954.

Introduction to *Hawaii, 1961* by W. W. Davenport, et al., pp. 5 - 8. Fodor's Modern Guides. New York: David McKay, 1961.

Introduction to *A Hawaiian Reader*, edited by A. Grove Day and Carl Stroven, pp. xi - xvii. New York: Appleton-Century-Crofts, 1959.

Introduction to *Adventurers of the Pacific* by A. Grove Day, pp. vii - xiii. New York: Meredith, 1969.

Introduction to *Here's Hawaii* by Bob Krauss, pp. 7 - 9. New York: Coward-McCann, 1960.

Introduction to *Modern Japanese Prints* by Oliver Statler, pp. xv - xvii. Tokyo: Charles E. Tuttle Co., 1956.

Introduction to *The Spell of the Pacific*, edited by Carl Stroven and A. Grove Day, pp. vii - xi. New York: Macmillan, 1949.

Introduction to *Years of Infamy: The Untold Story of America's Concentration Camps* by Michi Weglyn, pp. 27 - 31. New York: Morrow. 1976

"Is America Burning?" *New York Times Magazine*, July 1, 1973, pp. 10 - 11.

"Islam: The Misunderstood Religion." *Reader's Digest* 66 (May, 1955), 67 - 75.

"Israel: Nation Too Young to Die." *Look* 31 (August 8, 1967), 64 - 68.

"Japan." *Holiday* 12 (August, 1952), 26 - 41.

"Kabuki Is a Must for America." *Theater Arts* 38 (March, 1954), 74 - 75.

"Lament for Pakistan." *New York Times Magazine*, January 9, 1972, pp. 11 - 13.

"Legacy: The Australian Way." *Reader's Digest* 68 (March, 1956), 57 - 60.

Letter to Clarice B. Taylor, *Honolulu Star-Bulletin*, July 28, 1961, p. 18. Concerns reception in Honolulu of New York interview of previous April.

"Madame Butterfly in Bobby Sox." *Reader's Digest* 69 (October, 1956), 21 - 27.

"Madrid's Fabulous Prado." *Reader's Digest* 94 (June, 1969), 145 - 51.

"Magic Malaya." *Reader's Digest* 73 (September, 1958), 228 - 40.

"Main Line." *Holiday* 7 (April, 1950), 34 - 37; abridged in B. A. Botkin, *Sidewalks of America*, Indianapolis: Bobbs-Merrill, 1954.

"Mexico's Mild-Mannered Matador." *Reader's Digest* 79 (July, 1961), 202 - 4.

"Miracles of Santiago." *Reader's Digest* 87 (July, 1965), 228 - 34.

"My Other Books." *Harper's Magazine* 222 (January, 1961), 42 - 44.

"Mystery of Angkor." *Holiday* 12 (November, 1952), 44 - 47.

"Of Men and Ships: Favorite Tales of the Sea." *Life* 53 (December 21, 1962), 96 - 98.

"On Wasting Time." *Reader's Digest* 105 (November, 1974), 193 - 96.

"One and a Half Cheers for Progress." *New York Times Magazine*, September 5, 1971, p. 9; abridged, *Reader's Digest* 99 (December, 1971), 209.

"One Man's Primary, and How He Lost." *New York Times Magazine*, May 21, 1972, pp. 28 - 29.

"One Must Respect Korean Culture." *Reader's Digest* 64 (April, 1954), 15 - 19.

"One Near-Square Who Doesn't Knock the Rock." *New York Times Magazine*, October 31, 1965, pp. 56 - 57.

"Out to Pasture." *Nation's Business* 37 (April, 1949), 32 - 33. Story.

"Pakistan: Divided It Stands." *Reader's Digest* 65 (November, 1954), 136 - 46.

"Peace of Mind." *Look* 35 (July 27, 1971), 22.

"People of the Pacific." *Saturday Review* 43 (November 12, 1960), 41 - 43.

"Perfect Teacher." *Coronet* 30 (June, 1951), 21 - 24.

"Portraits for the Future." *Saturday Review of Literature* 34 (August 4, 1951), 19 - 21.

Postscript to *Something is Missing* by Arthur Goodfriend. New York: Farrar, Straus & Young, 1950.

Publishing on a Sub-Tropical Island." *Publisher's Weekly* 194 (July 1, 1968), 26 - 27.

"Pursuit of Happiness by a GI and a Japanese." *Life* 38 (February 21, 1955), 124 - 26.

"Report from the Frenzied Fifties." *New York Times Magazine*, August 13, 1961, p. 15.

Review of *Race Relations in World Perspective* by Andrew Lind. *Honolulu Star-Bulletin,* June 12, 1B, 1956. With Mari Michener.

"Revolution in Middle-Class Values." *New York Times Magazine,* August 18, 1968, pp. 20 - 21.

"Riddle of Pandit Nehru." *Reader's Digest* 69 (July, 1956), 96 - 102.

"Sea of the Talented Travelers." *Saturday Review* 37 (October 23, 1954), 47 - 48.

"Should Artists Boycott New York?" *Saturday Review* 44 (August 26, 1961), 12.

"Soccer's Wild World Cup Scramble." *Reader's Digest* 96 (June, 1970), 173 - 74.

"Some Practical Applications." In *Through A Quaker Archway,* edited by Horace M. Lippincott. New York: Yoseloff, 1959.

"South Pacific." *Saturday Review* 42 (October 17, 1959), 41.

" 'South Pacific' vs. 'My Fair Lady.' " *New York Times,* September 23, 1956, II, 1.

"Soviet Jewry: 'We Want Moral Outcry.' " *New York Times,* September 16, 1972, p. 29.

"Speaking of Books: What Transpired." *New York Times,* December 17, 1967, VII, p. 2.

"Statehood is Concrete Answer to Reds." *Honolulu Advertiser,* Statehood edition, June 23, 1959. sec. 12 - A, p. 8.

"Straight Talk About Today's Youth." *Reader's Digest* 104 (March, 1974), 166 - 69.

"Thailand, Jewel of Asia." *Reader's Digest* 65 (December, 1954), 57 - 66.

"The Empty Room." *Ladies' Home Journal* 64 (September, 1947), 72 - 73. A story.

"The Gift of Phan Tat Thanh." *Reader's Digest* 69 (September, 1956), 163 - 64.

"The Mature Social Studies Teacher." *Social Education* 34 (November, 1970), 760 - 67. Fiftieth anniversary edition.

"The Red Kimono." *New York Times Magazine,* November 26, 1972, p. 35.

"The Way It Is in Korea." *Reader's Digest* 62 (January, 1953), 15 - 20.

"The Writer's Public Image." *Esquire* 64 (December, 1965), 150. Letter.

"This Great Big Wonderful World." *Holiday* 19 (March, 1956), 40 - 51.

"This I Believe." *Reader's Digest* 65 (July, 1954), 143 - 44. Collected in *This I Believe,* edited by E. R. Murrow, pp. 96 - 97. New York: Simon & Schuster, 1954.

"Those Fabulous Italian Designers." *Reader's Digest* 95 (September, 1969), 157 - 62.

"To Moscow: A Mission for Peace." *Reader's Digest* 101 (September, 1972), 111 - 17.

"Today's Wild West: The Great Australian North." *Reader's Digest* 68 (April, 1956), 63 - 70.

"Tough Man for a Tough Job." *Life* 32 (May 12, 1952), 103 - 6. Condensed
    in *Reader's Digest* 62 (January, 1953), 15 - 20.
"Unusually Close Working Relationship: James A. Michener and Albert
    Erskine." *Publisher's Weekly* 201 (April 10, 1972), part 2, 104 - 5.
"Weapons We Need to Fight Pornography." *Reader's Digest* 93
    (December, 1968), 125 - 30.
"What Every New Candidate Should Know." *New York Times,* September
    23, 1962, VI, 23; reprinted as "Confessions of a Political Candidate."
    Reader's Digest 81 (November, 1962), 199 - 204.
"What Hawaii Means to Me." *Honolulu Star-Bulletin,* July 10, 1954, Satur-
    day section, p. 5.
"What To Do About the Palestinian Refugees?" *New York Times
    Magazine,* September 27, 1970, pp. 22 - 25.
"What's Good About Today's Youth?" *U.S. News* 75 (December 10, 1973),
    48 - 50.
"When Does Education Stop?" *Reader's Digest* 81 (December, 1963),
    153 - 56.
"While Others Sleep." *Reader's Digest* (October, 1957), 68 - 75.
"Why I Am Running for Congress." *Saturday Evening Post* 235 (May 5,
    1962), 8.
"Why I Collect Art." *Reader's Digest* 96 (May, 1970), 147 - 52.
"Why I Like Japan." *Reader's Digest* 69 (August, 1956), 182 - 86.
"Writer's Wars." *Saturday Review* 38 (January 22, 1955), 44.
"Writing a Book in Hawaii." *Paradise of the Pacific* (Honolulu) 71
    (November, 1959), 154 - 56.
"Yancey and the Blue Fish." *Ladies' Home Journal* 66 (November, 1947),
    48 - 49. Story.

4. Articles on Education

"Bach and Sugar Beets." *Music Educators Journal* 25 (September, 1938), 29.
"The Beginning Teacher." In National Council for the Social Studies, *In-
    Service Growth of Social Studies Teachers,* 10th Yearbook, 1939, pp.
    1 - 37.
"Discussion in the Schools." *Social Education* 4 (January, 1940), 4 - 5.
"Functional Social Studies Program." *Curriculum Journal* 9 (April, 1938),
    163 - 64.
Future of the Social Studies. National Council for the Social Studies, Cam-
    bridge, Massachusetts, 1939. Editor.
"Idealism Today." *High Points* 31 (May, 1949), 13 - 21; condensed, *Educa-
    tion Digest* 15 (December, 1949), 44 - 47. Reprinted in E. R. Davis
    and W. C. Hummel (eds.), *Reading for Opinion,* New York: Prentice-
    Hall, 2nd ed. 1960, pp. 252 - 59.
"Improved Unit Method." *Harvard Education Review* 10 (March, 1940),
    211 - 24.

"Music and the Social Studies." *Social Studies* 28 (January, 1937), 28 - 30.
"Participation in Community Surveys as Social Education." In National Council for the Social Studies, *Utilization of Community Resources in the Social Studies*, 9th Yearbook, 1938, pp. 144 - 63.
"P.E.A. Report." *Social Education* 4 (December, 1940), 530 - 31.
"Sex Education: A Success in Our Social-Studies Classes." *Clearing House* 12 (April, 1938), 461 - 65.
"Steps in Unit Learning and Teaching." Eastern Commercial Teachers' Association, 15th Yearbook, 1942, pp. 58 - 68.
"Teachers in the Community." *Social Studies* 33 (May, 1941), 219 - 21. Summary in *Progressive Education* 17 (December, 1940), 546 - 47.
Unit in the Social Studies. Introduction by H. E. Wilson. Harvard Workshop Series No. 1. Cambridge, Massachusetts: Harvard University Graduate School of Education, 1940. With H. M. Long.
"What Are We Fighting For?" *Progressive Education* 18 (November, 1941), 342 - 48.
"Who Is Virgil T. Fry?" *Clearing House* 16 (October, 1941), 67 - 70; condensed, *Education Digest* 7 (November, 1941), 4 - 6; reprinted, *Clearing House* 19 (October, 1944), 69 - 72; reprinted, *Clearing House* 23 (September, 1948), 12 - 16; *Education Digest* 20 (May, 1955), 32 - 34; *Scholastic*, 67 (September 22, 1955), 97; condensed, *NEA Journal* 50 (September, 1961), 23 - 24.

5. Unpublished Materials

Conversations by A. Grove Day with James A. Michener.
Private correspondence, A. Grove Day and James A. Michener.
Note: For the purpose of collecting data on the activities of a leading author of today, the Library of Congress is amassing the unedited papers of Mr. Michener over a long period. These will be preserved but are not generally accessible.

SECONDARY SOURCES

"Again the Warm Voice of Asia." *Newsweek* 43 (January 25, 1954), 92 - 95, and condensed as "Michener of the South Pacific" in *Reader's Digest* 64 (April, 1954), 20. Mainly a review of *The Bridges at Toko-Ri*.
"Artists and Writers." *Newsweek* 59 (May 14, 1962), 102. Quotes Michener on the pleasures of collecting Japanese prints and modern American painters.
"Author Enacts Own Plot." *Life* 39 (Novermber 7, 1955), 55. A brief, well-illustrated account of Michener's third wedding.
"Author Explains: Why Michener Wrote *The Bridge at Andau*." *Newsweek*, 49 (March 4, 1957), 104 - 5. Contains useful information on his activities while covering the Hungarian revolution.
BARRETT, M. E. and M. "On Our List." *Good Housekeeping* 144 (April,

1957), 275 - 77. Has some personal news and a photograph of the Micheners.

"Biographical Note." *New York Herald-Tribune Book Review* (October 7, 1951), p. 6. Useful information previous to the publication of *The Voice of Asia*.

"Biographical Note." *Saturday Review of Literature* 34 (April 28, 1951), 10. Covers life up to publication of *Return to Paradise*.

BREIT, HARVEY. "Talk with Mr. Michener." *New York Times*, May 22, 1949, VII, 26. Mentions *South Pacific* and the author's ideas on the novelist's function in society.

CLURMAN, ROBERT. "Talk with Mr. Michener." *New York Times Book Review*, March 3, 1957, VII, 18. Deals with experiences in collecting material for *The Bridge at Andau*.

Current Biography. New York: H. W. Wilson Co., 1948, 448 - 50. An early source of information derived from Michener himself.

FRANKEL, H., ed. "On the Fringe." *Saturday Review* 48 (July 24, 1965), 62. Comments in an interview after publication of *The Source*.

FREED, A. "Windfall for Texas." *Art in America* 57 (November, 1969), 78 - 85. An account of the reception of the Michener Collection by the University of Texas.

HAVIGHURST, W. "Michener of the South Pacific." *English Journal* 41 (October, 1952), 397 - 402; also in *College English* 14 (October, 1952), 1 - 6. The only previous appreciation of Michener's novels published by an English professor; gives useful judgments on the early books.

HAYES, JOHN P. "James Michener." *Writer's Digest* 52 (April, 1972), 20 - 22; (May, 1972), 22 - 25. Lengthy interview on life and work after publication of *Kent State*.

HUTCHINS, J. K. "Man Behind *The Bridges*." *New York Herald Tribune Books*, July 19, 1953, p. 2. Deals mainly with the preparation of Michener's Korean War novel.

"On an Author." *New York Herald-Tribune Books*, May 20, 1951, p. 3. Deals with the writing of *Return to Paradise*.

INOUYE, HON. DANIEL K. "James A. Michener." *Congressional Record*, Proceedings and Debates of the 87th Congress, Second Session, September 17, 1962. Speech in House of Representatives by Congressman from Hawaii. Pays high tribute to Michener as an author, a representative of America in Asia, and a candidate for the House of Representatives.

"James A. Michener Collection of Japanese Prints at the Hawaiian Academy of Arts." *Paradise of the Pacific* (Honolulu) 72 (November, 1960), 66 - 67. A brief description with photographs.

"James Michener Puts His Birthday Gift in Writing." *People*, 2 (September 16, 1974), 54 - 57. Brief interview on the occasion of the publishing of *Centennial*.

"James Michener Speaks Out: excerpts from remarks at press conference,

April 27, 1971." *Publisher's Weekly* 199 (May 10, 1971), 17 - 18. Remarks at time of publication of *Kent State*.

KRAUSS, BOB. "Success Story of a Story." *Paradise of the Pacific* (Honolulu) 71 (November, 1959), 157. Reprinted from column in *Honolulu Advertiser*, September 12, 1959. Reports an interview concerning *Hawaii* just previous to the publication of that novel.

KUNITZ, STANLEY J. *Twentieth Century Authors: First Supplement*. New York: H. W. Wilson Co., 1955, pp. 665 - 66. Furnished the best biographical information to that date.

LINDLEY, MARION WONG. "Reactions to Michener's *Hawaii*." *Social Process in Hawaii* 24 (1960), 41, 75, 83, 101. Collects a few comments of local readers on the novel.

MERAS, P. "Desire to Inform." *Saturday Review* 51 (May 4, 1968), 29. Interview mainly concerned with comments on the writing of *Iberia*.

NATHAN, G. J. "*South Pacific* and Its Criticism." In *The Magic Mirror*, pp. 250 - 57. New York: Knopf. Is less concerned with analyzing the musical comedy than with blasting other schools of Broadway reviewers, but he does call *South Pacific* an "infinitely more intellectual musical than most."

NATHAN, P., ed. "Rights and Permissions." *Publisher's Weekly* 193 (June 24, 1968), 60. Random comments on the apparent popularity of several of Michener's books.

NEWQUIST, ROY. "An Interview with James Michener." *Writer's Digest* 48 (August, 1968), 38 - 42. Interview by literary editor of *Chicago American* after publication of *The Source*.

NICHOLS, L. "Talk with Mr. Michener." *New York Times Book Review*, July 12, 1953, p. 16. A discussion of the writing of *The Bridges at Toko-Ri*.

"People Are Talking About. . . ." *Vogue* 129 (April 15, 1957), 85. Contains a good portrait of the Micheners not long after publication of *The Bridge at Andau*.

"People Are Talking About. . . ." *Vogue* 148 (November 1, 1966), 180 - 81. A chatty interview with the Micheners in a smart magazine.

"Personal Glimpses." *Reader's Digest* 82 (January, 1963), 134 - 35. Gives a brief version of the anecdote concerning Michener's masquerade that enabled him to view the Barnes Collection.

POPPY, JOHN. "Hawaii." *Look* 30 (September 6, 1966), 48 - 55. Review of book and film, with photographic interpretation by Dennis Stock.

PRESCOTT, ORVILLE. "Novelists and War." In *In My Opinion*, pp. 146 - 64. Indianapolis: Bobbs-Merrill, 1952. Attempts to place Michener in the group of World War II authors; Prescott was one of the first to acclaim *Tales of the South Pacific*.

"Pulitzer Boy." *New York Times*, May 16, 1948, VII, 8. A brief early biography.

SHADDINGER, ANNA E. *The Micheners in America*. Tokyo: Charles E. Tuttle Co., 1958. A prime source for data on Michener's parentage.

SUTTON, HORACE. "The Strange Case of James Michener." *Paradise of the Pacific* (Honolulu) 75 (September-October, 1963), 21 - 22. Gives special attention to Michener's relations with Hawaii and contains some biographical information supplied by A. Grove Day.

TAYLOR, CLARICE B. "Michener and Names." *Paradise of the Pacific* (Honolulu) 71, (October, 1959), 54 - 55. Mentions the search for names of some of the characters in *Hawaii*.

————. "More on Michener's *Hawaii*." *Honolulu Star-Bulletin*, June 5, 1960, Women's Section, p. 8. Written by the author's research assistant on his giant novel, notes that her predictions made the previous year have been realized (see below).

————. "A Preface to a Novel," *Honolulu Star-Bulletin*, Hawaiian Life supplement, June 6, 1959, pp. 2 - 3. A valuable account of Mrs. Taylor's conversations with Michener and predicts that the novel will arouse much comment in Honolulu.

WARFEL, HARRY R. *American Novelists of Today.* New York: American Book Co., 1951, pp. 299 - 300. A standard account, now somewhat dated.

WHITBREAD, J. "Private Life of James (*Hawaii*) Michener." *Good Housekeeping* 150 (February, 1960), 28. A brief interview with Michener at his home in Bucks County.

Index

Fictional places and characters are not indexed.

DATE DUE			

DEMCO 38-297